WOMEN DEVELOPMENT IN INDIA

WOMEN DEVELOPMENT IN INDIA

E.A. NARAYANA
E.V. LAKSHMI

Foreword by

C.V. RAGHAVULU

REGAL PUBLICATIONS
New Delhi - 110 027

WOMEN DEVELOPMENT IN INDIA

ISBN 978-81-8484-92-6

Typeset by
THE LASER PRINTERS
8/15, 3rd Floor, Subhash Nagar, New Delhi-110027

Printed in India at
NEW ELEGANT PRINTERS
A-49/1, Mayapuri Phase I, New Delhi-110064

Published by
REGAL PUBLICATIONS
F-159, Rajouri Garden, New Delhi-110027 • Phone : 45546396
E-mail : regalbookspub@yahoo.com

Contents

FOREWORD

Women living in many parts of the world face severe deprivations. They are among those hit hardest by the inadequate rate of progress. While gender disparities and institutionalized discrimination tell part of the story, the limited access of women to life-saving resources reflects the other part of it. In India, there has been increasing awareness about the need for incorporating gender concerns in public policy. The policy-makers in India, as in many other parts of developing world, have also been sensitized about the contribution that women can make to development and social progress. In the drive towards women empowerment, reservation of positions in local bodies—now contemplated at 50 per cent—has been provided on a statutory basis. Despite a number of initiatives in the public domain through gender-specific polices aimed at bringing women into the mainstream, India slipped to the bottom half of the World Economic Forum's Global Gender Gap Index 2009 rankings at 114 among 134 countries—one rank lower than the previous year's position. The ranking examines the distribution of resources and opportunities among men and women. It is, therefore, necessary to take a serious look at the development profile of women, assess the empowerment index, and attempt a critical analysis of the existing policy responses including those related to implementation, as also the adequacy of the machinery which is entrusted with the responsibility of policy execution. In this contest, the book on Women Development written by Prof. E.A. Narayana and Dr. E.V. Lakshmi has great relevance.

The authors dealt with wide range of issues relating to women development. The rich empirical data is used for analysis. This publication shows a comprehensive study of Women Development Organisations in India. It will be found very useful to research students and teachers interested and connected with women development. As the development of women is a major concern for the government, this publication which combines sociological, developmental and administrative aspects of women development will greatly help the policy-makers and administrators. I congratulate Prof. Narayana and Dr. Lakshmi for publishing their research work in a book form for wider circulation and use.

C.V. RAGHAVULU
Ex-Vice-Chancellor
Acharya Nagarjuna University

ACKNOWLEDGEMENTS

The authors received the help and assistance of many individuals in the completion of this work. They deem it a pleasure to express their thankfulness to all those who are connected with this work.

The authors express their deep sense of gratitude to Prof. C.V. Raghavulu, Professor of Political Science and Public Administration (Retd.) and former Vice-Chancellor of Acharya Nagarjuna University, Guntur, for writing Foreword by sparing his valuable time.

They wish to thank Prof. D.S. Naidu, Prof. M. Madhusudan and other faculty members of the Department of Politics and Public Administration, Andhra University, Visakhapatnam, for their support to write this book.

They express their thanks to the officers and staff of the women development organisations for providing information on various aspects of their agencies. They owe a lot to both official and beneficiary respondents who spared their time and gave their opinion.

The authors thank their son Dr. Aravind and daughter Dr. Haritha for their backing and moral support. Their sincere appreciation goes to Sri M. Suribabu and Ms. M. Sravani for the neat documentation of the manuscript.

Finally the authors thank the publisher, Regal Publications, for the publication of the book in the present form with attractive get up.

E.A. NARAYANA
E.V. LAKSHMI

ABBREVIATIONS

AARRO	: Afro-Asian Rural Reconstruction Organisation
ACDPO	: Assistant Child Development Project Officer
ANC	: Ante-natal Care
APWCFC	: Andhra Pradesh Women's Cooperative Finance Corporation
AWC	: Anganwadi Centre
AWTC	: Anganwadi Training Centre
BCs	: Backward Classes
BPFA	: Beijing Platform for Action
CAPART	: Council for Advancement of People's Action and Rural Technology
CDPO	: Child Development Project Officer
CIRDAP	: Centre for Integrated Rural Development for Asia Pacific
CSWB	: Central Social Welfare Board
CSWI	: Committee on Status of Women in India
DBCCSS	: District Backward Classes Cooperative Service Society
DMSVK	: Durgabai Mahila Sisu Vikasa Kendram
DPEP	: District Primary Education Programme
DRDA	: District Rural Development Agency
DSCCSS	: District Scheduled Castes Cooperative Service Society

DWCD	: Department of Women and Child Development
DWCDA	: District Women and Child Development Agency
DWCRA	: Development of Women and Children in Rural Areas
ICDS	: Integrated Child Development Services
IMY	: Indira Mahila Yojana
IRDP	: Integrated Rural Development Programme
KVIC	: Khadi and Village Industries Commission
MSY	: Mahila Samrudhi Yojana
MTPA	: Medical Termination of Pregnancy Act
NABARD	: National Bank for Agriculture and Rural Development
NBCFDC	: National Backward Classes Finance Development Corporation
NCLP	: National Child Labour Project
NCW	: National Commission for Women
NFLS	: Nairobi Forward Looking Strategies
NGOs	: Non-Governmental Organisations
NIPCCD	: National Institute of Public Cooperation and Child Development
NIRD	: National Institute of Rural Development
NORAD	: Norwegian Agency for International Development
NPAW	: National Plan of Action for Women
NPPW	: National Perspective Plan for Women
NREP	: National Rural Employment Programme
NSCFDC	: National Scheduled Castes Finance Development Corporation
NSKFDC	: National Safai Karamchari Finance Development Corporation
PNC	: Post-natal Care

PRIs	:	Panchayati Raj Institutions
RBI	:	Reserve Bank of India
RLEGP	:	Rural Landless Employment Guarantee Programme
RMK	:	Rashtriya Mahila Kosh
SCs	:	Scheduled Castes
SCSP	:	Scheduled Castes Sub-Plan
SGSY	:	Swarnajayanti Gram Swarojgar Yojana
SHGs	:	Self Help Groups
STEP	:	Support to Training and Employment Programme for Women
STs	:	Scheduled Tribes
TRYSEM	:	Training of Rural Youth for Self Employment
UNO	:	United Nations Organisation
WDC	:	Women Development Corporation
WDO	:	Women Development Organisation
WHO	:	World Health Organisation
WID	:	Women in Development
YWCA	:	Young Women's Christian Association

INTRODUCTION

Women form 50 per cent of the world population and contribute 50 per cent of the food production. They do two-thirds of world's work hours. In other words, the sphere of activities of women is larger and wider than that of men, almost in all the societies of the world.[1] But nowhere in the world do women enjoy equal status with men. The world's poorest women are not merely poor. They live on the edge of subsistence. They are economically dependent and vulnerable, politically and legally powerless—as wives and mothers they are caught in a life cycle that begins with early marriage and too often ends with death in child birth. They work longer hours and sometimes work harder than men, but their work is typically unpaid and under-valued. They are grossly under-represented in institutions of government. It is seen that women have been denied equal opportunities all over the world for personal growth and social development. It is necessary to ensure that this large segment of the world's population gets its rightful share out of all the development programmes and it assumes its rightful role in the society.

U.N. Endeavours

Recognition and appreciation of the role of women as agents

and beneficiaries of development activities had emerged. The international community has endorsed several plans of action and conventions for full, equal and beneficial integration of women in all development activities.

The charter of the United Nations signed in 1945 is the first international agreement that proclaimed gender equality as a fundamental right. Ever since there had been many conventions, programmes and goals to help humankind by conferring on them human right which are "universal, indivisible, interdependent and inter-related."[2]

In order to promote development of women and protect their rights, the General Assembly of the UN adopted "convention on the elimination of all forms of discrimination against women" on 18th December, 1979, which came into force on 3rd September, 1981. The convention also took notice of particular problems faced by rural women and their significant role in survival of their families. So all state parties to the convention agreed to take appropriate measures to enable rural women to participate and benefit from rural development.

The declaration of 1976-85 as the Decade for Women was another landmark endeavours of the United Nations Organisation. The Decade for Women proclaimed in Mexico that the problem of status of women was a global issue. The conference also observed that in order to enhance the status of women the entire human race had to participate. "It has been established, accordingly, that this is not a problem that has to be or can be resolved by women alone, but rather as a part of the entire complex of economic, political and social problems of the world and of each country respectively with active participation of men and women as agents and beneficiaries of development". In the Declaration of Mexico on the "Equality of Women" and their contribution to Development and Peace is also expressed the recognition that women of the entire world, whatever differences exist between them, share the painful experience of receiving or having received unequal treatment, and that as their awareness of this phenomenon increases they will become natural allies in the struggle against any form of oppression.[3]

In the same year of the Declaration of the Decade for Women, the International Labour Organisation also adopted a Declaration on Equality of Opportunity and Treatment for Women Workers and it adopted a Plan of Action "to eliminate all forms of discrimination against women in all sectors of social and economic activity and at all levels of skill and responsibility." In the first half of the UN Decade for Women, considerable efforts had been made by UN and its various specialized agencies to ensure social development for creating conditions in which women would find enough space to realize their potentials as that of men. It is also implied that in the development process women and men would not be objects. They would be the subjects.

The world conference of the U.N. Decade for Women adopted a Programme of Action in Copenhagen in 1980. The Programme of Action formulated a more realistic approach to women's role and position. The Copenhagen Conference also emphasized that to provide equal opportunity to women their employment in various sectors of the economy should be ensured. The measures on which it emphasized were:

1. to ensure that women and man receive equal remuneration for work of equal value to improve the working conditions and occupational mobility of women workers;
2. to ensure equal rights and opportunities for gainful employment of rural women both in agricultural and non-agricultural jobs under proper working conditions; and
3. to promote occupational mobility for women by providing maternity protection, childcare facilities, technical training and health protection.

The Nairobi Forward Looking Strategies (NFLS) adopted at the UN Decade for Women End Conference in June 1985 is a unique document in the history of international community's efforts for women development. This document contains a conceptual framework or a future vision for the advancement of women.[4] For the first time, the NFLS succeeded in designing an inter-governmental programme at the global level, by bringing women and development issues centre-stage in international negotiations. The main themes of the UN Decade for Women, Equality, Development and Peace, were refined and redefined at the international policy level in this document to enable the formulation of national policies, programmes and projects affecting women. Under the equality theme, equal participation of women with men is envisaged within existing national institutions and structures by introducing specific policy measures.

The United Nations Fourth World Conference on Women in Beijing in 1995 put on the agenda the question of women's equality, an essential component of human rights, as a condition of social justice and as a prerequisite for peace and development. The conference addressed itself to removing all obstacles to participation of women in all spheres of public and private life and came out with a definite international agreement regarding the status of women. The agreement referred to as Beijing Platform for Action (BPFA), identified twelve critical areas for concern.[5] These are:

(1) Institutional Mechanisms for the Advancement of Women;
(2) Human Rights of Women;
(3) Women and Poverty;
(4) Women and the Economy;
(5) Education and Training of Women;
(6) Women and Health;
(7) Women in Power and Decision-making;
(8) Violence against Women;
(9) Women and Armed Conflict;
(10) Women and Media;
(11) Women and the Environment; and
(12) The Girl Child.

Each country committed itself to the development of a National Plan for Action (NPA) in which both the country's specific situation of women and related policy commitments should be elaborated upon. Subsequently in June 2000, at a special session of the U.N. General Assembly, representatives of government and NGOs met to asses of progress made by governments as well as NGOs and other private sector bodies regarding the fulfilment of commitments made in the BPFA, to reaffirm the commitments and to take note of the obstacles in the fulfilment of these commitments. At the same time the implementation of the Nairobi Forward Looking Strategies for the Advancement of Women which was adopted at the Third World Conference for Women in 1985 was also reviewed. This process formally called "Women 2000: Gender Equality, Development and Peace for the 21st Century" is commonly known as Beijing Plus Five.[6] The government as well as NGOs took the initiatives in preparing the BP 5 reports which focused attention on change in policies, laws, institutions, programmes, the generation and dissemination of knowledge and to some extent resource allocation. At BP 5 regional meeting in Kathmandu, poverty, violence and lack of political participation were identified as issues of special concern for South Asian women.[7]

The United Nations gave an official and global recognition to women to fulfil the long felt need that half of humanity can no longer be ignored at different levels of policy-making, administration and implementation[8]. National governments, donor agencies and women groups all over the world have started showing concern about the status and role of women in every aspect of human and economic development. In fact, development of women has become an important indicator in judging the development process itself. Needless to say human resource development, and particularly women resource development, is most significant for this process. The Government of the country, voluntary organizations and the people have shown their concern for multifaceted development of the women and for that purpose various kinds of programmes at micro and macro-levels have been evolved and undertaken to improve the conditions of women.

In India also women constitute 50 per cent of the population, that is, one half of the country's human resources. As citizens, workers and mothers, their contribution to economic and social development is crucial requisite for economic development and social progress. Towards this end and in order to empower women, an enabling environment, with requisite policies and programmes, institutional mechanisms at various levels and adequate financial resources has been created. The Government of India has consciously fostered an enabling policy environment in which women issues are properly reflected, articulated and seriously addressed.[9] Several women specific and women-related policies have been initiated and programmes have been undertaken by the government to give the much needed impetus to holistic development of women and their economic and social empowerment. The adoption of National Plan of Action for Women in 1976 is a clear proof for the concern of Government of India towards women's issues.

The Government had launched several schemes to provide income generating opportunities and social and economic securities to women. In fact, after independence, the Constitution guaranteed equality of men and women. The laws concerning marriage, divorce, inheritance, maintenance, dowry, widow remarriage, sati, etc., have been passed from time to time. The introduction of concept of equality through various provisions in the Indian Constitution and the various laws concerning women are intended to prevent discrimination and exploitation. In effect, a basic framework for women's development has been provided in India.

The state had thus, introduced radical changes in the life conditions of men and women in the society through its expanding bureaucratic organizations and implementation of various development programmes. All such programmes right from the Community Development Programme to the latest Development of Women and Children in Rural Areas (DWCRA) have created new administrative structures while expending tens of thousands of rupees. Though these programmes and governmental organisations true to the spirit and nature of the state, could raise some hopes among the women, they in practice, helped the dominant classes of the society, defeating the very purpose for which they were introduced. The Constitution guaranteed equality of men and women and various laws has been passed. However, women are not at par with men. All the legislative measures have put a wide gap between theory and practice and patriarchal domination in all spheres of life of women. The so-called constitutional guarantees coupled with the introduction of various development programmes have not altered their basic life conditions and their position reminded the same. Besides the socio-economic problems from which these people already suffer as a consequence of their subordinate class position, factors like their unorganized state, the insecure job conditions, lack of skills, low wages, and casual nature of employment further reduced them to a subservient position in the society.

Women are backward, they are exploited, oppressed and deprived in every sphere of life, whether socially, economically, politically or culturally. The patriarchical structures, gender-based disparities and hierarchies in the family and community continue to exist in the Indian society.[10] Demographically, steady decline in sex ratio of the women, lower expectancy in life and high death rates, chronic mal-nutrition amongst women are confirmed by national surveys. The majority of women are illiterate. Even literates are backward in many aspects. Since the levels of their education is very low, most women are employed in the primary sectors and get very low wages. The process of development itself has unleashed changes, which have widened and accentuated socio-economic inequalities. The evaluation studies of development interventions also showed that many projects had very mixed and in many cases detrimental consequences for women. The development projects ignored the possibility of unequal relations between men and women. Men frequently were the primary beneficiaries of development assistance, as a result, women, particularly of the poorest groups, found their access and control over resources actually weakened. The planners and project officials underestimated women's economic and social contribution to productive and reproductive activities. Not only were women made relatively worse-off than their men but often became absolutely worse of being effectively subordinated to men in the development process. The overall conclusion of such studies was that the majority of women's work was not recognized as an integral part of the national economic production and that in consequence they were being neglected by governments, planners and development theorists alike. True development, argue the feminists, cannot happen when the needs, talents and potentialities of half of the world's population are seen as secondary and marginal.

Thus, all the development programmes, constitutional provisions and laws passed by the Government have not proved effective. This situation makes one suspect that something has been going wrong with the policies formulated for women development, in the implementation of women development programmes, and with the institutions created for implementation of women development programmes. The present study modestly attempts to examine the institutional mechanism at the local level for women development.

The concept of development, theories on development, development models, the relevance of these theories and models to women's development, studies on women issues, objectives of the study and research methodology are explained in this chapter.

Concept of Development

Women's question is now not only a women's concern but an important issue in the development debate and policy. The traditional view of women's concerns, seen by planners and social scientists as a welfare aspect rather than developmental or as peripheral rather than central to the development process, have undergone changes. These changes have been due to the changes in the perception about historical and ideological dimensions of women's roles and status in Indian society. An attempt is made in this section of the chapter to examine the concept of development and the various theories of development.

Development is one of the most widely used term in the contemporary world. However, development means different things to different people. In general terms, development means removal of poverty, improvement of productivity and consequently raising the quality of life in a given society. This means better education, health and nutritional status for population backed by purchasing power and access to well developed social services in order to reach the level when one is said to meet the indicators of development or social goals. A society will be developed if it has abolished mass poverty.[11] Broadly speaking there is no disagreement that development would imply that the majority of people have their survival needs met (food, clothing and shelter) and that they would come to enjoy increasingly higher levels of living in terms of education, health, communication, etc.

Development is process as much as an end product. This means that in an attempt to jump from here to there, a lot of changes have to take place. Changes in education, changes in production, changes in family and various other organizations, changes in value all have to take place. Thus, when we think of development as a process it is definitely not synonymous with growth. It is not expansion or more of everything you have but many changes in the very structure of society. This list of desirable changes is endless; employment opportunities; more education; participation in government; national independence; social and economic equality; new institutions and attitudes; social discipline, etc. Development as a process necessitates changes in fundamental attitudes to life and work, in social, political and cultural institutions.[12] It is a difficult process because all things cannot obviously be altered at once and all desirable achievements cannot be simultaneous.

Theories of Development

Many changes took place over the past few centuries in developed countries to bring them up to where they are at present. Different explanations emphasize one or other change as the most important-external factors such as trade or other things such as invention, or political factors such as wars or State Policy or many factors acting in combination. There is the understanding that these factors of change become 'development' only when they become cumulative and self-perpetuating.[13] Other countries are viewed as not having had one or the other of this catalytic agents of change and development lies mainly in trying to replicate those conditions that will propel the country forward. Whatever be the means that were elaborated, the most important transformation was understood to be industrialization. Manufacturing increased the volume, value and number of products that economy could produce. Technology was necessary to do this. Economic theories of development, therefore, concentrate heavily on industrialization and technology. The Indian Plan model sought to increase investment in industries that help the future production of consumer goods by increasing the supply of tool-making industries, called "heavy industries". This had the implication of foregoing any increase in consumer goods right now in order to produce more later within the country.

There were other theories such as that several industries must expand at once or that some imbalance is necessary. Another version of the initial imbalance theory is that dual economy approach build an advanced sector while tolerating a backward sector. In the first phase, an industrial sector expands but at the same time agricultural output is needed to support the labour withdrawn from agriculture. In the second phase, as labour transfer increases, competition for labour between industry and agriculture will make capital more attractive. This will lead to commercialization of agriculture and the transition to a highly industrialized economy will be completed.[14]

Various kinds of launching strategies are advocated such as market-oriented agriculture instead of agriculture for own consumption, building transport, power, etc. encouraging exports to finance, import of technology, etc. These theories are flawed in many ways.

(1) All of them originated in developed market economies that ignore the diversities in various under-developed countries.
(2) Various factors are assumed to be constant, whereas they are variable (for example, international relations, national politics, population, etc).
(3) It is assumed that under-developed countries are exactly in the state, where the now developed countries were at the beginning of their development.
(4) These theories totally ignore the institutional factors.
(5) There is no particular definition of development or any operational ways of dealing with the qualitative variables such as organizational changes in production and other institutional changes.

Today's under-developed countries, it has now become clear, cannot replicate the same stages or processes of development that the developed countries went through the simple reason that the matrix of international relations, both economic and political have altered irreversibly.

Women's Development

Current theories of development have been inadequate in

general but particularly inadequate for women. The major thesis of development hitherto has been that every one can reach the goal through abundance, the larger the cake, the more there will be for every one. Not only does this not take place automatically, but, what is worse, the process also reinforces inequalities in ways that entrench them deeper. The human development paradigm, which puts people at the centre of its concerns is now a universally acknowledged strategy for the development of a nation. The growing consensus among development thinkers is that people are—and should be—the starting point, the centre and the goal of each development intervention.[15] The real wealth of a nation is its people, both men and women, and the purpose of development is to create an environment to enable them to enjoy long, healthy and creative lives. However, the harsh reality is that "in no society do women enjoy the same opportunities as men."[16]

All men, women and children shall equally or adequately be benefited from development. They all shall have a say in the changes taking place. If development is a tremendously complex social process, then the extent to which it meets social goals agreeable to all the members in terms of their ultimate interests is alone the true test of development. The evidence from development literature of Asia, Africa and South America point to two major trends:

(a) The disparity in opportunities for women in all those needs that ensure survival and growth, i.e. the comparative aspect.[17]
(b) The increasing degree of new forms of oppression and subordination brought about by the changes taking place in the society.[18]

The disparities as well as negative effects also exist in the developed countries though in a different form.

Conventional approaches to women's development and empowerment have all started with the premise that poverty was the problem, and that economic betterment would resolve not only the issue of lack of purchasing power, but also empower women and lead to an improvement in their social and familial status. The reality is that such a sequence of economic improvement 'trickling down' from above and resulting in social betterment has not taken place.[19] Development has to be broad-based which not only meets at least the basic needs of the entire population but also ensures wider participation of the majority, particularly women as partners of development.[20]

After ten five-year plans over the last five decades even the government has now come to concede that conventional strategies for women's betterment need re-assessment and reshaping. Any development strategy or plan has to take into consideration women's status and disabilities and should provide such measures and incentives, whereby constitutional principles are able to provide the needed equality for their development.

Approaches to Women Development

Several approaches have been tried for the benefit of women. They are social welfare approach, development approach and empowerment approach.

Social Welfare Approach

The women issues with welfare approach that primarily gave emphasis is on the fulfilment of the practical needs surrounding their reproductive role, like delivery of food, family planning, health care, etc. The social welfare measures were initiated for women because of the vulnerable position of woman as 'weaker sex' unable to protect and support herself economically. In the earlier days even socio-economic programmes sponsored by the Central Social Welfare Board for women were in the ambit of social welfare. Thus, social welfare measures were undertaken in the context of women merely because of their weak physiological, economic and social position.

When we started having a closer look at our welfare and development programmes, particularly in the context of weaker sections, it was found that primarily the poverty is the consequence as well as cause of several factors that limit life. It was also found that poverty induced cycle impinges hardest on women, which leads to a chain of consequences such as infection, nutritional deficiency, ill-health, slow learning, small body size, repeated child bearing, unpaid and unorganized work, low earning capacity, and unemployment which in turn perpetuates poverty. In this life cycle the matters like girl's education, gender bias, food, security, safe environment, safe motherhood, vocational training, support services to save energy and time, employment opportunities, etc., were perceived as the areas concerning women.

Shift from Social Welfare to Development

There was, however, a shift from welfarism for the weaker and down-trodden to development approach. Self-reliance of the so-called welfare beneficiaries became the motto of development. Provision of basic social service coupled with income-generation and employment were the other hallmarks of the development process. Another prominent trend was the shift from clubbing various categories of destitute and handicapped persons together on doles to classifying them on the basis of special needs of persons with reference to age, sex, physical and mental conditions, etc. Thus beginning in the Fifth Five Year Plan, the social development plan divided itself into various sub-sectors—welfare and development of children, development of youth, women development, etc.

Recognizing the peculiar situation in which the Indian women are placed because of the historical reasons and their physiological and economic conditions, women's development has become a priority area in the development plans. The bifurcation of the Ministry of Social Welfare into Department of Women and Child Development and Ministry of Welfare was based on the clear demarcation perceived by the planners between welfare and development. One other reason for introducing the concept of development has been the emphasis laid on women's participation in development because of their sheer number. Their number is also having certain political connotations in as much as no political party can afford to ignore this big chunk of population.

Empowerment Approach

The empowerment approach considered women's improved condition and position to be ends in themselves rather than only a means to broader development goals. Unlike the equity approach, this approach focused on meeting women's strategic needs through a bottom-up self-reliant endeavour. Empowerment can be considered as a change in the context of a woman or man's life that enables her/him increased capacity to lead a human life, fulfilling characterized by external qualities such as health, mobility, education and awareness, status in the family, participation in decision-making, and level of material, security, as well as internal qualities such as self-awareness and self-confidence.[21] It entails greater access to knowledge and resources, greater autonomy in decision making to enable them to have greater ability to plan their lives or have greater control over the circumstances that influence their lives. Empowering women necessitates transforming and restructuring of society to ensure equity and social justice through eradication of all customs and prejudices that stand in the way of unrestricted enjoyment of human rights by all.

Studies on Women Issues

The studies on women particularly in India, were scant up to the declaration of International Women's Year, 1975. This declaration had given an inspiration to governments, academic bodies and individual researchers to take up research work on the issues pertaining to women. As a result, several studies had appeared with regard to her status in the family as well as in the society, her level of education, health, employment and her place in the political field. A brief review of literature on women issues is made in this section of the chapter.

"Education of Women in India" written by Lakshmi Mishra provides the necessary historical data regarding the growth of women's education during the period 1921-66, an eventful period for women's education.[22] This book also gives us the background materials on the conditions and forces that influenced the education of women before 1921. There is also a detailed statistical account of the progress of education for women. It also touches on the contemporary forces moulding women's education.

The book, Status of Women in India, by H.C. Upadhyay depicts various patterns of women's struggles against the age-old discrimination. It also covers the development of women's movement in every part of the country. The writer exposes that women are not only economically dependent but also politically powerless.[23] He concludes that all the rights guaranteed by the constitution have benefited very small section of women.

Harshad Trivedi's work on Scheduled Caste Women seeks to study the status of women with reference to ignorance, poverty and superstitution and deals specifically with data collected from a few states.[24] It focuses on the exploitation of the scheduled caste women for prostitution. Among other things the status of women and the economic and occupational life of the family are covered and the book provides a comparative assessment of the change in status of scheduled caste women.

In the book, The Position of Women in Hindu Civilization, Altekar examines the history of women, their status and position in India while tracing the changes in their position, power and status in the course of time.[25] The writer opines that at one stage women did enjoy considerable freedom and privileges in both the family and society. However, gradually their position has been adversely reversed.

Gail Omvedt, in the book, We Will Smash This Prison, explains the awakening of women's movement in India, concentrated particularly in the state of Maharashtra. The book is a first person account of a feminist activist.[26] Gail Omvedt emphasizes that women's oppression is due to acute poverty and certain social issues like caste system, which affect the whole community. According to the writer, due to these factors women are denied access to resources.

Vina Majumdar's edited volume on "Symbols of Power" is a collection of research studies on the political status of women in India.[27] The book helps to shatter some of the comfortable myths regarding the status of women in Indian society and shows that the fact that women have been granted formal political rights and that quite a few of them are occupying positions of power tends to cover the stark reality of the situation of gender injustice. The essays include an analysis of women's participation in the electoral process of the country and the politicalisation of women in India.

Devaki Jain describes in her book, "Women's Quest for Power", the growing awareness of women and provides as much as five detailed examples of women's efforts to organize, participate and vocalize their demands for better food, clothing and shelter.[28] This is an excellent documentation of women-oriented development projects. The experiences presented, analysed and evaluated are useful for debates on the role of women in the development process.

The two studies of Rekha Mehra and Saradamoni in their book, "Women and Rural Transformation," provide a critical view of rural development programmes and planned policies for social and legal change.[29] Both the studies start with the premise that the policies for rural development and other social and legal changes, necessary for the take-off stage of development are invariably based on middle class male criteria. In operation, therefore, the policies fall to effect any change in the socio-economic lives of the women, or when it does so, it is for the worse.

The volume of Kalpana Shah attempts to understand the working of the Akhil Hind Mahila Parishad, one of the important voluntary organisations of the country.[30] At a larger level the author gives an analysis of the relationship between ideologies, leadership and programmes of the women's movement. She further examines the central issues of development and explains how the welfare programme undertaken by a middle class women's movement unwittingly strengthens the traditional image of women and, therefore, performs a very restricted and perhaps even a regressive role.

Gita Sen and Caren Grown discuss the major issues of development, social and economic crisis from the vantage point of the poor and oppressed women.[31] The writers present an argument that women are socially disadvantaged in most of the societies and women even carry the additional burden imposed by gender inequality. Their book also focuses on the built-in inequalities of a patriarchal society and women's economic deprivations were aggravated by the colonial system. The writers even try to explain how social norms restrict women's movements in the society. The book also points out how the present global economic and political crisis acutely affected women in the third world countries.

The monograph of Neera Desai and Vibhuti Patel is a country-wide report on the impact of the International Decade for Women on the Indian women with the view of examining the achievements and limitations.[32] It takes into consideration the various aspects of Indian women like their lives, status and struggles; and studies with reference to the changing socio-economic and political reality. It critically reviews the demographic, employment and unemployment situation, socio-cultural and mass media and critically evaluate the policies and programmes of development for the welfare of women. It also examines the various trends of women's groups and organisations.

The anthology of articles on women's oppression, patterns and perspectives, by Susheela Kaushik, deals with the political concepts and values like democracy, equality, social justice and some institutions like authority and private property because they are interrelated with the plight of women in India.[33] It is an attempt to subject the empirical studies on women to academic scrutiny, which would ultimately help to reach a general theoretical perspective on the question of women.

Leela Dube and Rajini Parliwala focus in their volume on living conditions of working women in different countries of Asia.[34] The book gives an analysis of household family and kinship while examining the productive and reproductive work of women. However, irrespective of the stage of economic development in different countries of Asia, she assumes that patriarchy is the structure underlying the subordination of women.

Neera Desai and Maithreyi Krishna Raj in their comprehensive study of women and society of India from a feminist perspective, underline the way the major social change in the society has affected women's position, especially in the development process and interaction with the pre-existing social structure.[35] They explain the position of the women through explanations of the historical, socio-economic and politico-cultural factors that are at work in society and the influence that religion, caste and a dominant patriarchal family have exerted on second sex. The book also depicts the interaction between the patriarchal structure and emergence of industrial capitalism within a given economic order. An in-depth study is made pertaining to the economic structure and women's role in it, the educational system and its biases, family and its role in controlling women's fertility, sexuality and individuality. The book also seeks to define the subjection of women in Indian milieu.

In his book, "Women's Quest for Economic Equality", Victor R. Fuchs explains that women's weaker economic position results primarily from conflicts between career and family, conflicts that are stronger for women than for men.[36] Fuchs assembles different kinds of evidences to suggest that, an average woman feels a stronger desire for children than men do, and have a great concern for their welfare after they are born. This desire and concern create an economic disadvantage for women, even women who never marry and never have children in future. In his masterful conclusion, Fuchs ponders over the future of women's quest, describing four possible scenarios showing why the decisions that individuals-women and men-make with respect to work, marriage, fertility and children affect the entire society. He argues that the country must explicitly and vigorously attack gender inequality.

Indu Prakash Singh, in her book "Indian Women: The Power Trapped", attempts to categorize the gruesome oppression which Indian women encounter in five different ways.[37] This categorization of oppression or victimization of women is necessary to understand the problem besetting Indian women and not to get bewildered in the maze of it. The book also creates new concepts like feminicidealisation, femistigamatisation among many others to grapple with the dynamics of patriarchy. The book highlights the crucial role women played in the chequered history of ours. It also focuses on the plight of girl child, victims of prostitution, rape, dowry, state violence and intrigue, child marriage, bigamous marriage, social directorship, etc. As a solution to the oppression of women, hopes are pinned on the enlightened women and men. It exhorts them to attack the problem before it is too late.

The edited volume of R.B. Mishra and Chandrapal Singh explains changing attitudes, values, behavior patterns and economic changes witnessed by Indian women in general.[38] It also encompasses numerous problems such as depressed conditions, exploitation, injustice and other related problems of daily life, which Indian women are experiencing today, in spite of different measures and steps taken in regard to their development. The book also focuses on fluctuating situations in which Indian women of today are living.

The book on NGOs and Women's Development is the outcome of Vanitha Viswanath's field research conducted during the period of 1986-87 in the state of Karnataka.[39] It is a comparative analysis of two rural development NGOs namely, India Development Service (IDS) and Gram Vikas (GV). The author collected the information and data for this book through participant observation techniques, unstructured interviews with individual women and also from group meetings.

The study of Kiran Devendra on the changing status of women examines the role assigned to them by tradition, religion and law and the stage of economic development.[40] A review has been made of their participation in the freedom movement leading to their partial emancipation after the independence of India and later the gradual removal of constraints which impeded a more forthcoming role on the part of Hindu women. The present study concentrates on the changing status of Hindu women in response to various governmental enactments promulgated in accordance with the demands of the small but important urban-educated female social group as a pioneering force.

O.P. Ralhan has made an attempt to expose the position of Indian women through ages in his five volumes.[41] Ralhan opined that it is a march towards progress in every sphere of their lives in the present day society. The different volumes of the book deal with Mahatma Gandhi and women, Indian political leaders and women, women and modernity and eminent Indian women in politics. The volume cover how women in India have participated in day-to-day national activity. The pages in these volumes have recorded how a woman played her role in the formation of the society.

R.K. Tandon, in his book "Status of Women in Contemporary World" has tried to explore the status in terms of a role, or the pattern or behavior expected of the occupant of the status—the woman.[42] He has made a review of some of the developed, developing and under-developed countries in terms of the position occupied by women in different social structures.

The book, Women and Social Order: A Profile of Major Indicators and Determinants, by Sarala Ranganathan, tries to provide useful insights into the position of women *vis-a-vis* the interaction they experience in the workplace.[43] She explains that the many forms of repression and subjugation of women have been the result of the male dominated social order. The parameters of the status and standing of women are defined to a large extent by the social mores and sociological trends of the day. The materials brought together in the present publication serve to indicate in meaningful terms, the indicators and determinants of women and the prevailing social order. The selected articles, papers, essays, reviews and the excerpts have for their subject a wide range of issues that concern the women.

In her book on "Women in Medieval Times" Padma analyses their position and status in the society from 11th to 14th centuries A.D. An attempt is also made at the history of Medieval Andhra from a gender perspective to understand the position of women in a better way.[44] In this anthology of Andhra Pradesh, different aspects of women like marriage and polity, education, property rights, women in performing arts, women and the temple and ornamentation of the period are discussed thoroughly.

Mira Seth compiled tremendous data in her book on women and development.[45] She analyzes various issues such as historical position of women in Indian society, women development policy and planning, etc. Special attention has been devoted to the problems and issues relating to girl child, women's health, education and employment.

Usha Sharma in her book on "Women's Emancipation" explains how family planning across the globe has undermined public health care and maternal and child health in many countries.[46] She tries to suggest that the solution to this crisis does not lie in narrow quantitative approaches to population size and natural resources that lead to wiping out poor women of colour and their children. The solution to current dilemmas calls for emancipation of women by providing them proper places in the society. The case is argued on the grounds that modern family planning programmes have rarely given women genuine choices, control over their bodies or a sense of self-empowerment.

Vijay Sharma in her book "Protection to Women in Matrimonial Home", discusses, analyzes and debates the issues relating to the status, position and protection of women in her matrimonial home.[47]

The Book of Susmita Chandra on "Women and Economic Development" provides an in depth analysis and study of the role of women in economic development at national as well as state levels.[48] It also presents a new dimension to the concept of development by giving emphasis on real or human development rather than the concept of mere development and opens avenues for further research in the field of women studies.

The book of Anju Bhatia is a comprehensive study on the functioning of NGOs in one of the most under-developed districts of India.[49] Probably the first of its kind, the study brings out in detail various aspects of the functioning of NGOs, profiles and portrays the psyche of their personnel and also presents the views and opinions of their beneficiaries.

The international community has also constructed brick by brick a comprehensive information and data base on the status of women world-wide.[50] The multilateral agencies of the UN system, the inter-governmental and non-governmental organizations, the media and the academic have all pooled their intellectual resources to produce global statistics on very aspect of women's lives in their national scene.

There also appeared many other works, dealing with one or other aspect of women and they are good in their own way, but there is hardly any work done dealing exclusively with the governmental machinery and the changes it brought about in the daily life of Indian women and the family and affecting their status within society. The present work attempts not only to fill this gap but also to examine institutional mechanism engaged in women development and its role in women development.

Objectives of the Study

Women all over the world are a handicapped and exploited section. The poverty and extreme discrimination in India add a sharper edge to the overall problems of women. The investigations of the Committee on the Status of Women in India had revealed that large masses of women in this country had remained unaffected by the rights guaranteed to them by the constitution and the laws enacted since independence.[51] The development and welfare of women requires, removal of certain obstacles and provision of certain facilities if women are to overcome the disadvantageous situation. The systematic efforts are now made in India for redistribution of wealth and of welfare services to the weaker and backward sections of society including women. The machinery of government is being used extensively for this purpose. A review of the administration of women welfare and development programmes in India also indicates that there is an organizational network to provide welfare services for women in a sustained manner.

The UNO observation on the eve of IWY that the administrative machinery is not adequate for the emancipation of women. The success of any women development programme significantly lies with the ability of organisations to uplift the status of women. Hence, the present study has been undertaken to fill-up the gap in the existing literature and to examine the role and function of governmental machinery in women's development. The main objectives of the present study are as follows:

1. To examine the social, economic and political status of women in India;
2. To examine the women development policies and programmes;
3. To identify the women development organizations and the women development programmes being undertaken by them;
4. To determine the contribution made by governmental organizations in the field of women development;
5. To study the structure of the women development organizations in terms of governing body, staffing pattern, qualifications and professional skills of staff, etc.;
6. To study whether the women development organizations have been able to play a catalytic role in reaching out to women by forming linkages and collaborative mechanisms with other agencies;
7. To analysis the problems and constraints faced by women development organizations as implementing agencies;
8. To ascertain the views of the officials on the working of governmental organizations engaged in women development; and
9. To ascertain the views of beneficiaries on various women development programmes and their implementation by governmental organizations.

Research Methodology

Different methods have been employed to collect the required data pertaining to the study. The secondary data have been collected from the libraries of Indian Institute of Public Administration, New Delhi, National Institute of Rural Development, Hyderabad, Osmania University, Hyderabad, Kakatiya University, Warangal and Acharya Nagarjuna University, Guntur. The main source is, however, the main library of Andhra University and the library of the Centre for Women Studies of Andhra University.

The primary data have been collected by both formal and informal techniques. Two structured interview schedules have been made use of for the purpose of collecting the data. To pursue the objectives of the present study, four governmental organisations working for the development of women in the district of Visakhapatnam in Andhra Pradesh had been selected. The information on governmental organizations engaged in women development and their programmes in the district has been collected. Any assessment of an organisation's success on achieving its goal would require information about the structure of the organisation and its administrative set-up. Therefore, in this study, a priority has been given to understanding the structure and the functional potential of the organisation. The major indicators considered for analysis are the size of the staff, job tenure, resource management, and the mechanism of programme implementation. Details about these and the other quantitative aspects of the programmes as to the scope and coverage, number of beneficiaries, budget, etc. were gathered from official publications of the governmental organisations and the records maintained by the selected organisations. The interview schedule for officials has been administered to the officials of the government organisations engaged in women development in the district. In all, 52 officers of the District Women and Child Development Agency, District Rural Development Agency, District Scheduled Castes Co-operative Service Society and District Backward Classes Co-operative Society were interviewed. The interview schedule on beneficiaries of women development programmes of these four organisations has been administered to 425 beneficiaries. The purpose was to determine the relevance, utility and value of the programmes and the working of governmental organisations in the opinion of the respondents.

The choice of the sample from the target population proved to be a difficult task. Firstly, the number of beneficiaries and clientele of the programmes is very large. Secondly, the organisations do not maintain regular records about their clients. Thirdly, clientele groups varied from one programme to the other. Finally, the target population and actual beneficiaries are scattered and dispersed all over the district. These factors compelled and restricted the interviews to those available and obliging. Hence, accessibility of the respondent was the main criteria in determining the sample.

Plan of the Study

This study has been divided into seven chapters. The first chapter "Introduction" covers the statement of the problem, objectives of the study and research methodology. The research methodology covers the methods of data collection and scope of the study. A review of literature on women issues has been included in this Chapter.

Second Chapter deals with the status of women in India. It deals with two aspects. One is the status of women during ancient, medieval and modern periods and the other is present status of women. An analysis of education, health, employment and political empowerment of women has been done.

Chapter three signifies the women development policies and programmes. Chapter four refers to the institutional mechanism for women development at all the three levels, i.e. central, state and district levels. Chapter five deals with the governmental organisations engaged in women development in Visakhapatnam district. The organisational structure, infrastructural facilities, personnel, and functions of women development organisations have been examined in this chapter. The women development programmes implemented by them in the district have also been examined in this Chapter. The opinions of the officials on their organisations and women development programmes have been analysed in Chapter six. The field data on sample beneficiaries' responses have been analysed in the same Chapter. Chapter seven gives a summary of the findings. The concluding remarks are also made in this chapter.

NOTES AND REFERENCES

1. H.C. Upreti, "Role of Rural Women in Development; Some Structural and Cultural Constraints", *Report of the Seminar on Role of Rural Women in Development*, NIPCCD, New Delhi, 1988, p. 93.
2. J. Bhagyalakshmi, "Women's Empowerment; Miles To Go", *Yojana*, Vol. 48, No. 10, August, 2004, p. 38.
3. V. Tomsic, "Policy of Non-Alignment Struggle for the NIEO and the Role of Women in Development", paper presented at Golden Jubilee symposium on Women, Work and Society, I.S.I., New Delhi, 1982, pp. 5-6.
4. Krishna Ahooja Patel, *Women and Sustainable Development: An International Dimension*, Ashish Publishing House, New Delhi, 1995, p. 39.
5. United Nations Department of Public Information, The *Beijing Declaration and Platform for Action*, New Delhi, 1995.
6. United Nations Division for the Advancement of Women, *Beijing Plus Five Draft Political Declaration*, 1999.
7. His Majesty's Government of Nepal, *Beijing Plus Five Country Report*, Kathmandu, 1999.
8. S. Sita Lakshmi and K. Thangamani, "Organisational Support for Rural Women", *Report of the Seminar on Role of Rural Women in Development*, NIPCCD, New Delhi, 1988, p. 119.
9. Maya Ghosh, "Human Face of Indian Women: A Policy Approach towards correcting imbalance", *Administrative Change*, Vol. XXXII, No. 2, Vol. XXXIII, No. 1, January-December, 2005, p. 87.
10. G. Narayana Reddy, *Women and Child Development: Some Contemporary Issues*, Chugh Publicaitons, Allahabad, 1987, p. 40.
11. Robins Sherman, and Davis Kemal, "Income Distribution and Socio-Economic Mobility", *Journal of Development Studies*, Vol. 13, No. 4, 1977.
12. Phillip Klein, "An Institutionalist View of Development Economics", *Journal of Economic Issues*, Vol. XI, No. 4, 1979.
13. Maithreyi Krishna Raj, *Women and Development: The Indian Experience*, Subhadra Prakashan, Bombay, 1988, p. 16.
14. David Colman and Frederick Nixon, *Economics of Change in Less Developed Countries*, Halstead Press, John Wiley and Sons, New York, 1978.
15. Michael M. Cernea, *Putting People for Sociological Variables in Rural Development*, Oxford University Press, New York, 1985.
16. United Nations Development Programme, *Human Development Report, 1995*, Oxford University Press, Bombay, p. 29.
17. R.L. Sivard, *Women—A World Survey: World Priorities*, Washington, D.C., U.S.A., 1985.
18. Irene Tinker and B.O. Bramsen, (eds.), *Women and World Development*, Overseas Development Council, U.S.A., 1972.

19. Sakuntala Narasimhan, *Empowering Women: An Alternative Strategy for Rural India*, Sage Publications, New Delhi, 1999, p. 17.
20. Paul D. Chowdhry, *Women Welfare and Development*, Inter-India Publications, New Delhi, 1992, p. 134.
21. B. Ackerley, "Testing the Tools of Development Credit Programmes: Loan Involvement and Women's Empowerment", *IDS Bulletion*, Vol. 26, No. 3, 1995, pp. 56-57.
22. Lakshmi Mishra, *Education of Women in India, 1921-66*, Macmillan, Bombay, 1966.
23. H.C. Upadhyay, *Status of Women in India*, Anmol Publications, New Delhi, 1977.
24. Harshad Trivedi, *Scheduled Caste Women: Studies in Exploitation*, Concept Publishing Company, New Delhi, 1977.
25. A.S. Altekar, *The Position of Women in Hindu Civilization*, Motilal Banarsidas, Delhi, 1978.
26. Gail Omvedt, *We Will Smash This Prison*, Orient Longman, New Delhi, 1979.
27. Vina Majumdar (ed.), *Women in Changing Society*, Allied Publishers, Bombay, 1979.
28. Devaki Jain, *Women's Quest for Power: Five Case Studies*, Vikas Publishsing House, New Delhi, 1980.
29. Rekha Mehra and K. Saradamoni, *Women and Rural Transformation*, Concept Publishing Company, New Delhi, 1983.
30. Kalpana Shah, *Women Liberation and Voluntary Action*, Ajanta Publications, New Delhi, 1984.
31. Gita Sen and Caren Grown, *Development Crisis and Alternative Vision: The Third World Women's Perspectives*, Institute of Social Studies Trust, New Delhi, 1984.
32. Neera Desai and Vibhuti Patel, *Indian Women: Change and Challenge in the International Decade 1975-85*, Popular Prakashan, Bombay, 1985.
33. Suseela Kaushik (ed.), *Women's Oppression, Patterns and Perspectives*, Vikas Publishing House, New Delhi, 1989.
34. Leela Dube and Rajini Parliwala (ed.), *Women and Household in Asia: Structures and Strategies—women, work and family*, Oxford University Press, London, 1986.
35. Neera Desai and Maithreyi Krishna Raj, *Women and Society in India*, Ajantha Publications, Delhi, 1987.
36. Victor R. Fuchs., *Women's Quest for Economic Equality*, Harward University Press, London, 1988.
37. Indu Prakash Singh, *Indian Women—The Power Trapped*, Galaxy Publications, New Delhi, 1991.
38. R.B. Mishra and Chandrapal Singh (eds.), *Indian Women: Challenges and Change*, Commonwealth Publishers, New Delhi, 1992.
39. Vanitha Viswanath, *NGO's and Women's Development in Rural South*

India: A Comparative Analysis, Vistaar Publications, New Delhi, 1993.

40. Kiran Devendra, *Changing Status of Women in India*, Vikas Publishing House, New Delhi, 1994.
41. O.P. Ralhan (ed.), *Indian Women Through Ages*, Anmol Publications, New Delhi, 1995.
42. R.K. Tandon, *Status of Women in Contemporary World*, Commonwealth Publications, New Delhi, 1998.
43. Sarala Ranganathan, *Women and Social Order: A Profile of Major Indicators and Determinants*, Kaushik Publishers, New Delhi, 1998.
44. A. Padma, *Women in Medieval Times*, G.V. Graphics, Hyderabad, 2001.
45. Mira Seth, *Women and Development: The Indian Experience*, Sage Publications, New Delhi, 2001.
46. Usha Sharma, *Women's Emancipation: Rights* Vs. *Population Control*, Authors Press, Delhi, 2001.
47. Vijay Sharma, *Protection to Women in Matrimonial Home*, Deep & Deep Publications, New Delhi, 1994.
48. Susmita Chandra, *Women and Economic Development: A Case Study of U.P.*, B.R. Publishing Corporation, Delhi, 2001.
49. Anju Bhatia, *Women's Development and NGOs*, Rawat Publications, New Delhi, 2000.
50. United Nations, *World's Women: Trends and Data, 1970-90*, New York, 1990.
51. Government of India, *Towards Equality: Report of the Committee on the Status of Women in India*, Ministry of Education and Social Welfare, New Delhi, 1975.

Status of Indian Women

In the context of women's development, one has to keep in mind the past and the present status of women. The status of women in any society is determined by the interplay of various socio-economic factors. Some of these may be 'objective' in nature like education, employment, income, etc. or 'subjective' depending on the social values prevailing in the society.[1] The status of women in India has changed from time to time. Their position has been variously estimated and diametrically opposite views are held regarding her place in different stages of civilization. The utility of women in domestic life, company and affectionate care of children have always proved a great asset to her partner in life and have, to a considerable extent, determined her status at different stages of civilization. The status of women in our country is culture, region and age specific.[2]

In this chapter an attempt is made to present contemporary position of women in India. In order to have a better understanding of the present social structure and position of women therein, it is imperative to know the operation of various historical, political, cultural and economic factors moulding the society. Indian history, as much as history of other nations, indicates a dismal picture as also conflicting situations in regard to the status of women.[3] And such an historical perspective is all the more necessary in the case of a society with a continuous history of more than three thousand years. The present chapter has been divided into three very broad periods. They are:

1. Ancient and Medieval India,
2. Colonial India, and
3. Independent India.

ANCIENT AND MEDIEVAL INDIA

The norms and values, class or caste base of Indian society provide a fundamental structural context for understanding women's status. Hence, a brief description of these norms and values is given before the description of the position of women in ancient and medieval India.

Norms and Values

The Indian society like a number of classical societies was patriarchal. The patriarchal values regulating sexuality, reproduction and social production (meaning total conditions of production) prevailed and were expressed through specific cultural metaphors. Overt rules prohibiting women from specific activities and denying certain rights did exist. But more subtle expression of patriarchy was through symbolism giving messages of inferiority of women through legends highlighting the self-sacrificing, self-effecting pure image of women and through the ritual practices which day in and day out emphasized the dominant role of a woman as a faithful wife and devout mother.

The basic rules for women's behaviour as expressed in the Laws of Manu insist that a woman must constantly worship her husband as a god, even though he is destitute of virtue or a womaniser. The women should be kept in dependency by her husband because by nature they are passionate and disloyal. The ideal women are those who do not strive to break these bonds of control. The salvation and happiness of women revolve around their virtue and chastity as daughters, wives and widows.

In India, for centuries, women have been pushed aside from the race of development in the name of customs, traditions and religion. As a result, they have been denied the opportunities for their social, economic and political development leading to a lower status in society.[4] The social customs, religiously sanctioned rituals, the authoritarian structure of the family organisation, the accepted mode of socialization of young girls and the very rigidly defined roles and activities of women have contributed to the social degradation of women in the Indian society.

Caste System

In order to properly estimate the position of women in ancient society, a brief reference to the stratificatory system as expressed through varna and caste system is also necessary. The varna principle of categorisation of society into four groups, viz., Brahmans, Kshatriyas, Vaishyas and Shudras existed in vedic society. The features of the caste system have direct relevance to women. Features like caste endogamy as a mechanism of recruiting and retaining control over the labour and sexuality of women, concepts of purity and pollution segregating groups and also regulating mobility of women are very crucial. The concept of anuloma and pratiloma marriages by definition denigrate women. A marriage where a boy of upper caste marries a girl of lower caste is approved and called anuloma while marriages of women of ritually pure groups with men of lower ritual status were considered pratiloma. Most serious punishments like excommunication and even death could be evoked for transgressing the norms.

The other very important feature of the caste system is its control over women's labour. Caste not only determines social division of labour but also sexual division of labour. Certain tasks have to be performed by women while certain other tasks are meant for men. In agriculture, for instance, women can engage themselves in water-regulation, transplanting, weeding, but not in ploughing. With upward mobility of the group, women are immediately withdrawn from the outside work. Physical mobility is also restricted through caste norms.

The linking of women and shudras together is one more evidence of the low position of women. Prescriptions and prohibitions for shudra and woman were the same on many occasions. The prohibition of the sacred thread ceremony for both women and shudras, similar punishment for killing a shudra or a woman, denial of religious privileges, etc. are some of the illustrations which indicates how caste and gender get entrenched.[5] In short, the caste system not only provided a legitimisation to feudal relation of production but ideologically also provided justification for the subordination of women. The growth of a class society, which manifested itself in the form of varnas and the decline in position of women have occurred simultaneously.

Vedic Age

In the vedic age the women were highly esteemed and they enjoyed equal socio-cultural status. The early Rigvedas mentioned of women as equals who participated in all the household activities related both to social and economic spheres. No important function could be performed by man alone. Man was considered incomplete without the woman in those days. The women had the rights to read and recite the vedas and other sacred as well as secular texts. Several of them played very important roles in the formulation of social policies and code of conduct. Maitrayee, Gargi and Leelavati were not only highly learned women, they were equally well versed in higher mathematic astronomy and the humanities. Women were eulogized in the hymns. Feminine deities like Saraswati, Kali, Lakshmi, Durga are worshipped even today. Woman was regarded as the base of all power or 'shakti'. Many traditions and customs which persist even today bear evidence of such exalted status of women in the past.

However, in the later vedic period, the status of women underwent significant changes. Degeneration on society brought about many social evils. The women were deprived of the status that was once enjoyed by them. Equality of socio-cultural opportunities to express themselves was also denied. The birth of a daughter, which was not source of anxiety during the vedic period, became a source of disaster for the father during the post-vedic phase. Thus, it was said that the birth of a son is bliss incarnate, while that of a daughter is the root of family misery. Education of women, which was an accepted norm during the vedic period, slowly began to be neglected and later on girls were totally denied any access to-education. Upanayana or the sacred thread ceremony, which was performed to initiate a person into the vedic studies, was prohibited in the case of women and shudras by the Manu codes, thus closing the doors for many formal education to women. By circa 8th century AD the marriageable age for girls was lowered to 9 to 10 years, which gave a final blow to any effort at educating women.

In one of Manu's codes, it has been mentioned, "Be a girl or be a young woman or be advanced in years, nothing must be done even in her own dwelling place according to her pleasure. Again Manu says, she should do nothing independently even in her own house. In childhood, she is subjected to her father, in youth to her husband and during her widowhood to her sons; she should never enjoy independence. Awesome practices of sati, female infanticide, child marriage, parda and suppression of widows got ultimately accepted as the cherished norms of the society. Thus, a woman become subordinate and subservient to man.

The heterodox religions like Jainism and Buddhism which sprang up challenging the Brahmanical (vedic orthodox) religion, too were based on the philosophy of avoidance of materialism. Women were regarded as a part of materialism, as both Gautam and Mahavir discarded their wives Yashodhara and Yashoda, respectively, and children in their so called pursuit for 'Truth'. Moreover, nuns in both these religions were second to the male monks. They walked behind the monks in processions and were not given any position of authority. Amongst the Jains, even today the nuns outnumber the monks but still women play a second fiddle to the monks. The nuns who are joining this religion do so not because of any religious conviction and faith but compulsion. As dowry is every high amongst Jains not many parents can marry off their daughters. Religion comes handy, by accepting them as nuns as it cannot provide a "dignified" life outside its confines.[6]

Another liberal current to which to some extent widened the horizon for women was the Bhakti movement—the medieval saints movement. The saints emphasised salvation through devotion to a deity, wherein no intermediary such as a pandit or a purohit was required. The Bhaktas vehemently attacked ritualism and overlordship of the Brahmans, used the vernacular as a language of communication and opened the gates of religion for women. Not surprisingly it is the Bhakti movement which produced women saints like Meerabai and Lalla in the North, Andal and Akka Mahadevi in the South and Bahanabai in the West. As the movement did not basically challenge the unequal social structure and limited it only to individual salvation, it could not fundamentally affect gender subordination.

In conclusion, in the post-vedic period women's position in the society declined. Patriarchal values relating to sexuality and regulation of her movement, thus controlling her purity, got entrenched during this phase. A woman during this vast span not only occupied an inferior position but was made to feel that her position was subordinate to men in the society.

COLONIAL INDIA

In colonial India, imperial interests dictated economic policy and their impact in a gender—asymmetrical society descended with extra severity on women. After industrial revolution in England, the rulers turned India into a colony, which produced raw material for Britain. Industrial capitalism, transplanted on the Indian soil by the colonial rule, created major discontinuity for Indian economy. Women as major partners in the economic activities of the household lost out more than men as the occupations in which they were engaged declined drastically. Besides spinning and weaving women were involved in rice dehusking, selling milk and butter-ghee, marketing of vegetables and fish, rearing of silk worms to weaving and spinning silk, etc. The advent of rice mills in the 20th century led to mass displacement of women. Every mill displaced 500 hand pounders, while a huller displaced 40 workers. By 1824 with Bengal importing British yarn, millions of people were out of jobs, half of them being women.

The position of women was, however, improved during the British period because of two major movements. These were the Social Reform Movement of the nineteenth century and the Nationalist Movement of the 20th century. Both these movements raised the question of equal status of women.

The issues, which attracted the attention of the nineteenth century social reformers were Sati, the ill-treatment of widows, the ban on widow marriage, polygamy, child marriage, denial of property rights and education to women. The social reformers felt that these social evils should be eradicated by raising consciousness and making people sensitive to the injustice perpetrated on women. The social reformers reasoned that reform in the social position of women would reform the entire society.[7] It was argued that since the family was and is the basic unit of social organisation in India, the contribution of women to the stability of the family, and through it to society, was crucial.[8] Moreover, women had considerable influence on the socialization of children, and were central to child-rearing and housekeeping. Therefore, apart from influencing their own sphere of activity, they also influenced the sphere of male activity—mainly through ideas and values—which pertained to cultural transmission and provided support to the male. It was for this reason that they propagated the cause of women's education. They thought that by giving women the access to education and by enacting progressive legislation, social change could be initiated.

Another very powerful force, which helped change the position and attitude towards the women, was the Nationalist Movement particularly during the Gandhian phase. Gandhiji, apart from being a political leader was also a critic of some of the outmoded social institutions. He vehemently criticised the custom of child marriage, prohibition of widow remarriage, temple prostitution and the custom of purdah. He had immense faith in the woman's inner strength and her moral appeal. In the various satyagrahas which were launched, not only the upper class urban women participated but at many places simple unsophisticated rural women also assumed leadership.[9]

In short, the social reformers laid great stress on the education of women as a liberalising actively. Gandhiji also stressed the need for educating women. His call to women to join the political movement brought women out of their homes in large numbers from all parts of India and from varied backgrounds, and had a catalytic effect. The impression that had gained currency all over India was that Gandhiji was a social reformer with a special message for women. This is reflected in the manner in which Durgabai Deshmukh organised a meeting between Gandhiji and the local devadasis and Muslim women at Kakinada on 2nd April 1921. She was twelve years old then. She felt that if Gandhiji could only talk of these women they would become interested in changing their way of life and social customs. M.N. Srinivas contends that Gandhiji's success in attracting women to the political struggle was partly due to the confidence and respect he enjoyed among men.[10] The pre-independence period, thus, marked the beginning of awareness of the sufferings of women. During this phase a favourable climate was also created to improve the status of women through legal reforms. Many laws were enacted which tried to eradicate certain social evils. The act legalising remarriage of widows was passed as early as 1856. There were many other laws which were passed during 1920-40. To mention a few, the Child Marriage Restraint Act, popularly known as Sarda Act, prohibited marriages below the age of 14 years for a girl; The Hindu Women's Right to Property Act recognised women's right to property in joint family property. Besides the social legislation, there were other laws which affected women's work status, such as limiting hours of work in organised industries, prohibiting night work, restricting work in the mines, establishment of creches, etc.

INDEPENDENT INDIA

Women Status in Independent India

The independent India has seen tremendous functional changes in the status and position of women in Indian society. The Constitution of India has granted franchise to Indian women. This has brought women on an equal footing with men. The adult franchise has done much to remove sex discrimination. The Constitution has laid down as a fundamental right the equality of the sexes. But the record of decades after independence shows that we have progressively but unmistakably regressed from the position that we had attained.

There has been a differential impact of factors of change on different sections of women. This has further resulted in creating contradictory images of women. Middle-class educated women, particularly in large urban agglomerations, who are working and moving freely, generate an impression that Indian women's status has substantially improved. Moreover, there is evidence of capable, efficient, powerful women at times with political clout, which reinforces this impression. But in small towns or rural areas or in city slums, women still suffer social and economic oppression. In small towns and villages, upper caste women even today are confined to home bound activities and involved in responsibilities and interests limited only to their kith and kin. The growing instances of suffering socially and economically by women of scheduled castes and scheduled tribes generate despair, frustration and expose the inter-turning of caste, class and gender forces.

In general, education, employment, and political participation have been looked upon as enhancing women's status. This expectation is in keeping with the claims of the nineteenth century social reformers when they made appeals for educating women. Education was not merely expected to liberate a woman from some traditional values and customs but was also presumed to make her a willing partner in initiating and supporting social change. A somewhat similar pay-off has also been expected from voting rights, leading to access to deliberative processes in the political sphere. Thus, at different periods of time, education, franchise and employment are looked upon not merely, as significant in themselves but also steps towards achieving higher status for women. In the following pages, the present status of women in India in terms of sex-ratio, education, health, employment and political representation has been examined.

Sex Ratio

Sex composition of the human population is one of the basic demographic characteristics, which is extremely vital for any meaningful demographic analysis. Indian census has the tradition of bringing out disaggregated information by sex on various aspects of population. The first and foremost is the simple count of males and females. Changes in sex composition largely reflects the underlying socio-economic and cultural patterns of a society in different ways. Sex ratio, defined here as the number of females per 1000 males in the population, is an important social indicator to measure the extent of prevailing equity between males and females in a society at a given point of time. It is mainly the outcome of the interplay of sex differentials in mortality, sex selective migration, sex ratio at birth and at times the sex differential in population enumeration. The sex ratio of women in India is low. This is revealed through a study of the sex ratio existing in our country from 1901 onwards. In 1901, the sex ratio was 972 females for 1,000 men. This ratio has been continuously declining from 1901 onwards as seen from the following table.

TABLE 2.1

Sex Ratio (1901-2001)

Period	*Sex ratio (females per 1000 males)*
1901	972
1911	964
1921	955
1931	950
1941	945
1951	946
1961	941
1971	930
1981	933
1991	927
2001	933

Source: Census of India, 2001.

In 1951, there was a marginal increase of one point, but thereafter it again dropped for two consecutive decades to reach 930 in 1971. In fact, between 1961-71, the country saw the sharpest decline of 11 points in the sex ratio. Thereafter, it has fluctuated marginally around 930 in successive census.

TABLE 2.2

Sex Ratio of Total Population, 1991 and 2001

Sl.No.	*India/States/Union Territories**	*1991*	*2001*
	India	927	933
1.	Jammu & Kashmir	N.A.	900
2.	Himachal Pradesh	976	970
3.	Punjab	882	874
4.	Chandigarh*	790	773
5.	Uttaranchal	936	964
6.	Haryana	865	861
7.	Delhi*	827	821
8.	Rajasthan	910	922
9.	Uttar Pradesh	876	898

(Contd.)

Sl.No.	*India/States/Union Territories**	*1991*	*2001*
10.	Bihar	907	921
11.	Sikkim	878	875
12.	Arunachal Pradesh	859	901
13.	Nagaland	886	909
14.	Manipur	958	978
15.	Mizoram	921	938
16.	Tripura	945	950
17.	Meghalaya	955	975
18.	Assam	923	932
19.	West Bengal	917	934
20.	Jharkhand	922	941
21.	Orissa	971	972
22.	Chhattisgarh	985	990
23.	Madhya Pradesh	912	920
24.	Gujarat	934	921
25.	Daman & Diu*	969	709
26.	Dadra & Nagar Haveli*	952	811
27.	Maharashtra	934	922
28.	Andhra Pradesh	972	978
29.	Karnataka	960	964
30.	Goa	967	960
31.	Lakshadweep*	943	947
32.	Kerala	1,036	1,058
33.	Tamil Nadu	974	986
34.	Pondicherry*	979	1,001
35.	Andaman & Nicobar Islands*	818	846

Source: Census of India, 2001.

There are considerable variations from one state to another. The only state in which the sex ratio (proportion of females) is above 1000 is Kerala with a figure of 1,034. The states of Karnataka, Tamil Nadu, Andhra Pradesh, Orissa, Jammu & Kashmir and Himachal Pradesh have a sex ratio between 950 and 1,000, and all the rest are below 950. In other words, in most of the Northern and North-Eastern States, Haryana, Punjab, Uttar Pradesh, Assam, Nagaland, Sikkim and West Bengal males outnumber females by almost 10 per cent, in Andhra Pradesh and Karnataka 4 per cent and in Tamil Nadu and Orissa 2 per cent.

It may also be observed that strangely enough, the national sex ratio in rural areas is higher (938 females per 1,000 men) compared to the national urban average (894 females per 1,000 men). The rural sex ratios are better than that of the urban in spite of the fact that health facilities, especially in the private sector, are much better in the urban areas as compared to rural areas. The explanation for this seems to lie in migration of rural people to urban areas, especially the able bodied men who go in search of employment in the cities, leaving the women folk behind in their houses.

The development process of independent India at a pace never achieved before, have also not succeeded in stopping the decline of sex ratio. The incident of the poverty is not as important and determining a factor in the declining sex ratio as the mores of a predominant culture. High per capita incomes of Punjab and Haryana have not given them higher sex ratio.[11] In spite of the advances in medical sciences, the drop in death rate, the tremendous advances made in the eradiation of malaria and control of infectious diseases, like tuberculosis, as well as, increase in life expectancy for women, the sex ratios of our population continue to be adverse for women.

Several reasons are adduced to explain the consistently low levels of sex ratio and their further decline in the country. Some of the important reasons commonly put forward are listed below:

1. Neglect of the girl child resulting in their higher mortality at younger ages.
2. High maternal morality.
3. Sex selective female abortions.
4. Female infanticide.
5. Change in sex ratio at birth.

The imbalance in the number of males and females begins in the beginning. It is now a well established law of nature that the males exceed females at the time of birth. It is believed that generally 943-952 female births take place for every 1000 male births, which in effect would mean that there is a deficiency of about 50 females per 1000 males in every birth cohort. Many demographers believe that left on its own, this is an unalterable constant. The possibility of female foeticide or the existence of infanticide in some rare cases is also contributing to adverse female sex ratio.

The infant mortality rate is another factor that decides sex ratio. Though there is significant drop in infant mortality rates (IMR), largely due to the grand success of the Expanded Programme of Immunization started in 1978 and the universal immunization launched in 1985, which has succeeded in getting more than 85 per cent children immunized, the figures of girl child mortality are higher than boys. This factor contributes to the low sex ratio of women. This phenomenon can be attributed to the lower health care status of girl children, where delay often takes place in taking the girl child to the hospital, as also her lower nutrition status leading to poor health. A review of the status of the girl child indicates that it is the people's perception, in general, that the birth of a girl child is less desirable than that of a baby boy. It is ingrained in the Indian psyche, cutting across religious, caste and regional barriers, that the birth of a girl child evokes less happiness than that of a boy. If the first child born to the parents is a girl, she is less unwelcome than her subsequent sisters. The phenomenon of aborting female foetuses is occasionally resorted to in cities as well as in rural areas, if girl children are already present in a family. The passing of the Prevention and Regulation of Amniocentesis Act, 1993, has not been a great hindrance as doctors still use the procedure of ultrasonography to predict the sex of a foetus.

Education

Education is the heart of the development process. It is also an important instrument for attaining economic power and independence, for it opens of formal education attainment.[12] Education is an important input in the overall development of individuals enabling them to comprehend their social, political and cultural environment better and respond to it appropriately. Higher levels of education and literacy lead to a greater awareness and also contributes to the improvement of economic conditions. Improved levels of literacy is also one of the prerequisites for acquiring various skills.

Education develops the personality and rationality of individuals, qualifies them to fulfil certain economic, political and cultural functions and thereby improves their socio-economic status. It provides vertical mobility and can thereby help to equalise status between individuals coming from different social strata. The Universal Declaration of Human Rights regards education as one of the basic rights to every human being. As education is linked with the totality of the development process, several articles in the Indian Constitution emphasized certain key principles, which would underline the educational system in the country. The Directive Principles contained in Article 45 enjoined that the state shall endeavour to provide within a period of 10 years from the commencement of the Constitution, compulsory education for all children until they complete the age of 14 years.

Education is an important indicator of women's development. It is crucial for the country's development that we should have enlightened, educated and hence empowered women. The movement for improving women's status all over the world has always emphasized education as the most significant instrument for changing women's subjugated position in the society.

While education is essential for both boys and girls, the benefits of educating girls tend to be greater. Educated women pass on their knowledge to their peers and family members, particularly their daughters, thereby multiplying the effects of their education manifold.[13] Moreover, realising the importance or education, they also tend to assert that their daughters be educated also. There is a close and complex relationship among education, marriage age, fertility, mortality, mobility and activity. Women play a key role in the tasks of child-bearing and child-rearing and are the chief agents of socialization, particularly in the early formative years of a child, which contribute significantly to the healthy foundation of an efficient society. Education enhances a women's sense of her own health needs and perspectives and her power to make any health and family planning decisions. Education helps reduce child and maternal mortality and morbidity rates.

There is a clear link between higher literacy rates and lower infant mortality rates. This fall in infant mortality rates is more in higher female literacy states than in lower female literacy states. Studies by Dreze and Sen and Deolalikar show a clear correlation between women's educational status and infant and child morality.[14] Broader access to education is also a factor in internal migration and the composition of working population. In other words, the educational level of women is particularly important because educational attainment can affect age at marriage, reproductive behaviour, the use of contraceptives, the health and nutritional levels of the family, proper hygienic practices, migration trends and above all, their own status.

After independence, the Government of India appointed various commissions and committees to promote the cause of women's education. National Committee on Women Education regarded women's education as a major and a special issue.[15] It recommended that every state should be required to prepare comprehensive development plans for the education of girls and women in its area. According to the National Policy on Education, education should be used as an agent of basic change in the status of women.[16] The National Perspective Plan for Women's Education formulated some important objectives for women's education so that women may also participate in the area of social, cultural, economic, political and educational fields.[17]

As a result there is a phenomenal expansion of the formal educational system since independence. There has been noticeable progress in literacy rate of the general population. Literacy rate has increased from 18.33 per cent in 1951 to 65.38 per cent in 2001. Male literacy rate has increased from 27.16 per cent in 1951 to 75.85 per cent in 2001, whereas female literacy rate has increased from 8.86 per cent in 1951 to 54.16 per cent in 2001. There has been a continuous progress in total male and female literacy rates in the previous decades.[18] However, nearly 50 per cent of the female population is still steeped in ignorance and illteracy.[19] Women have been benefited much less from educational opportunities. The female literacy rate is low when compared to the literacy rate of males. The census-wise figures for literacy are given in the table 2.3.

The male-female combined literacy rate in 1901 was 5.39 per cent, the female literacy rate being only 0.63 per cent. Right up to the 1941 census, it had increased only up to 7.30 per cent, which was a little less than 50 per cent of the total literacy rate of 16.10. The gender gap works out to 100 per cent. Over the six census conducted in India since independence, the literacy rate for female

TABLE 2.3

Census-wise Literacy Rates: 1901-2001

Year of Census	*Total population (in lakhs)*	*Percentage of Literacy*		
		Male	*Female*	*Total*
1901	2,520.90	09.83	0.63	05.39
1911	2,513.20	10.56	1.05	5.92
1921	2,789.80	12.21	1.81	7.16
1931	3,186.60	15.59	2.93	9.50
1941	3,610.90	24.90	7.30	16.10
1951	4,392.30	27.16	8.86	18.33
1961	5,481.60	40.40	15.34	28.31
1971	6,833.30	45.95	21.97	34.45
1981	8,463.00	56.50	29.85	43.67
1991	8,463.00	64.13	39.29	52.51
2001	10,286.00	75.65	54.16	65.38

Source: Census Reports, Registrar-General and Commissioner, Census Operations, Government of India, New Delhi.

has increased from 8.86 (1951) to 54.16 (2001). The low female literacy rates bring down the total literacy rate of the country. In terms of sheer volume, although the number of literate women has increased from 155 lakh in 1951 to 2,250.41 lakh in 2001, we still have 1,895.55 lakh illiterate women. This is definitely the largest number of illiterate women existing in any country of the world. The efforts of the government to increase female literacy through formal and non-formal education has been tremendous. In spite of these gains we are still lagging behind in our achievements as compared to important developing countries.

There is a wide gap in the male-female literacy rates. The literacy rates for the country and the gap in male-female literacy rates are given in the Table 2.4.

If we look at the gap in male-female literacy rates it is understood that the gap has increased from 18.30 per cent in 1951 to 26.62 per cent in 1981, though the gap in male-female literacy rates is observed to be reducing from 1981, it still constitutes 21.70 per cent by 2001.

TABLE 2.4

Literacy Rate in India : 1951-2001

Census year	*Persons*	*Males*	*Females*	*Males-females gap in literacy rates*
1951	18.33	27.18	08.86	18.30
1961	28.30	40.40	15.35	25.05
1971	34.46	45.88	21.97	23.81
1981	43.57	56.38	29.76	26.62
1991	52.21	64.13	39.29	24.84
2001	65.38	75.85	54.16	21.70

Major Reasons for Low Literacy

Most parents believe that education is good for girls, but many parents especially among the poor do not send their daughters to school because these daughters are needed for agricultural and household production tasks as well as for domestic chores such as cooking and looking after younger siblings. In a poverty situation schooling is seen as a poor investment which provides no definite access to better employment.[20] One important social factor affecting girl's participation in education is early marriage. The availability of certain facilities will also affect the education of girls.

A survey sponsored by the Committee on the Status of Women in India revealed some significant attitudes to the education of girls. While a statement that girls should not be given any education at all was categorically rejected by the majority, many felt that higher education for girls depended on whether certain facilities are available such as more girls schools, more women teachers and nearness of schools to their homes, better transport and toilet facilities.[21] While the latest government document states that 95 per cent of the population is within a kilometre of a primary school and 80 per cent has the same facility as far as middle school is concerned, the same document admits the lack of vital facilities in schools such as potable water, buildings, blackboards and so on.[22] In the light of these facts, major reasons for low literacy rate among women are listed below:

1. Need for girls to help in the farms or family occupation or household chores or responsibility of looking after younger siblings.
2. High intensity of poverty and parents inability, to bear educational expenses.
3. Early marriage and dowry.
4. Lack of access to schools.
5. Shortage of women teachers.
6. Lack of infrastructure facilities which lead to low enrolment and large dropouts.

Health Status

Health is the basic factor that affects the physical and mental efficiency of human beings and acts as a reinforcing force for life. In the 30th World Health Assembly in 1977, it was decided that the main social goal of the governments and of the World Health Organisation should be the attainment by all the people of the world by the year 2000, of a level of health that will permit them to work productively and to participate actively in the social life of their community.[23]

Across much of Africa, Asia and Latin America, drastic population growth and poverty have contributed to extremely severe health problems that stand as an enormous obstacle to sustained development and social progress. Apart from the health problems in general, the gender biases in health are even more glaring. Gender focussed understanding of health problems becomes all the more important because women face specific health problems and their health concerns are often neglected, especially in developing countries like India, where health consciousness is very low among women.

It is vital for a woman's health and life that she has access to medical and health care needs for preventive, as well as curative health, so as to be able to play her full part in the development of this country. An important indicator of women's health is her life expectancy at birth. The available data, which traces life expectancy for men and women, indicate that women had lesser life expectancy than men up to 1971-81. It is only now that women have a slight edge over men. There is an increase in the life expectancy of women from 31.7 years in 1941-51 to 64.2 years in

1991-2001. This has been due to the multifaceted health initiatives taken by health agencies. It is a very significant achievement. The steeply declining death rates have contributed towards increasing life expectancy. However, India still has a long way to go to achieve the standards of the developed world and even to some important developing countries.

The women's health status is low during her optimal reproductive years. It is useful to understand how the institution of marriage affects this status. It is important to remember that throughout our cultural history, marriage has been considered as essential and even obligatory for women. The women could choose to remain unmarried during the *Rigvedic* Age and devote their lives to the pursuit and spread of learning. Overwhelming evidence, however, indicates that in spite of this choice they continued to marry. There were early marriages till the age of marriage for boys and girls was raised. Efforts to raise the age of marriage have borne fruit as it steadily rose from a low 13.1 in 1901 to 20.5 years in 1993.

The presence of anaemia among adolescent girls and adult women has very harmful effects on them during pregnancy. Many studies indicate that where maternal haemoglobin is below 11 grams per decilitre, there is significant rise in pre-natal mortality. Maternal immune depression and increase in morbidity due to infection have been reported in women with low haemoglobin levels of below 8 gm/dl.[24] They also give birth to low weight babies who have higher mortality rates. The national data seems to reveal a maternal mortality rate of 408 per 1,00,000 births.[25] The maternal mortality rates are higher in the 15-19 year age group for understandable reasons of low health status, lack of knowledge about pregnancy and related problems. The national data further show that 17 per cent of MMR deaths occur due to anaemia, 9.9 per cent due to toxaemia, bleeding occurs in 28.9 per cent cases, abortion in 17.6 per cent cases and the rest occur due to other causes. The maternal mortality rates of India are very high compared to the developing countries of the West and East Asia.

In India nearly 1,00,000 women die every year due to abortion and childbirth, a figure 100 times higher than in developed countries. Two-thirds of pregnant women in India are anaemic complications of pregnancy due to high fertility lead to many complications of pregnancy resulting in a high percentage of deaths. Pregnant women lose immunity to malaria and are most susceptible to viral infections. It also participates the development of overt leprosy and diabetes and childbirth triggers episodes of major psychiatric pathology. Besides maternal mortality deaths, a tremendous wastage of female reproductive energy occurs due to high rates of illegal abortions, neonatal, postnatal and prenatal mortality rates.

Women have also special occupational health hazards. Every woman is a working woman in India, whether she works at home or outside. The mental and physical health hazards are innumerable and varied. Most of them are concentrated in the informal sector where the nature of occupation exposes them to severe back pain as in rice planting, weaving, coir, jute, carpet-making, construction industry and cooking of food which is almost entirely the women's preserve. Respiratory diseases occur because of consumption of kitchen smoke while cooking, or due to the burning firewood, and during spinning and carpet making. Women are also exposed more to rheumatism through exposure to water and parasitic infections like malaria and insect bites through agricultural labour.

The changing patterns of economic development have put a heavy burden on women which is reflected in their health status. The growth of small and cottage industries do not come under the purview of any kind of safety legislation. Women work in industries like tanning, tobacco, cashew, coir, textiles, garment, fish processing and canning, etc. In all these industries, they toil to long hours at low paid, unskilled jobs. Low wages, long and erratic working hours and deplorable working environment, coupled with the several household and productive tasks have adverse effects on women's health. The scenario for women's health, though it has improved since independence as indicated by their longer life expectancy, is far from satisfactory. New initiatives and new funding has gone primarily into programmes concentrating on her maternal role. There is no concept of a life-long view of women's health. Health programmes for the girl child are minimal, and programmes to prepare her for young womanhood most inadequate. Young girls nutritional status is inferior compared to young boys and what is important is that even in spite of nutritional interventions for pregnant and lactating mothers through the ICDS, the actual percentage of such women taking advantage of this scheme is inadequate.

Recent trends in public and policy awareness about women's health needs and concerns, and actual access by women to the means and services to address those concerns show complex and contradictory tendencies. Although women became central targets of the family planning programme from the late 1960s, it is well known that their reproductive health needs were neither acknowledged as a policy concern nor set within an overall integrated approach to their health. The field of women's health in India was full of resounding policy and research silences, misdirected and partial approaches, and insufficient attention to critical issues.[26]

Problems of irregular bleeding and amenorrhoea were left unaddressed despite growing evidence of the prevalence of under- and mal-nutrition and iron deficiency anaemia among girls and women. The cross linkages between anaemia and vulnerability to malaria continued to be ignored by policy and programme. In a country, where abortion had been legal since the early 1970s, it continued to be unsafe for an over-whelming majority of those who needed the service.

Undoubtedly the weak policy and funding support that bedevilled public health infrastructure and services in this period was experienced most seriously by the poor and by women especially among the poor. Official statistics on illness shows that women in India tend to under-report illness. Records of the health care system, whether public or private, show that health services are availed at much less by women than by men.[27]

Women have been the major targets of family planning programmes. The family planning programmes are population control-oriented and do not place any emphasis on women's health and emotional and psychological welfare. They do not raise the status of women by reducing unwanted pregnancy but make them victims of experimentation and state policy. In sum, there is a deterioration in health condition of women and this is precisely what a declining sex-ratio indicates. The health services for women shall be improved so that there is a substantial change in their social status. Basic services such as routine ante-natal care

(ANC), post-natal care (PNC) infant care, immunisation and treatment of ailments should be delivered to all women.

Women Employment

The vital role of women in the Indian labour force and their contributions to the national economy have been established beyond doubt. Several committees have made recommendations regarding the employment of women. The Committee on the Status of Women had made far-reaching recommendations. It had suggested the development of training and employment programmes. Action plans were proposed to take care of promotion of self-employment for women as well as greater opportunities in other areas. Special training programmes were also considered. Action plans, developmental efforts and welfare services had led to the expansion of employment opportunities for women.

Gainful employment of women is identified as a major entry point in promoting their economic conditions. Realising this fact some young women entered the fields of industry, public service as well as business and are successful in these fields. For the last two decades women's work participation rate increased from 22.73 per cent in 1991 to 28.6 per cent during 2001. But the number of employed women is very less when compared with men. The Census of India 2001 statistics show that out of a total of 32.62 crores of economically active females population only 6.03 crores, i.e. 18.5 per cent is employed, whereas out of 34.97 crores of economically active males, 23.63 crores representing 67.6 per cent is employed in paid jobs. The employment of women in the different branches of the public sector and various government agencies indicates concentration of women in state government and local bodies. The share of employment of women in central government services is very low as compared to men. If we see women's status as indicated in all sectors of employment, it would be clear that women are concentrated in low paid jobs and are low in the hierarchies of status. This compares very adversely with women's attainments in developed countries. Despite the attention of the centre and state governments on women's problems "India ranks quite low in terms of female work participation, as compared to other countries.[28] Female work participation is low because of Indian cultural and traditional reasons.

The Organised Sector

In the organised sector women were employed more in the public sector than in private sector. Women are employed in community, personal and social services in the public sector while they have the highest percentage of employment in the manufacturing sector in the private sector followed closely by community, personal, social services and agriculture. Employment in organized sector has done much to draw women out of the family and household which had hitherto made up their world. The wages earned through industrial employment have given them a measure of independence, besides contributing handsomely to household earning. However, their prospects in the organized sector have come under a cloud even before the full impact of such employment has become manifest. Rapid changes in technology, automation and the curtailment of employment have drastically reduced their opportunities for work in the organised sector. In traditional industries such as jute, mining and cotton textiles, which were the major employers of women's labour, they have suffered a sharp setback. There has been a marked reduction in their employment in mining, the loss being most pronounced in coal. Women who constituted about a quarter of the work force in coal mines around independence now make up one-fourth of their original strength. The situation is not very different in jute and textiles, which apart from closing their doors to women, have themselves become declining industries.

The problem is compounded by the fact that growth industries, such as petrochemicals, fertilizers and engineering, offer no scope for women. There seems to be no place for them in high technology industries, except in some sections of assembly and packaging, which are low technology jobs. The introduction of micro-electronic and information technologies would make their position even more vulnerable. Women with their low skills would be of no use in this new order.

Another noticeable trend in women's employment is the growing presence of women in the service sector, especially in transportation, communications and financial services. Overall, the opportunities are better in the banks, public financial institutions, insurance, post and telegraphs and the travel and tourism industry. Two observations are pertinent in this context. The service sector is open only to women with education. It holds out no hope for women workers pushed out of sunset industries, who have neither education nor any well-developed skill. It is to middle class women with a background of education that the service sector has become accessible. The second point is that even in this sector, it is the jobs at the lower end of the spectrum, where skills are low and levels of pay relatively poor, which are available for women. In the service sector, women are concentrated in information handling and secretarial and clerical jobs.

Although the organised sector has offered employment opportunities to women, industries do labour under severely restrictive notions as to what is properly women's work. The labour market in this sector is sharply segmented, with lower-end jobs being regarded as the proper domain for women. The division of labour in all kinds of industries—including the most modern—is circumscribed by custom and tradition. The report of the National Committee on the Status of Women in India shows that out of 200 operations in the textile industry, women are employed in only four or five operations

The fact that modern technology has brought many arduous manual jobs well within women's reach is not reflected in the actual division of labour in the industry. Even now, occupations are categorized as men's or women's on the basis of conventional norms rather than any assessment of changes made possible by new technology. The low premium on women's skill continues to colour the character of women's employment. Women are normally found in unskilled, semi-skilled or low grade office jobs, or in assembly and tail-end tasks associated with packing, filling and checking.

Unorganised Sector

Majority of women are in the vast rural and urban unorganised sector. According to an estimate by National Commission on Self-Employed Women, 94 per cent of the female work force operates within this highly exploited sector. In the rural unorganized sector, women have a noticeable presence in several segments. They participate extensively in agriculture, animal husbandry, dairying, social and agro-forestry, fisheries, handicrafts, khadi and village industries, handloom weaving and seri-culture. In agriculture, where their participation is substantial, their activities range from sowing to weeding, transplantation and harvesting. In agro-forestry, they are engaged in the collection of minor forest produce and medicinal herbs, as well as in afforestation programmes. Besides land-based occupations, women contribute in no small measure to village industries. The majority of working women are in self-embroider making garments, rolling bidis and incense sticks and in a variety of other activities.

In the urban informal sector, women are working as petty traders. They are also engaged in producing and selling a variety of goods such as vegetables, fruits, flowers, cooked food, groceries, etc. or work as domestic workers. In both rural and urban areas, they are also engaged as construction workers. In addition to this, women spend on an average seven to ten hours a day in domestic chores.

The nature of the work that women perform in the unorganized sector ranges from wage employment at one end to self-employment, family labour and piece-rated work at the other. The self-employed may be classified in three categories. The first are the small traders, vendors and hawkers, selling vegetables, fruits, eggs, household goods and so on. The second are the home-based producers, such as potters, milk producers, processors of agricultural products and handloom workers. The third category is made up of those, who sell their labour or service. A sizeable section of the self-employed is urban.

The women workers in unorganized sector experience acute subjugation and vulnerability. Certain features typify women's work. Custom and tradition prescribe the jobs in which women would be employed. Division of labour is gender-specific. Whether in agriculture, construction, weaving or village industries, women carry out jobs which are tedious, arduous and low-skilled, while men corner the more skilled and less onerous tasks. Handloom weaving is an excellent example of such a hierarchical, gender-controlled division of labour. Women carry out the entire range of tasks involved in preparing the yarn for the loom, while men are in charge of the actual weaving. This situation is more or less replicated in all village industries, where women perform tedious, unskilled work while men take on the skilled jobs.

In addition to this, women also put in much longer hours of work. This is primarily because of the nature of their labour. They work with the lowest forms of technology and carry out the least skilled jobs. They also have to combine gainful labour with child-bearing, child-rearing and the performance of domestic chores. Quite a lot of their time is taken by domestic work involving the collection of food, fuel, water and fodder. Putting together these basic necessities is back-breaking labour for a great many women.

A further discriminating feature is differential wages. It is now a common place that women get paid much less than men, often for performing similar work. Their earnings are low because wages are discriminatory and work is seasonal. They are the lowest segment of the workforce and are afforded hardly any statutory protection either with regard to wages or hours of work and are the first to be dislodged when work is scarce.[29] Definitely much of the work that women perform as part of family labour or as self-employed and home-based producers is either not recognized as work or is dubbed a subsistence and therefore, a subsidiary activity.

The committee appointed to look into the conditions of self-employed women and women in the organised sector published their findings in a report entitled *Shramshakti* in 1988.[30] The report highlighted the dismal working conditions of women, occupational hazards, long working norms and precarious wage conditions without any welfare programmes or protective legislation. The invisibility of these women workers has been pointed out not only in this study but in other researches too.[31]

The presence of a vast multitude of women as workers and producers in the unorganized sector, where earnings are low, employment seasonal and insecure, supportive services woefully inadequate or even non-existent, growth opportunities few and collective organization weak, has brought into sharp focus the failure of the mainstream to alleviate their predicament. While it is true that workers, irrespective of sex, are exploited in the unorganized sector, women suffer more by the fact of their gender. There is enough evidence to substantiate the view that developmental processes have only pushed women to states of survival until recently, their contribution to the economy has gone unnoticed. The national database pays little attention to their presence or contribution.

Middle class women, who are urban, educated and upper caste, took up work outside the home in significant numbers. The acceleration of work participation of middle class women began in the 1970s for various reasons, such as the growing economic crisis, the widening public sector, and the emerging concert of the use of higher education through work participation.[32] Available studies refer to middle class women working largely in white collar jobs as clerks, secretaries, telephone operators and so on, and in the professions like school and college teaching, medicine and research. They are found mostly in lower or middle level jobs, and with fixed hours of work. Generally the educated working woman is married, has two or three children, and stays in a nuclear household.

The significant issues in some of these studies refer to the motivations of women for work and the linkage between work and status. One of the major reasons for women to work is economic necessity. Without the salary of these women, the family would not be able to meet some of their basic needs, such as housing and children's education in "good" schools, and developing children's personality and talent by providing them opportunities to participate in dancing, painting, music or sports activities. Today, with the rising cost of living the cost of all these activities has also risen. The Committee on the Status of Women states:

> "rising prices and levels of unemployment, added to the increasing cost of education and housing and absence of social security, have increased the degree of economic pressure on the major section of this class."[33]

Social changes and rapid urbanisation process make women to have more commitments and responsibilities.[34] More and more lower class, rural and tribal women seek employment both in organised and unorganised sector. Many micro-studies have demonstrated the inverse relationship between income level of the household and women's participation.[35] The lower the income level, the greater is the pressure on women to seek work to sustain themselves and their families. The relationship between earning income or being employed by itself is not an indicator of status. As the reasons for earning are more for improving or maintaining the standard of living of the family or to cushion it against inflationary pressures, women's own interests are not fully served. The girls earning to collect their own dowry or remain unmarried to support parents are fairly common. The research done on this class of women, shows clearly that employed women spend almost entirely what they earn for the improvement of family welfare, barring some exceptions.

Recent emphasis on vocational training and job-oriented courses in higher education for girls have an underlying assumption that girls will be working for money, perhaps they may not do so immediately after marriage, but the possibility of their entry at a later stage can not be ruled out. Mathews noted that, in the fishing industry, young unmarried girls from poor families who had dropped out from school had to fill in the gap between school and marriage. As she states:

> "In this interlude the girls are compelled to search for jobs to support their poor parents and, in many cases, the responsibility of earning some money and saving part of it for dowry falls on the girls themselves."[36]

Further, parents are aware that the capacity to earn is a good asset for girls in times of personal crisis. In some ways this capacity enables women to stand firm in a difficult material situation. Parents, even in the poorer sections of society, realize the linkage between education, training and employment. They give considerable emphasis to girls' education for upward mobility, particularly in terms of occupation. The employment of women by and large has not meant any change in the relationship inside the family or in their own identity. Karlekar, while analysing the earning ability of Balmiki women, observes that it 'led neither to economic independence nor affected the traditional structure of male-female relationships within the family.[37]

Political Status

The position of women in politics has always been marginal. Their participation in political life has been negligible all along.[38] Today, at the world level only 10 per cent of Parliamentary positions and six (6) per cent of Cabinet Ministerial posts are occupied by women.[39] Only a few countries have crossed 30 per cent representation of women in their Parliament. The UNO has been working since its inception for the improvement of women by providing equal opportunities in every field. The UNO constituted a commission on the status of women, followed by regulations about the remuneration and political rights of women. The member-countries also initiated measures to provide opportunities for women's participation in politics. Despite all these efforts, there are a number of countries where women do not even have the right to vote.

India is one of the very few countries in the world that openly encouraged women's participation in politics. In fact, right from the days of freedom struggle the Indian women have been consistently encouraged to take part in active politics. But due to the vitiated political milieu, resulting from increasing politicisation and criminalisation of politics, the level of political participation of women has been adversely effected despite the fact that there has been a marked increase in the level of literacy and political awareness of women. The Indian women did not, however, have to struggle for the right to vote. It was granted to them through constitution, which recognizes that all men and women possess equal rights.

Before beginning discussion on political participation of women in democratic institutions of free India, it is worthwhile to throw some light on the role of women in politics, during pre-independence days. The struggle for freedom, broadly speaking, marked the beginning of a political awakening among women in India. However, an effort towards improvement of women's status has been an integral part of the process of national regeneration that began as early as in the 19th Century with Raja Rammohan Roy. The Indian National Congress championed the principle of equal political rights for women as early as in 1918. A large number of educated women actively participated, shoulder to shoulder, along with men in the struggle for independence when it was intensified in the later phase of the movement.[40] It is too well-known to remind that it was the male dominated Indian National Congress which first appealed to women for their political participation. It was not that the women joined the Indian National Congress purely at their own volition or initiative. Nevertheless, their participation remained confined to a microscopic minority of educated urban women. Mahatma Gandhi was quite instrumental in bringing thousands of women out of their homes to join the freedom struggle. He believed that uplift merit of status of women was a necessary pre-condition to regeneration of Indian society. So he mobilized women into national movement apart from working for their emancipation.

On the eve of independence, the Indian women's participation in freedom struggle was given recognition, when various women's organisations scattered throughout India were asked to participate in the framing of the Constitution. Fourteen women were included as members of the Constituent Assembly. The Constitution had incorporated the notion of equality before law irrespective of gender. In fact, in many matters they have been provided special privileges and protections. In this respect, India's Constitution is, in fact, unique in the world. With the grant of constitutional gender-equality in free India came legal support through a series of legislations. While dealing with gender issues, it is important to mention that the Constitution of India has guaranteed equality before law and equal protection of law (Article 14) and prohibits discrimination on the ground of sex alone and it has empowered the State to make special provisions for women and children (Article 15). It has made provisions to prohibit traffic in human being and to provide for just and humane conditions of work along with maternity relief (Article 23 and Article 42). It is a constitutional duty of every citizen to renounce practices derogatory to the dignity of women (Article 51A). In this respect, India's Constitution has a place of distinction among the comity of nations.

The Indian Constitution made a deliberate radical departure from the age-old poor social status of women by granting them equal, social and political status. Constitutional equal status means that every adult female, whatever be her social position or accomplishments, has now the opportunity to function as a citizen and individual partner in the task of nation building.

In view of the constitutional obligations, during the post-independent era, women have been recognized as a separate target group and the government has directed its efforts towards mainstreaming of women into the national developmental process. This period has witnessed far reaching changes in almost all spheres—political, economic and social. In terms of constitutional, legal and administrative measures, many commendable initiatives have been taken. Prominent among them are the constitutional provisions for gender equality and justice, enactment of new laws and amendment of existing laws to protect and promote the interests of women, setting up of women-specific administrative and economic structures, such as Women and Child Development Department at the Union and State Government levels, National Commission for Women, Women Development Corporations, orienting plan strategy to include women specific and women-related programmes and launching of special schemes like Rashtriya Mahila Kosh, Mahila Samridhi Yojana, Indira Mahila Yojana, etc.

In Independent India women have important political and administrative positions. For instance, Indira Gandhi guided the destiny of the country as Prime Minister for more than 15 years. Women have also served as Governors, Chief Ministers, ministers in central and state governments, presiding officers of legislative bodies, judges of high courts and secretaries to the government. Though the constitutional equality is granted to women and women have held important positions, in practice, women are not treated well in all fields including politics.

It was believed that though very few women were actually joining politics, given time the overall change in terms of education and employment opportunities would necessarily percolate into the political sphere too and their representation would increase. However, the position of Indian women in the Parliament has always remained at a very low level never going beyond 10 per cent at any point of time.[41] An Inter-Parliamentary Union report in February, 1997 revealed that women hold 7.2 per cent seats in the Lok Sabha, 7.8 per cent in the Rajya Sabha. The track record of women candidates in the last fourteen Lok Sabha elections speaks for itself.

TABLE 2.5

Number of Women Elected to Lok Sabha

General Elections	*No. of Women Elected*	*Percentage*
First	22	4.4
Second	27	5.4
Third	34	6.7
Fourth	31	5.9
Fifth	22	4.2
Sixth	19	3.4
Seventh	28	5.1
Eighth	44	8.1
Ninth	28	5.29
Tenth	39	7.02
Eleventh	40	7.36
Twelth	44	8.07
Thirteen	49	9.02
Fourteenth	45	8.25

TABLE 2.6

Women Members of Rajya Sabha and their Percentage

Year	*Number*	*Percentage*
1956	20	8.62
1958	22	9.52
1960	24	10.25
1962	18	7.62
1964	21	8.97
1966	23	9.82
1968	22	9.64
1970	14	5.85
1972	18	7.40
1974	18	7.53
1976	24	10.16
1978	25	10.24
1980	29	11.98
1982	24	10.16
1984	24	10.24
1986	28	11.98
1988	25	10.59
1990	24	10.34

(Contd.)

Year	*Number*	*Percentage*
1992	17	7.29
1994	20	8.36
1996	19	7.81
1998	19	7.75
2000	22	9.01
2002	25	10.20
2004	28	11.43

When India became a sovereign republic, the first Lok Sabha had only 22 women though there was no dearth of suitable candidates at that time. The second Lok Sabha had 27 women (5.4 per cent). In the third Lok Sabha this was improved marginally to 34 (6.7 per cent), whereas the fourth one saw a slump with only 31 women (5.9 per cent). There was a sharp decline when Indira Gandhi was at the peak of her career and only 22 (4.29 per cent) women were elected to the fifth Lok Sabha. There was a further decline in the sixth Lok Sabha (with 3.4 per cent). There was a small increase in 1980 in the seventh Lok Sabha with their figures going up to 28 (5.1 per cent). This situation improved somewhat and the figure went up to 44 (8.11 per cent) in the eighth Lok Sabha, the highest so far. This declined in the ninth Lok Sabha to 28 (5.29 per cent). It went up a little in the tenth, eleventh, twelfth and thirteenth Lok Sabha. The number of women in the fourteenth Lok Sabha has, however, declined to 45 (8.25 per cent). The political parties remain reluctant to field female candidates for election unless they are judged potential winners. In the case of Rajya Sabha also the percentage of women members has never crossed 12 per cent. Thus, the participation of women has dwindled in the country's political life.

Women's marginal political presence is often attributed to their apathy and unwillingness, the influence of patriarchal culture, the negative female response to increasing criminalization of politics or the general stigma associated with women politicians. In addition to those stated above, there are some other factors too. In the empowerment route, participation of women, at different levels, have many obstacles as follows:

1. Relatively short historical tradition of women's political participation (especially during the freedom struggle);

2. Prevailing negative attitudes towards women's active participation in public life;
3. Difficulty in combining a political career with parental and conjugal role of women;
4. Economic dependency on male or lack of financial means;
5. Poor female education and lack of awareness of their rights. Illiteracy happens to be an important stumbling block towards empowerment; and
6. Women's reluctance for power games or indifference to political participation due to the system of *Purdah.*

Political empowerment of women is not to be viewed in isolation. Structural changes in the formal power institutions, economic independence, increasing awareness through education and gender equality in the social and cultural ethos are important prerequisites for political empowerment of women. The political participation of women generally suffers on two counts: first, because the society as a whole is impoverished, and second, because they are women.

The strategy should be to empower a still greater number of women in the decision-making process. Governments, political parties and other organisations should encourage women's participation in politics and in the exercise of political responsibilities. The women's organisations should exert pressure on political parties to open up opportunities to women as candidates for elections and encourage female functionaries in political parties. In addition, political parties need to express clearly their commitment to end discriminations against women and to ensure women's development as an integral component of their policies of national development and as their party ideology. As a supplementary measure, political parties need to encourage women at all decision-making levels, if necessary, by providing affirmative measures to strengthen and consolidate women's presence at various organizational and decision-making levels. Alternatively, they can also form their own political party and try to capture power through political socialization and mobilization of women. There is no need to depend on male dominated political organisations for graceful and rightful political participation of women.

Lack of education and political awareness partly accounts for deprivation of women. In such a situation, the main objective of women's education should be on mainstream gender issues and strengthening the capability of women to make them aware of their rights so that they are able to face the challenges in securing gender equality. These facts inevitably lead us to conclude that there is need for positive action in favour of women.

Women's participation in political process is important for strengthening democracy and for their struggle against marginalisation, triviasation and oppression. There can be no true democracy, or no true people's participation in governance and development without equal participation of men and women in all spheres of life and at different levels of decision-making. The goals of development may not be fully realized without women's full and active participation not only in the development process but also in the shaping of its goals. Needless to reiterate that parliamentary democracy is the rule of majority. Fifty per cent of women's population cannot be left behind in the country's march towards attaining the goals of justice, liberty and equality under the socialist, egalitarian and democratic framework of India's Constitution.[42] It is in this context, the concept of political empowerment of women assumes special significance. Empowerment is envisaged as an aid to help women achieve equality with men, or at least reduce the gender-based discriminations considerably. Empowerment would enable women to perform certain social roles that they cannot perform without it. Gender equality—political, economic or social—is enshrined in the Fundamental Rights under the Constitution together with equality of opportunity to employment and appointment to office. Political equality includes not only equal right to franchise but also more importantly, the right to gain access to the institutionalized centres of power.

Political status of women implies a degree of equality and freedom enjoyed by women in shaping and sharing of power and importance given by the society to the role of women. The equality is inseparable from active political participation. Participation of women in political life is integral to the advancement of women. Their political participation means not only using the right to vote, but also power-sharing, co-decision-making, and co-policy-making at all levels of governance of the State. Women's equal status in every sphere is inextricably linked to country's progress and development. Emergence of women as a strong group would change the prevailing political practices, the nature and content of debates in the legislature and women's issues can be taken are of from feminist perspective both in policy formulation and implementation.[43] Political representation of women is not possible in the normal election processes and, therefore, reservation is suggested to enable women to contest in less competitive seats.

The Committee on the Status of Women recommended for all Women Panchayats and in 1978 the Committee on Panchayat Raj Institutions recommended reservation of two seats for women in each panchayat. In the 1980s and 1990s women's issues had a focus on empowerment. The "National Policy for the Empowerment of Women" underscored empowering women through convergence of services, resources and infrastructure and outlined several priority areas like economic empowerment, special support service, health, nutrition, prevention of atrocities and violence, natural resources and environment, media and advocacy and political participation of women by recommending 30 per cent of seats for women in all levels of legislation, i.e. panchayats to Parliament. In pursuance of the above, one-third of the seats in local bodies have been reserved for women through the 73rd and 74th Constitutional Amendment Acts. This indeed makes a beginning for the effective participation of women in the decision-making process at the grass-root level.[44]

The 73rd constitutional amendment has been hailed as a watershed achievement in empowerment of women, as over one million rural women have joined village panchayat posts as *Sarpanch* or *adhyaksha* or members of community administration. According to Majumdar, a feminist author, this legislation brought about the 'political dynamism' of female voters. She concludes, "It is time for India to try out some new experiments in achieving real democracy. . ."[45] The kind of political empowerment is unprecedented even from the Western standard. For the first time in the history of this country, low caste people are substantially represented in statutory panchayats. Although most women are illiterate and poor and belong to the category of other backward classes, and yet, many of them have proved their mettle and won acclaims as able administrators. For instance, Fatima Bee of Kalva village in Andhra Pradesh, who is unlettered and had never seen a city, became sarpanch of the village through reservations under the panchayat legislation, and flew to New York in 1998 to receive the "UNDP Race Against Poverty" award from the Secretary General for her work relating to the programme of poverty alleviation.

In terms of percentages, women's representation in different bodies may not seem significant, but statistics do not always reflect the reality of changing perceptions at the community level. Quite recently, in Andhra Pradesh, for instance, about 25,000 rural women turned up for *Mahasabha* gatherings and passed resolutions demanding their rights as citizens despite the fact that they were very poor and illiterate. It is a political awareness rather than conventional schooling or education in terms of degrees or number of years of schooling that makes a real difference.

The constitutional amendments had the persuasive influence in the demand for similar provision in the state and union legislatures. All the political parties have committed to reserve one-third of seats for women in Lok Sabha and state legislatures by a constitutional amendment. But when the Women Reservation Bill was introduced in the Parliament, the parties were not serious in approving the bill. Female protagonists of reservation of seats for women in Parliament and State Assemblies are terribly worried over such a fate of the bill. Making a strong reaction to it, they often say that the bill is pending because it is against the established values of a male dominated society. However, the charge is frivolous because the bill was not moved by a female-headed or dominated government. It is also said that the low female representation in the decision-making organisations is because the political parties harbour very conservative view about women. Different parties champion the cause of women in their manifestos, but during election time they give tickets mostly to men. All political parties do have a women's wing, but the access to the inner ring of the party, which is the core of the power structure of the party, is not very easy for women for various reasons. Increasing lumpenisation and use of muscle power in political game keep the women away. The criterion for political parties for their selection of contestants is the 'winnability factor' rather than their identity in the constituency. Some political parties deny tickets to women on the ground of non-winnability factor.

There is strong apprehension about the necessity of reservation for women in the highest legislative body at this juncture. Many people, even those who are strong votary of gender equality, feel that it would be premature to initiate affirmative action for women through passing the women's reservation bill. The level of literacy for women is quite low and the country is way behind in matters of development compared to most developing countries, leaving the developed world aside. Indian democracy has not really come to the stage for such an action. There is no need to caricature or emulate blindly what is seen in some developed countries. India should wait and watch for some more time and assess the effectiveness or success of reservation for women at the local level government.

Different political parties, however, are opposed to the passing of the bill for some other reasons. The political parties, which stand for the cause of backward communities, minorities and other socially and economically under-privileged sections of society, apprehend that through reservation for women the political interests of the under-privileged would suffer. This was one of the important reasons why most leaders of the Rashtriya Janata Dal, Janta Dal (U), Samata Party, Bahujan Samaj Party, Samajvadi Party and other parties and politicians with socialist leaning opposed introduction of the bill in the Lok Sabha. Thus, the Women Reservation Bill proved to be a source of intense controversy from the beginning and every effort to introduce and pass it by successive governments saw much of the same drama.[46]

In sum, baring vedic period when Indian women enjoyed an enviable status, the Indian women through the ages have passed through a period of low status and discrimination as much as women in other countries.[47] The patriarchal structures, gender based disparities and hierarchies in the family and community continue to exist in the Indian society.[48] The above analysis on the status of women also makes it clear that women have remained outside the mainstream of development of Indian society. The measures taken from time to time have no doubt led to a significant improvement in the status of women over the years. However, much more still needs to be done as the position of women in society continues to be alarming. Many of the legislations enacted continues to be violated with impunity. Women in India continue to bear the burden of poverty, illiteracy economic marginalisation, lack of access to resources, exclusion from decision-making, social stereo-typing, discrimination and violence at both household and societal level. Their position, as compared to men is inferior, be it the fields of literacy, educational status, health, administration, work participation, politics or even sports, as is clearly revealed by various indicators.

Notes and References

1. N. J. Usha Rao, *Women in a Developing Society*, Ashish Publishing House, New Delhi, 1983, p. 7.
2. Kiran Devendra, *Changing Status of Women in India*, Vikas Publications, New Delhi, 1994, p. 1.
3. D. Paul Chowdhry, *Women Welfare and Development*, Inter-India Publications, New Delhi, 1992, p. 34.
4. Anju Bhatia, *Women's Development and NGO's*, Rawat Publications, New Delhi, 2000, p. 42.
5. A.S. Alteker, *The Position of Women in Hindu Civilization*, Motilal Banarsidas, Delhi, 1962, pp. 204, 317 and 326.
6. Indu Prakash Singh, *Indian Women: The Power Trapped*, Galaxy Publications, New Delhi, 1991, p. 2.
7. Karuna Chanana, "The Education of Women in Pre-Independence India," in A.M. Shah, B.S. Baviskar, E.A. Rama Swamy (Eds.), *Women in Indian Society*, Sage Publications, New Delhi, 1996, p. 122.
8. Vina Mazumdar, "The Social Reform Movement in India from Ranade to Nehru" in B.R. Nanda (ed.), *Indian Women: from Purdah to Modernity*, Vikas, New Delhi, 1976, p. 66.
9. Neera Desai and Maithreyi Krishna Raj, *Women and Society in India*, Ajanta Publications, Delhi, 1987, p. 37.
10. M.N. Srinivas, *Changing Position of Indian Women*, Oxford University Press, Delhi, 1978, pp. 26-27.
11. Mira Seth, *Women and Development: The Indian Experience*, Sage Publications, New Delhi, 2000, p. 87.
12. M.M. Rehman and Kamalakant Biswal, *Education, Work, and Women: An Enquiry into Gender Bias*, Commonwealth Publishers, New Delhi, 1991, p. 6.
13. Neeta Tapan, *Need for Women Empowerment*, Rawat Publications, New Delhi, 2000, p. 124.
14. See Jean Dredz and Amartya Sen, *India Development and Participation*, Oxford University Press, Delhi, 2002; and Anil B. Deolalikar, *Attaining*

the Millenium Development Goals in India, Oxford University Press, Delhi, 2005.

15. Government of India, *Report of the National Committee on Women Education*, Ministry of Education, New Delhi, 1959.
16. Government of India, *National Policy on Education (1986)*, Ministry of Education, New Delhi, 1986.
17. Government of India, *National Perspective Plan for Women's Education 1988-2000 A.D.*, Ministry of Education, New Delhi, 1988.
18. K. Pandimuruga Chinnan, "Women's Education as a Tool for Rural Development", *Kurukshetra*, Vol. 53, No. 11, September 2005, p.21.
19. K. Rajyalakshmi, "Development Through Education" in Rajakumari Chandrasekhar (ed.), *Women Resources and National Development: A Perspective*, Gauraw Publications, New Delhi, 1992, p. 116.
20. Neera Desai and Maithreyi Krishna Raj, *op. cit.*, p. 149.
21. Government of India, *Towards Equality: Report of the Committee on the Status of Women in India*, Ministry of Education and Social Welfare, New Delhi, 1975.
22. Government of India, *Challenge of Education*, Ministry of Education, New Delhi, 1985, pp. 27-34.
23. S. C. Bhatia, *Social Justice in Health*, IUACE, New Delhi, 1988, p. 26.
24. Prema Ramachandran, "Nutrition in Pregnancy" in G. Gopalan and Surinder Kaur (eds.), *Women and Nutrition in India*, Nutrition Foundation of India, New Delhi, 1986, p. 160.
25. Government of India, *Annual Report 1999-2000*, Ministry of Health and Family Welfare, New Delhi, 2000.
26. Gita Sen, "Whither Women's Health", *Seminar*, 537, May 2004, p. 42.
27. Neera Desai and Mithreyi Krishna Raj, *op. cit.*, p. 229.
28. See Kamalnath, "Female Work Participation and Economic Development—A Regional Analysis", *Economic and Political Weekly*, Vol. 5, No. 27, May 23, 1970, and Leela Gulati, "Female Work Participation", *Economic and Political Weekly*, Vol. 10, No. 2, January 17, 1975.
29. Uma Ramaswamy, "Women and Development" in A.M. Shah B.S. Baviskar, E.A. Ramaswamy (Eds.), *Women in Indian Society*, Sage Publications, New Delhi, 1996, p.87.
30. See Government of India, *Shramshkati: Report of the National Commission on Self-Employed Women and Women in the Informal Sector*, Department of Women and Child Development, New Delhi, 1988.
31. See Andrea Manefee Singh and Anita Kelles Vitanen (eds.), *Invisible Hands: Women in Home-based Production*, Sage Publications, New Delhi, 1987.
32. Neera Desai, "Women's Employment and their Familial Role in India" in A.M. Shah, B.S. Baviskar and E.A. Ramaswamy (eds.), *op. cit.*, p. 100.

33. Aileen D. Rose, *Hindu Family in an Urban Setting*, Oxford University Press, Delhi, 1961, p.198.
34. R. Chinnadurai, "Women Entrepreneurship and Service Sector", *Kurukshetra*, Vol. 54, No. 1, November 2005, p. 19.
35. Devaki Jain and Nirmala Benerjee (eds.), *Women in Poverty—The Tyranny of Household*, Vikas, New Delhi, 1985.
36. Molly Mathews, *Woman Workers in the Food Processing Industry in Kerala* (mimeo.), Indian Institute of Regional Development Studies, Kottayam, 1983, p. 26.
37. Malavika Karlekar, *Poverty and Women's Work: A Study of Sweeper Women in Delhi*, Vikas, Delhi, 1982, p. 14.
38. Ravinder K. Verma and Gyanender K. Verma, "Women in Bihar Politics", *Economic and Political Weekly*, April 13, 1996, p. 935.
39. Usha Narayanan, "Women's Political Empowerment: Imperatives and Challenges", *Mainstream*, April 16, 1999, p. 1.
40. For details see Tara Ali Baig (ed.), *Women of India*, Publications Division, Government of India, New Delhi, 1990.
41. Roopa Sharma, "The Women's Reservation Bill: A Crisis of Identity", *The Indian Journal of Public Administration*, Vol. XLVII, No. 1, January-March 2005, p. 51.
42. J.P. Singh, "Indian Democracy and Empowerment of Women", *The Indian Journal of Public Administration*, Vol. XLVI, No. 4, October-December 2000, p.618.
43. Snehalata Panda, "Reservations for women in Union and State Legislators", *The Indian Journal of Public Administration*, Vol. XLVII, No. 4, October-December 2001, p.702.
44. Yogendra Narian, S.N. Sahu and L. Lakshmi, "Political Empowerment of Women", *The Indian Journal of Public Administration*, Vol. LI, No. 1, January-March, 2005, p. 41.
45. Vina Majumdar, "Historical Soundings", *Seminar*, 457, September, 1977, p. 19.
46. Gail Omvedt, "Women in Governance in South Asia," *Economic and Political Weekly*, Vol. 40, No. 39, October 29, 2005, p. 4750.
47. Kalpana Shah, *Women's Liberation and Voluntary Action*, Ajanta Publications, New Delhi, 1984, p. 1.
48. G. Narayana Reddy, *Women and Child Development: Some Contemporary Issues*, Chugh Publications, Allahabad, 1987, p. 40.

Women Development Policies and Programmes

In the beginning attempts to bring about improvement in the condition of women by educating them and raising their social status were made by social reformers of the 19th century.[1] The principal social reformers are Raja Ram Mohan Roy, Keshab Chandra Sen, Iswarchandra Vidyasagar, Pandita Rama Bai, Swami Dayananda, Syed Ahmed Khan and Maharshi Karve. Their reforms included abolition of sati and child marriage, removal of restrictions on widow remarriage and provision of educational opportunities for women. The process of women emancipation gathered momentum during the years of freedom struggle under the leadership of Mahatma Gandhi, Annie Besant, Maniben Patel, Pushpaben Mehta, Miraben and Sushila Nayar. Under the leadership of Mahatma Gandhi in Indian politics, women participated enthusiastically in all the movements launched by the Congress. Their warm patriotism and unabashed enthusiasm won for them the love and respect of their fellow countrymen. In this circumstance, when the Constitution of free India came into force, the rights of women were readily recognized.[2]

The Government also enunciated numerous measures over the years for improving the conditions of women through its various commissions, committees, institutions and policy documents. The various policy measures on the women development are presented in this chapter in the form of the following aspects.

1. Constitutional Provisions
2. Legislative Measures
3. Appointment of Committees and Commissions
4. Women Development Plans
5. Creation of Institutions
6. Support to Voluntary Organisations
7. National Policy for Empowerment of Women

A brief description of various women development programmes is also given in this chapter.

Constitutional Provisions

The framers of the constitution were conscious of the social maladies, particularly with reference to the Indian women. They realised the unequal status of women and assured that women get equal rights. Equality became an article of faith in the Indian constitution not merely as the concept of social justice but as a pre-condition for socio-economic development of the nation.[3] The preamble to the Constitution of India resolved to secure to all its citizens justice—social, economic and political; liberty of thought, expression, belief, faith and worship; equality of status and opportunity; and to promote among them fraternity assuring the dignity of individual and the unity of the nation. To attain these objectives, the constitution guarantees certain fundamental rights and envisages directive principles.

The fundamental rights enshrined in Articles 14, 15 and 16 guarantee the principle of equality before law, equality of sexes and equal opportunities in all walks of life.[4]

Article 14 ensures that the state shall not deny to any person equality before the law or equal protection of the law within the territory of India.

Article 15 prohibits discrimination against any citizen on grounds of religion, race, caste, sex, place of birth or any one of them.

Article 15(3) empowers the state to make any special provision for women and children. This has resulted in legislations like the Factories Act, Mines Act, etc.

Article 16(1) states that there shall be equality of opportunity for all citizens in matters relating to employment or appointment in any office under the state.

Article 16(2) guarantees that no citizen shall, on grounds of religion, caste, sex, place of birth, residence or any of them, be ineligible for or discriminated against in respect of any employment or office under the state.

The obligation not to discriminate in matters relating to employment or appointment to any office under the state has thus at least normatively ensured a significant position and status of Indian women. Indian women are the beneficiaries of the fundamental rights in the same manner as Indian men.[5]

The Directive Principles of State Policy embody the major policy goals of the welfare state. The state is expected to take notice of these principles while formulating laws. The Directive Principles of State Policy, which have a special bearing on the status of women are:

Article 39(a) directs the state to frame its policy for ensuring that the citizens, men and women, equally have the right to an adequate means of livelihood.

Article 39(d) directs the state to ensure equal pay for equal work for both men and women.

Article 39(e) directs the state to ensure that the health and strength of workers—men and women—are safeguarded and children of tender age are not abused and that they are not forced by economic necessity to enter avocations unsuited to their age.

Article 42 directs the state to ensure just and humane conditions of work and maternity relief.

Article 44 provides that the state shall endeavour to secure for the citizens a uniform civil code throughout the territory of India.

Article 51A(c) provides that it shall be the duty to every citizen of India to renounce practices derogatory to the dignity of women. This is also considered a directive to improve employment opportunities and conditions of women workers.

It is beyond doubt that the Constitution of India marks a heyday for Indian women. The women's right of equality with men embodied in India's constitution, its fundamental rights and directive principles of state policy are a clear declaration of just equal humane society.[6] The judiciary on its own way has helped the process of equality between men and women in independent India. A new social life based on equality between men and women has definitely emerged. It is accepted that a change in the status of women is a good indicator of the pattern and direction of social change. If the direction of that change is towards a more egalitarian distribution of roles between men and women in tune with the constitutional directives, the direction of change is welcome one. Thus, the Constitution not only grants equality to women but also empowers the state to adopt measures of positive discrimination in favour of women.[7]

Legislative Measures

Besides providing a formal structure of equality, the government as it is found in many of third world countries used law as a major instrument to change society. One of the major planks of government activities with regard to women is legislation.[8] Many legislations have been passed since independence which have been considered quite revolutionary. The laws passed in favour of women after 1947 are:

(1) Special Marriage Act (1954)
(2) Hindu Marriage Act (1955)
(3) Hindu Succession Act (1956)
(4) Hindu Minority and Guardianship Act (1956)
(5) Adoptions and Maintenance Act (1956)
(6) Suppression of Immoral Traffic Among Women and Girls Act (1956)
(7) Maternity Benefit Act (1961)
(8) The Dowry Prohibition Act (1961)
(9) Medical Termination of Pregnancy Act (1971)
(10) The Family Court Act (1984)
(11) The Indecent Representation of Women's Act (1986)
(12) The Commission of Sati (Prevention) Act (1987)
(13) The Protection of Women from Domestic Violence Act (2005)

The Hindu Marriage Act of 1955 came into force on 10th May

1955. Some of its salient features are the abolition of caste restriction as a necessary requirement for a valid marriage among the Hindus; the enforcement of monogamy; and permissibility of divorce or dissolution of marriage. Most of the provisions in the Act are of a permissive and enabling nature. The result of Hindu Marriage Act, 1955 is that 88 per cent of the Indian population is now governed by the principle of monogamy.

The Hindu Succession Act of 1956 relaxed the property laws for women. It conferred equal share of a female in the property. The Act confers absolute right over the property possessed by a female Hindu before or after the commencement of the Act. Suppression of Immoral Traffic among Women and Girls' Act (1956) was amended twice in 1978 and 1986. It prohibits trafficking in women and girls for purposes of prostitution as a means of livelihood. The amended Act has made the penal provisions more effective.

A much needed legislation has been promulgated in the Dowry Prohibition Act of 1961. Every bride, previously had to be given away decked in ornaments and with cash. Though this custom was relaxed and tolerant in ancient times, it became more and more a must in medieval and British Indian times. Parents became avaricious and claimed huge dowries for their sons. Mahatma Gandhi tried his best to stop unlimited amount of money being spent in marriages, or the giving of dowries, but the people still persisted. In 1961 the Dowry Prohibition Act was passed to stop this practice. Now any parent agreeing to give property or valuable security for the purpose of marriage becomes an offence.

The Maternity Benefit Act, 1961 made the benefits applicable to women working force in all factories, establishments, mines and plantation. The Medical Termination of Pregnancy, 1971 Act legalizes abortion by a qualified doctor on humanitarian and medical grounds. This is primarily a welfare measure to protect the health of women though it has also a family planning aspect. Women can now have induced abortion through qualified doctors. The service is free in public hospitals. The Commission of Sati (Prevention) Act, 1987 was passed by Parliament to provide for prevention of Sati and its glorification.

The Protection of Women from Domestic Violence Act, 2005 provides protection for women from violence of any kind occurring within the family and matters connected therewith or incidental threats. The Act covers all those women who are in a relationship with the abuser where both parties live together in a shared household and are related by consanguinity marriage or through a relationship in the nature of marriage or adoption. The domestic violence includes actual violence or abuse that is physical, sexual, verbal, emotional or economic. Harassment by way of unlawful dowry demands to the women or her relations also come under domestic violence.

The Act provides relief to the women and her children if they are subject to domestic violence. The Act stops committing any further acts of domestic violence. The victims of domestic violence have the right of assistance of a protection officer and service provider. The Act empowers Magistrate to pass protection order in favour of the aggrieved person to prevent the respondent from aiding or committing an act of domestic violence or any other specified act. The Act also provides for the appointment of protection officers and registration of non-governmental organisations as service providers for providing assistance to the aggrieved person with respect to her medical examination, obtaining legal aid, safe shelter, etc.

A series of labour legislations have contributed to the improvement in the status of women. The Factories Act, Minimum Wages Act, Labour Welfare Regulation Act, Contract Labour Act, Employees State Insurance Act, Plantations Labour Act and some other legislations seek to protect interests of women and provide for benefits to women. The Factories Act, 1948 empowers state governments to prohibit employment of women in dangerous. The Labour Act, 1951 makes it obligatory for the factories and plantations employing not less than fifty women to provide creches. A few enactments lay down the general rule that women should not be permitted to work between 7.00 p.m. and 6.00 a.m. The latest addition to the list of legislations are the Constitution 73rd and 74th Amendment Acts which seek to provide reservation of at least 33 per cent representation in the panchayati raj institutions and urban local bodies for women.

These Acts were passed to bring about significant change in the status and the position of women in India. The violation of these Acts can be challenged in the court where they exist.

However, these Acts were not effective in ensuring equality of status and opportunity for women. The Dowry Prohibition Act in the statute book is, for instance, ineffective in practice mainly because any dowry given may be construed as "presents" which are not prohibited by law if made at the time of marriage.

The experience shows that the legislative action has not effectively changed women's situation. When there arises tensions between conflicting rights, women rights are mostly seen as secondary.[9] A radical change in the attitude of women induced by an awareness of their rights which are constitutionally guaranteed and legally protected will be the first step in the complex process of transforming the social structure.

Appointment of Committees and Commissions

An important landmark in the history of women's welfare and development was the appointment of committees and commissions. A Committee on Status of Indian Women under the chairmanship of Phulrenu Guha, a social and political worker who later became the then State Minister of Social Welfare, was appointed in 1974. The main task of the Committee was to undertake comprehensive examination of all the questions relating to the rights and status of women in the context of changing social and economic condition in the country and problems relating to the advancement of women. The Committee generated considerable data about the needs, problems and programmes for women. The Committee presented the first comprehensive picture of the status of women which was a grim story of inequality. This Committee made extensive study of women's problems and made some comprehensive recommendations regarding what measure should be undertaken to enhance and improve the status of women in India. The Committee submitted its report entitled "Towards Equality" in 1975.

The Report of the Committee pointed out that dynamics of social change and development had adversely affected women and they manifested all signs of a backward group, that is, declining sex ratio, lower life expectancy, higher infant and maternal mortality, declining work participation, increasing illiteracy, rising migration, etc.[10] It emphasized the need for a national machinery to coordinate and intensity the efforts and measurer needed for women's development.

Another important step by the Government was the constitution of the National Commission on Self-employed Women. The Commission collected and presented very useful material on various aspects of socio-economic life of Indian women. This Commission made comprehensive study of women's status both at macro and micro levels. On the basis of the findings, the commission had made many important observations and recommendations. Some of them are given below:

(1) At various levels of planning, problems of women working in unorganized sector should be kept in view and appropriate strategies should be devised to protect them from exploitation to enhance their status and well-being. The strategy should aim at ensuring the fulfillment of their vital requirements of life and provide them various support services. The effort should be made to reach women in ever larger number.

(2) Every agency of the government should be responsible to ensure that their planned resources and programmes benefit both men and women equally.

(3) To improve the living conditions of women to reduce their drudgery and to provide social security to a women holistic and integrated approach should be adopted. This is specially necessary since women do not perform one action and, therefore, a straight jacket approach cannot be adopted.

In fact, the commission made sweeping and comprehensive recommendations touching every aspects of working women's lives and their activities.[11] The report of the commission has become the basis for planning of programmes and activities for self-employment opportunities for women.

The constitution of the National Commission for Women is another important measure for women welfare and development. Investigation and examination of all matters relating to the safeguards provided for women under the constitution and other laws are entrusted to the Commission. The Commission will examine the laws to suggest amendments. It will also oversee the implementation of the laws.

The International Decade of Women (1975-85) had given a momentum to women development to be adopted in the society and has focussed priority attention to women with effective mobilization of social awareness and pubic opinion on this front. As a result, we have a Blue Print of Action Points on National Plan of Action for Women (NPAW) duly adopted by both the Houses of Parliament and National Committee on Women with the chairmanship of the Prime Minister of India was formed for implementation. The NPAW was guiding document for the development of women.[12] It stressed the need to educate women and the need for equality of opportunity. It suggested that education would help Indian women to fulfill their multiple roles as citizens, house-wives, mothers, contributors to family income and builders of a new society.

In regard to health, the Plan asked for a basic change in the attitude towards girl's health so that they could be better mothers and there would be a fall in the death-rate of infants and mothers, to provide pre-natal and post-natal services. The National Plan also discussed programmes to help the aged and the needy women. A beginning has, in fact, been made in many states. To promote the working of welfare organisations which would mobilize public opinion for raising the status of women was also a programme of the National Plan. Every department or agency of the Government of India, which has any programme affecting women will be required to take into account the National Plan.

A National Perspective Plan for Women (1988-2000) was drafted advocating a holistic approach for the development of women. The Perspective Plan is an effort at evaluating the impact of developmental plans and programmes of Indian women, reviewing the existing policies and programmes and evolving future strategies for their development in order to ensure that they catch up with the mainstream of society by 2000 AD. The Perspective Plan covers areas like employment and training, rural development, agriculture, education, health and family welfare, legislation, political participation, media and communication, voluntary action, etc.

Five-Year Plans

The instrument of planning has been the most positive indicator of policy formulation for women.[13] The five-year plans have helped in the process of the development of women. Thanks to far-sighted approach of our first Prime Minister Jawaharlal Nehru, the question of the development of women was given due importance in the five-year development plans.[14] In each plan women development issues especially their economic and educational development and health received considerable attention and a number of welfare measures were undertaken to ameliorate their conditions.

The First Five-Year Plan emphasized services like family planning, health care, etc., for promoting the status of women. The Central Social Welfare Board was set up in 1953 with Durgabhai Deshmukh as its Chairman. The child development programmes were also introduced and a large number of mahila mandals were created in rural areas for the first time. The women voluntary workers were drawn from village level to the national level to man the various welfare programmes with government assistance. A network of voluntary workers came to the forefront.

The Second Five-Year Plan paid special attention to women. The plan envisaged equal pay for both men and women and provided maternity benefits and creches as supportive services for working women. The widening disparity between male and female education levels attracted the attention of the planners during the Third Five-Year Plan. They suggested "consequently by far the most important objective in the field of education during the Third Plan must be to expand facilities for the education of girls at various stages." Similarly, the Fourth Five-Year Plan (1969-74) continued the emphasis on women's education.

The Fifth Five-Year Plan (1974-79) emphasized training of women who were in need of income and protection. Functional literacy programmes got priority. This plan coincided with International Women's Decade and the submission of report of the Committee on the Status of Women in India. In 1976, Women's Welfare and Development Bureau was set-up under the Ministry of Social Welfare. It was to act as a nodal point to coordinate policies and programmes for women's development.

The Sixth Five-Year Plan (1980-85) can be taken as a landmark for the cause of women.[15] The sixth plan saw a definite shift from welfare to development. A separate chapter on "Women and Development" was included for the first time in the plan document. It was realised that no more piecemeal strategies but an integrated approach would deliver the desired goods. It reviewed the status and situation of women in general and came to the conclusion that in spite of legal and constitutional guarantees, women had lagged behind men in almost all sectors. It used the adverse and declining sex ratio for women and their lower life expectancy compared to men, as basic indicators of their low status and deprivation from development. It stressed that the main strategy for women' development was three-fold education, employment and health. For the first time, it clearly spelt out that economic independence would accelerate improvement in the status of women and suggested the setting up of cells at the district level for increasing women's participation through self-employment. It also wanted the government to review the adequacy of the implementing machinery of various special legislations passed for the protection of women's rights. It also stressed that science and technology, research and survey were to be instruments for assessing women's participation. It referred, as usual, to the need for increasing enrolment of girls at the elementary level, promotion of functional literacy and encouraging the promotion of education for women in backward areas. In health and family welfare, maternal and child welfare services were to be improved and extended and attention paid to women's nutrition. In employment, an effort was to be made to increase employment through greater skill training and support services. A working group was constituted by the Planning Commission on the employment of women. In labour welfare, the plan again talked of providing women workers' basic amenities at the work place, better living conditions, maternity benefits, education and creche facilities and for the first time, talked of training women in alternative employment.

The Seventh Five-Year Plan operationalised the concern for equality and empowerment of women articulated by the International Decade for Women. The Plan emphasized the need to open new avenues of work for women and perceived them as a crucial resource for the development of the country with a view to strengthening economic conditions. According to the Plan, new technologies for reducing drudgery of household work were to be explored. It also stated that lacunae in existing legislation would be removed. Women's corporations for promoting employment through skills training were planned for every state with the Centre and the State Government's equity participation at 50:50 funding. The Seventh Five-Year Plan stated, for the first time, that confidence building and awareness of their rights among women must be accelerated so that women realise their own potential for development and their rights to a share from this process. It also spoke for the first time, of the need for initiating integrated development projects for women covering health, education, nutrition, application of technology and science and creation of employment.

During the Eighth Five-Year Plan women were granted joint title of land, credit facilities, supportive services and other facilities. Women's development corporations were created in states. The need for changing societal attitudes towards women through awareness generation and women groups was stressed in the Plan. The need for free legal aid and home for distressed women was also recognized. Training institutions and family counselling centers were opened for integrating women into the mainstream of national development. The Plan perceives women as crucial resources for the development of the country. The Ninth Plan (1997-2002) stated categorically that for empowering women as the agents of social change and development, a 'National Policy for Empowerment of Women' would be formulated. In the field of development, the Plan discussed, for the first time, the need for reservation of seats for women in Parliament and the state legislative assemblies. The Plan also proposed to ensure 30 per cent representation of women in the public sector and provided a larger entry for women in the premier civil services. To increase women's participation in the industrial development of the country, the Plan proposed to set-up a 'Development Bank for Women Entrepreneurs' for assistance and share would be ensured through the rural development employment schemes. The most important resolve of the plan was to have a special women's component in the plan to ensure 30 per cent flow of funds to women development sectors.

The Tenth Five-Year Plan (2002-07) approach aimed at empowering through translating the National Policy for Empowerment of women into action and ensuring survival, protection and development of women though rights based approach.

If we analyse the trends of planning, it would be noticed that the First Five-Year Plan laid down stress on very important parameters of women welfare and development, i.e. education, health, employment, etc. The second, third, fourth and fifth plans carried on the same strategy. It was only in the mid-seventies, the setting up of a committee to survey the status of women in 1974, and preparation for celebrating the International Women's Year in 1975 that a heightened consciousness arose in government circles over intensifying the efforts towards the development of women. From the Sixth Plan onwards we find that every new exercise in planning stressed on this objective.

Establishment of Institutions

Another important landmark in the history of women welfare and development is the creation of institutions and setting up of organisations to implement various women welfare and development programmes. The Central Social Welfare Board was the first organisation set by the Union Government in 1953. The Central Social Welfare Board (CSWD) was given responsibility for promoting and developing welfare services for women and children. Women's Welfare and Development Bureau was set-up as a nodal point within the Government of India to coordinate the measures for women's welfare and development and to initiate policies and programmes for accelerating growth and development of women.

At the close of the Women's Decade (1975-84) in 1984 and following the President's announcement to the Parliament regarding a new policy for women, the Ministry of Social Welfare (created in 1979) came to be renamed as Ministry of Social and Women's Welfare.[16] The new national policy for women focused on women's development and other issues and also involve voluntary organisations both at the formulation and implementation levels. The new policy aimed at viewing women's development in a holistic and integrated manner.

In 1988, the Government of India constituted a separate department in the Ministry of Human Resource Development for the development of women and children. This department executes its policies through the Central Social Welfare Board, which concerns itself mainly with the welfare programmes for women. The department also plans and executes programmes for women, besides performing an overseeing function for implementing them through other ministries and departments. The creation of the Women's Welfare Department in the Ministry of Human Resource Development suggests that a new approach is being taken by the Government to tackle women's problems. The reason cited for the creation of this department is that by clubbing together related subjects, scare resources could be utilized properly for promoting women's welfare. It is also felt that tremendous human potential could be tapped by integrating this sector in the national development efforts. Women's welfare earlier in the Ministry of Social Welfare was treated as work geared towards the amelioration of living conditions of women. This included mostly programmes for destitute women. Now the focus has been broad-based to include women as a general category which should participate actively and contribute in the nation's development.

Women Development Corporations were set-up since 1986-87 in several states to identify and assist women entrepreneurs. Rashtriya Mahila Kosh was set-up as a registered society under the Registration of Societies Act, 1960 in March, 1993 to meet credit needs of poor women, particularly in the informal sector, who have little or no access to formal credit institutions.

Support to Voluntary Organisations

One of the instruments used in the post-independence period to develop programmes and services for women has been the grants-in-aid system administered through voluntary agencies. The First Five-Year Plan stated that the instrument of women development was to be through voluntary effort. The strategy of involving the voluntary organisations in the formulation and implementation of welfare programmes for women would ensure their compatibility with the social values and needs of various geographic regions in the country and also of the various strata of women in the country. The following are some of the Ministries and Departments, which give grants to voluntary organisations :

1. Ministry of Welfare
2. Ministry of Human Resource Development
3. Department of Women and Child Development
4. Department of Education
5. Ministry of Rural Development
6. Ministry of Agriculture
7. Ministry of Health and Family Welfare

In addition to the Union Ministries and Departments, some autonomous bodies give technical and financial assistance to voluntary organisations. These autonomous bodies are :

1. Central Social Welfare Board
2. National Council for Educational Research and Training
3. Council for Advancement of Peoples' Action and Rural Technology (CAPART)
4. Khadi and Village Industries Commission
5. Handloom, Silk, Coir and Handicrafts Boards
6. National Children Fund

There are several types of grants. Some of these are—

1. Development grants
2. Maintenance grants
3. Administrative grants
4. Recurring grants
5. Non-recurring or capital grants
6. Discretionary grants

Due to the encouraging policy of the Government and the initiative of the people themselves, the voluntary sector has borne rich fruit in the sense that there has been a profusion of voluntary organisations working for women. More than 10,000 voluntary organisations are registered with the Department of Women and Child Development. There are some organisations working exclusively in the field of education, health and rural development who are interested in helping women get their due share of national development. These organisations are so numerous and diverse that it is difficult to single out for mention. It is, however, important to put their services on record as they have been the greatest and most effective instrument for spreading awareness about their rights among women and rousing their level of expectation from society and government. In the field of education, in family welfare and health and employment in the informal sector as well as labour welfare, their contribution has been significant in terms of advising the government on mid-term course corrections and the formulation of the new schemes.

National Policy for the Empowerment of Women

Empowerment of women became one of the primary objectives of the Ninth Five-Year Plan. The year 2001 was observed as Women Empowerment Year by UN. The National Policy for the Empowerment of Women was evolved in the same year. The policy recognizes the causes of gender inequality which are related to social and economic structure. The policy underlines the need for mainstreaming gender perspective in the development process.[17] The objectives of the National Policy for the Empowerment of Women include:

(1) Creating an environment through positive economic and social policies for full development of women enable them to realise their full potential;
(2) The *de jure* and *de facto* enjoyment of all human rights by women on equal basis with men in all spheres—political, economic, social, cultural and civil;
(3) Equal access to participation and decision-making in social, political and economic life of the nation;
(4) Equal access to health care, equality education at all levels, career and vocational guidance, employment and equal remuneration;
(5) Strengthening of legal systems aimed at elimination of all forms of discrimination against women;
(6) Changing societal attitudes and community practices by active participation and involvement of both men and women;
(7) Mainstreaming a gender prospective in the development process.

(8) Elimination of discrimination and all forms of violence against women and the girl child; and
(9) Building and strengthening partnership with civil society, particularly women's organisations.

The policy also takes note of the commitments of the Ninth Five-Year Plan and the other sectoral policies related to empowerment of women. Besides empowering women to participate in decision-making process the policy also visualized the means of economic and social empowerment of women.

Steps will be taken for mobilization of poor women and convergence of services by offering them a range of economic and social options, along with necessary support measures to enhance their capacities. In order to enhance women's access to credit for consumption and production, the establishment of new and strengthening of existing micro-credit mechanisms and micro-finance institution will be undertaken so that the outreach of credit is enhanced. Equal access to education for women and girls will be ensured. A holistic approach to women's health which includes both nutrition and health services will be adopted and special attention will be given to the needs of women and the girl at all stages of the life cycle. Focussed attention would be paid to meeting the nutritional needs of women at all stages of life cycle.

All Central and State Ministries will draw up time bound action plans for translating the policy into a set of concrete actions, through a participatory process of consultation with Central and State Government Departments of Women and Child Development and National and State Commissions for women. The plans will specifically include the following:

(i) Measurable goals to be achieved by 2010;
(ii) Identification and commitment of resources;
(iii) Responsibilities for implementation of action points;
(iv) Structures and mechanisms to ensure efficient monitoring, review and gender impact assessment of action points and policies; and
(v) Introduction of a gender perspective in the budgeting process.

Institutional mechanisms, to promote the advancement of women, which exist at the Central and State levels, will be strengthened. These will be through interventions, as may be appropriate and will relate to among others, provision of adequate resources, training and advocacy skills to effectively influence macro-policies, legislation, programmes, etc., to achieve the empowerment of women.

National and State Councils will be formed to oversee the operationalisation of the Policy on a regular basis. The National Council will be headed by the Prime Minister and State Councils by the Chief Ministers and be broad in composition having representatives from the concerned Departments and Ministries, National and State Commissions for Women, Social Welfare Boards, representatives of non-government organisations, women's organisations, corporate sector, trade unions, financing institutions, academics, experts and social activities, etc. These bodies will review the progress made in implementing the policy twice a year. The National Development Council will also be informed of the progress of the programme undertaken under the policy from time to time for advice and comments.

National and State Resource Centres on women will be established with mandates for collection and dissemination of information, undertaking research work, conducting surveys, implementing training and awareness generation programmes, etc. These centres will link up with women's studies centres and other research and academic institutions through suitable information networking systems.

While institutions at the district level will be strengthened at the grass roots, women will be helped by Government through its programmes to organise and strengthen into Self Help Groups (SHGs) at the anganwadi, village and town levels. The women's groups will be helped to institutionalize themselves into registered societies and to federate at the panchayat and municipal levels. These societies will bring about synergistic implementation of all the social and economic development programmes by drawing resources made available through government and non-government channels, including banks and financial institutions and by establishing a close interface with the panchayats and municipalities.

The policy reaffirms its will to implement international obligations in all sectors of empowerment women. It is highly appreciable that a national policy on empowerment of women, who constitute half of the universe is formulated.[18] As the document rightly put it, "right from nutritious and equal share in square meal to equal status, everything is a scarce commodity to women."[19] This policy document is successful in identifying the areas where extra inputs are needed to ensure empowerment. Identifying various strata among women and exclusive attention to their problems is another novel feature of this policy.[20] The formulation and enactment of national policy for the empowerment of women was, therefore, indisputably an important milestone.

Women Development Programmes

Government programmes for women's development began as early as 1954. Apart from giving grants to voluntary agencies, the Central Social Welfare Board initiated some new programmes of assistance which were developmental in nature such as the scheme of welfare extension projects, socio-economic programmes and hostels for working women. Thereafter, the Ministry of Social Welfare also sponsored programmes and activities of women's welfare and development, through grants-in-aid. The other ministries such as Agriculture, Health, Rural Development, Labour, etc., also contributed for the development of women in addition to the programmes and services of the Department of Women and Child Development, which has the coordinating responsibilities. Some of the official programmes for the welfare and development of women are described briefly.

1. Socio-Economic Programme

The Central Social Welfare Board had started the socio-economic programme (SEP) in 1958. Under this programme, financial assistance is extended to voluntary organisations to undertake a wide variety of income-generating activities providing opportunities of 'Work and Wage' to needy women, like widows, destitutes, disabled, etc., particularly those coming from economically backward and under-developed areas for setting up industrial units, handlooms and handicraft units, dairy units and other allied economic activities like piggery, sheep and goat rearing, poultry, etc. During the Eighth Five-Year Plan (1992-97), an amount of Rs. 30.33 crore has been released to 2,457 units to benefit about 20,100 women. In 1996-97, 13 units have been sanctioned with the total expenditure of Rs. 6 crore.

2. Condensed Course of Education and Vocational Training (CCE & VT)

The CCE & VT scheme, in operation since 1968, has been revised from time to time to provide educational qualifications and relevant skills to needy women so that they become eligible for identifiable remunerative work opportunities. Under these programmes, voluntary organisations are given grant to conduct courses of two to three years duration for women of the age-group of 15 and above for passing primary, middle, metric and secondary level examinations. Under the Vocational Training Programme, grants are given to impart training to needy women of 15 year age-group in different vocations leading to wage and self-employment. Under these programmes, 5,823 courses have been sanctioned during the Eighth Five-Year Plan and a sum of Rs. 39.07 crore were sanctioned to benefit about one lakh women. In 1996-97, 598 courses were sanctioned with the total expenditure of Rs. 5 crore.

3. Short Stay Homes for Women and Girls

The Government of India launched a programme in 1969 in the Central Sector called the Short Stay Homes for Women and Girls to protect and rehabilitate those women and girls who are facing social and moral danger due to family problems, mental strain, social ostracism, exploitation or other causes. The services extended in these Homes include medical care; case work services occupational therapy; education-*cum*-vocational training and recreational facilities.

The need for providing Short Stay Homes for women and girls has been due to the changing pattern of life, rapid urbanization and industrialization and the resulting migration from rural to urban areas. The break-up of social institutions like the joint family, contributes considerably in creating problems of adjustment for women and young girls. Cases of marital conflict and emotional disturbance occur. An effort is made to help the women to rehabilitate themselves within a short period of time. These Short Stay Homes have been established by voluntary organisations.

At present, 273 Short Stay Homes receive grants from the Department, covering approximately 8,190 beneficiaries. Under the scheme the grant is being released at the revised financial norms on the recommendation of the State Government to the extent of Rs. 4,51,350 (Recurring and non-recurring). The recurring grant of Rs. 4,01,350 is given to the Home every year on the basis of 'C' class city. There is also a provision for some increase in subsequent years on the component of rent and the maintenance cost for residents. Provision have also been made for upgrading skills and capacities of staff and residents as well as education of the children of residents. The implementation of the scheme has been transferred to the Central Social Welfare Board.

4. Hostels for Working Women

Under the scheme of Construction or Expansion of Hostel Building for Working Women with a Day Care Centre implemented by the Union Department of Women and Child Development, financial assistance is given to voluntary organisations, local bodies and cooperative institutions engaged in the field of women's social welfare, and women's education. The public sector undertakings, women development corporations, educational institutions and state governments receive funds from the Union Department for the construction of hostels for women in order to enable women seek employment and participate in technical training. The objective of the scheme is to provide cheap and safe hostel accommodation to employed women living out of their homes. The target beneficiaries are single working women, widows, divorcee, separated and working women whose husbands are out of town. Women getting trained for employment and girl students studying in post school professional courses are also to stay in hostel. Since inception of the programme in 1972-73, 830 hostels for 58,744 working women have been sanctioned so far. Out of the 830 hostels, day are center facilities are also available for 7668 children in 293 hostels.

5. Employment and Income Generation-cum-Production Units

Under the scheme, which is assisted by Norweigian Agency for International Development (NORAD), projects of skill development and training of achieving self-reliance through income generation for women are supported. These projects of training for income generation are in the non-traditional trades of electronics, watch manufacturing or assembly, computer programming, garment making, handlooms, etc. During the year upto December, 1997 Rs. 1.56 crore has been sanctioned to benefit about 6,980 women through 45 projects. Between 1982-83 when the scheme was launched till 31st December, 1997, 1.40 lakh women have benefited through 887 projects.

6. Creches for Working and Ailing Mothers' Children

The central scheme of creches for working and ailing mothers' children is under implementation since 1975-76. The scheme is implemented through voluntary organisations. The scheme envisages day-care services for children of the age group 0-5 years. The services of the creches include health care, supplementary nutrition, sleeping facilities, immunization and play and recreation for the children.

7. Support to Training and Employment Programme for Women (STEP)

The STEP scheme launched in 1987, aims to upgrade the skills of poor and assetless women, mobilize, conscientise, provide training and subsequently employment on a sustainable basis in the traditional sectors of agriculture, animal husbandry, fisheries, handlooms, handicrafts, sericulture, social forestry, wasteland development, etc. In addition to the training and employment support, the programme advocates gender sensitization, women in development (WID) inputs and provision of support services. Since the inception of the programme about 3.32 lakh women have been benefited through 61 projects.

8. Setting up of Training-cum-Employment-cum-Production Centres

The second major programme of Training and Employment,

which is commonly known as 'NORAD assisted Training Programme for Women' extends financial assistance to public sector undertakings, autonomous bodies and voluntary organisations to train women in non-traditional trades like electronics, electricals, watch assembly and manufacturing, computer programming, printing and binding, handlooms, garment making, weaving and spinning, hotel management, fashion technology and beauty culture, tourism, bakeries and office management, etc. During the Seventh Plan an amount of Rs. 122 lakhs was spent on this programme.

9. *Mahila Samriddhi Yojana (MSY)*

In pursuance of government's policy to empower women by raising their socio-economic status, an innovative scheme of MSY was launched on October 2, 1993. The scheme aims at promoting self-reliance and a measure of economic independence among rural women by encouraging thrift.

10. *Indira Mahila Yojana (IMY)*

In order to coordinate and integrate components of all sectoral programmes and facilitate their convergence to empower women, IMY was launched as a strategy on August 20, 1995. It proposes to bring out a mechanism by which there could be a systematic coordination and a meaningful integration of various programmes of different sectors to meet women's needs.

11. *Special Thrust on Employment and Training for Women*

In line with the Eighth Plan strategy, the nodal DWCD has reset its priorities to accord special emphasis on employment and income generation activities for women. The ultimate objective in all these efforts is to make women economically empowered and self-reliant. For this purpose, the Department implements some programmes directly or through voluntary organisations and interacts with other departments and ministries to ensure flow of benefits to women through their programmes.

12. *Development of Women and Children in Rural Areas (DWCRA)*

The Development of Women and Children in Rural Areas

(DWCRA) was formulated as sub-scheme of the IRDP. The DWCRA was started as a pilot project covering 50 districts in all states in 1982-83. The DWCRA seeks to provide income generating activities to women and also provides an organizational support in terms of a receiving system for the assisted women so that they can become effective recipients of goods and services available in that area. While the target group of DWCRA is the same as IRDP, i.e. families having an annual income of less than Rs. 4,800 the methodology is through a group. The financial provisions under DWCRA are available only for the group. The following are the strategies to be adopted to attain the objectives of DWCRA.

(1) To create employment opportunities for rural women who are below the poverty line by providing skills, vocational training which are acceptable to the beneficiaries, enhancing productivity in their existing vocation and by introducing new activities so far not undertaken.
(2) To organise the beneficiaries according to group activity.
(3) To generate income for the rural poor.
(4) To organise production enhancing programmes in rural areas.
(5) To provide facilities for the children of working women by improved environment, care and food and by establishing crèche system

The scheme envisages formation of a group of 15-20 women. Women are expected to come together for an activity of mutual interest to all. The entry point for the group may not be income generating activities but it must be an essential ingredient of the total gamut of activities in which the group is involved. All viable economic activities can be undertaken under DWCRA. Activities should be identified by the group, suitably aided by the Gram Sevika, Mukhya Sevika and Assistant Project Officer (Women Development).

Notes and References

1. Anju Bhatia, *Women's Development and NGOs*, Rawat Publications, New Delhi, 2000, p. 45.
2. Sumitra Gupta, *Social Welfare in India*, Chugh Publications, Allahabad, 1989, p. 99.

3. Paul D. Chowdhry, *Women Welfare and Development: A Source Book*, Inter-India Publications, New Delhi,1992, p. 39.
4. Neeta Tapan, *Need for Women Empowerment*, Rawat Publications, Jaipur, 2000, p. 57.
5. Neera Desai and Maithreyi Krishna Raj, *Women and Society in India*, Ajanta Publications, New Delhi, 1990, p. 40.
6. Kiran Devendra, *Changing Status of Women in India*, Vikas, New Delhi, 1994, p. 68.
7. Sayed Afzal Peerzade and Prema Parande, "Empowerment of Women—As Lady", *Kurukshetra*, Vol. 54, No. 1, November, 2005, p. 7.
8. Neera Desai and Vibhuti Patel, *Indian Women: Change and Challenge in the International Decade, 1975-85*, Popular Prakashan, Bombay, 1990, p. 41.
9. Neeta Tapan, *op. cit.*, p. 62.
10. Government of India, *Towards Equality: Report of the Committee on the Status of Women in India, op. cit.*, pp. 281-82.
11. M.M. Rehman and Kamalakanta Biswal, *Education, Work and Women: An Enquiry into Gender Bias*, Commonwealth Publishers, New Delhi, 1991, p. 25.
12. J. Bhagyalakshmi, "Women's Empowerment: Miles to Go", *Yojana*, Vol. 48, No. 10, August, 2004, p. 39.
13. Mira Seth, *Women and Development: The Indian Experience*, Sage, New Delhi, 2001, p. 59.
14. Sarojini Varadappan, "Women's Development: A National Perspective" in Rajakumari Chandrasekhar (ed.), *Women's Resources and National Development: A Perspective*, Gaurav Publications, New Delhi, 1992, p. 8.
15. Shanta Kohli Chandra, "Women and Empowerment", *The Indian Journal of Public Administration*, Vol. XLIII, No. 3, July-September, 1997, pp. 395-99.
16. Government of India, Ministry of Social and Women Welfare, *Annual Report, 1984-85*, New Delhi, 1985, p. 1.
17. J. Bhagyalakshmi, *op. cit.*, p. 40.
18. M.V.S. Koteswara Rao, "National Policy for Empowerment of Women" in M. Lakshmipathi Raju (ed.), *Women Empowerment: Challenges and Strategies*, Regal Publications, New Delhi, 2007, p. 46.
19. Government of India, *National Policy for Empowerment of Women*, Department of Women and Child Development, New Delhi, 2001.
20. Sabala Sangh Saheli, *Development for Whom—A Critique of Women's Development Programmes*, Action India, Delhi, 1991.

Institutional Mechanism for Women Development in India

It is quite natural that when women become a subject of international interest, a mechanism had to be developed within the United Nations system. The UN system has a special bureau for women's affairs, which works through the governments. The Bureau in the United Nations could pass on the various mandates and declarations. The Bureau could not rest till it found its counterparts in member-states.[1] This is the main reason for having an institutional mechanism for women's development in member-states. The United Nations made a call on 12th July, 1963 to establish national machinery to monitor women welfare programmes. The First World Conference on the International Women's Year was held at Mexico in 1975 and a Plan of Action was adopted, which reads as follows:

> "The establishment of interdisciplinary and multi-sectoral machinery within government, such as National Commissions, Women's Bureaus and other bodies, with adequate staff and budget can be an effective transitional measure for accelerating the achievement of equal opportunity for women and their full integration in national life. The membership of such bodies

should include both women and men, representatives of groups of society responsible for making and implementing policy decisions in the public sector. Government ministries and departments (especially those responsible for education, health, labour, justice, communication and information, culture industry, trade, agriculture, rural development, social welfare, finance and planning) as well as appropriate private and public agencies should be represented on them."

The Fourth World Conference on Women in Beijing in 1995 adopted the Platform for Action for the Advancement of Women. The Beijing Platform for Action identified the creation and strengthening of national machineries as one of 12 critical areas of concern, requiring action by Governments. Accordingly, the Action should be taken by Governments to:

(a) Ensure that responsibility for the advancement of women is vested in the highest possible level of Government; in many cases, this could be at the level of a Cabinet Minister;
(b) Based on a strong political commitment, create a national machinery, where it does not exist, and strengthen, as appropriate, existing national machineries, for the advancement of women at the highest possible level of government; it should have clearly defined mandates and authority; critical elements would be adequate resources and the ability and competence to influence policy and formulate and review legislation; among other things, it should perform policy analysis, undertake advocacy, communication, coordination and monitoring of implementation;
(c) Provide staff training in designing and analyzing data from a gender perspective;
(d) Establish procedures to allow the machinery together information on government-wide policy issues at an early stage and continuously use it in the policy development and review process within the Government;
(e) Report, on a regular basis, to legislative bodies on the progress of efforts, as appropriate, to mainstream gender

concerns, taking into account the implementation of the Platform for Action; and

(f) Encourage and promote the active involvement of the broad and diverse range of institutional actors in the public, private and voluntary sectors to work for equality between women and men.

During its forty-third session in 1999, the United Nations Commission on the Status of Women recommended further action to be taken to create new or strengthened national machineries for the advancement of women and gender equality. Among the agreed conclusions of the session were measures to ensure a continued strong political commitment to the strengthening of national machineries and to placing them at the highest possible level of government, with the authority needed to fulfil their mandated roles and responsibilities.

India has been one of the most dynamic and energetic countries in following the various mandates and processes of United Nations. As a result of the UN General Assembly Resolution of 1963 the Government of India established in 1964 a Department of Social Welfare to look after women issues from the welfare point of view, the primary focus being on women in distress. India set-up a committee called the Committee on the Status of Women in 1974 to do a complete review and bring out a report on the status of women in India.

The Committee on Status of Women emphasized the need for a national machinery to coordinate and intensify the efforts and measure needed for women development.[2] As a result, a Women's Welfare and Development Bureau was established in 1976 in the Ministry of Social Welfare to aid the National Committee on Women, which was constituted in September, 1976 and also to act as a national point within the Government to coordinate policy and programmes and to initiate measures for women's development. It was also to work as a clearing house for information and was headed by a Joint Secretary. The Indian leaders felt the need for a human resource development approach for women. As a result of this feeling a separate department for women and child development was set-up in 1985 in the Ministry of Human Resource Development. New structures were also created in other ministries and departments to look after the issues and programmes relevant to women. Women development programmes have been integrated into the development projects of these departments and ministries. It was also thought of structures for women in Local Self-government Institutions.

There are, thus, different institutions created for the welfare and development of women at different levels, i.e. central, state and local levels on different occasions. These institutions have changed and been modified according to the demands. Some structures such as the National Committee on Women, the State Committees on Women, The National Steering Committee, etc., have come and gone. The Central Social Welfare Board along with the state level branches to encourage voluntary effort in the field of women's development, has been a part of it since long. Structures such as Women's Development Corporations, the National Commission for Women are recent entrants to the field. A description of some of the organisations is done in this chapter.

Central Social Welfare Board (CSWB)

The Central Social Welfare Board was created as the first nation-wide government structure for women welfare. It has a programme of grants-in-aid, for promoting welfare and development services for women, children and under-privileged groups. It owes much of its image and success to that great social reformer, social administrator par excellence and a matchless institution builder Smt. Durgabai Deshmukh.[3] The creation of CSWB in 1953 symbolized the government's welfare approach to women's problems. The CSWB provides services to women and children, primarily through women's organisations. The Board itself became not only a major national women's organisation but it worked for the welfare of women. Several programmes like welfare extension projects, socio-economic programmes, hostels for working women, public cooperation camps for women in border areas, financial assistance to homes for destitute women, establishment of after care homes for women, were a series of measures, which provided a strong base for women welfare through voluntary agencies. The Board has its state counterparts, and it aims at providing assistance to voluntary agencies, improving and developing welfare programmes and sponsoring them in areas where they did not exist.[4] The programmes of the Board encouraged growth of a large number of women's organisations. They provided status and activity to many of the erstwhile, active women social or political workers. The CSWB provides a forum for women social workers working in the field of welfare of women and children.[5]

The first Five Year Plan recognised the need for organising social welfare services as distinct from general services and for ensuring public cooperation and participation in the national plan. This could be achieved only through the efforts of voluntary organisations which had to be assisted. For this purpose in First Five-year Plan an amount of Rs. 40 millions was provided for welfare services for women. The Central Social Welfare Board was entrusted to administer this fund for assisting voluntary organisations engaged in the welfare of women and child welfare. Since then, financial assistance was available to the voluntary agencies engaged in women's welfare programmes. The total provision for the Second Plan for social welfare was Rs. 190 million out of which Rs. 92 million were allocated to CSWB.[6] In the Third Plan, the programmes of the CSWB envisaged a total outlay of Rs. 120 million. Similarly, the financial assistance was allocated to CSWB in the other five year plans.

Functions of Central Social Welfare Board

The special fields entrusted to the Board were the welfare of women, children and the handicapped. The functions assigned to the Board were generally to assist in the improvement and development of social welfare activities, and in particular.[7]

(i) to cause a survey to be made of the needs and requirements of social welfare organisations;
(ii) to evaluate the programmes and projects of the aided agencies;
(iii) to co-ordinate social welfare activities by various Ministries in the Central and State Governments;
(iv) to promote the setting up of social welfare organisations on a voluntary basis in places where no such organisations exist;
(v) to render financial aid, when necessary, to deserving

organisations or institutions on terms to be prescribed by the Board;

(vi) to organize a field counselling service as an effective supplement to the working of the grants-in-aid programmes to assess the programmes and projects of aided agencies;

(vii) to promote the setting up of the rural welfare projects to be administered through the agency of the State Social Welfare Advisory Boards;

(viii) to initiate the organisation of pioneering welfare services; and

(ix) to stimulate effective co-ordination among voluntary welfare agencies, especially at the national level and among agencies covered by the grants-in-aid programme.

The following activities are eligible for grants of CSWB:

Welfare Services for Children

(i) Residential institutions for the care, protection, education and rehabilitation of socially handicapped children e.g. orphans, destitute, foundlings, children of unmarried mothers, waifs and strays).

(ii) Temporary homes for children (e.g. uninfected children of leprosy and T.B. patients, children from broken homes, children of unattached women workers employed or under training).

(iii) Day care Centres including Creche, Balwadi, Nursery School or Pre-primary school.

(iv) Recreational and cultural centres and holiday homes for children of low income families.

(v) Infant Health Centres.

(vi) Child Guidance Clinics.

Welfare Services for Women

(i) Residential institutions and reception centres for the care and protection, training and rehabilitation of (a) destitute women and those in distress, and (b) rescued women.

(ii) Women's welfare organisations conducting social education (including domestic science and hygiene and extra-curricular activities for adolescent girls), literacy classes, arts and crafts, recreational activities, etc.

(iii) Maternity centres in places where such service is not easily available.

(iv) Condensed course of training for women.

(v) Hostels for working women (for low income groups).

(vi) Family counselling agencies.

Welfare Services for the Handicapped

(i) Institutions and services for the care and rehabilitation of the physically and mentally handicapped, and supply of aids to them.

(ii) Hostels for the working handicapped.

(iii) Small production units for the handicapped.

(iv) Special schools and residential institutions for children in need of special instruction (e.g. mentally retarded or those who have been under long hospitalized treatment, and orthopaedically handicapped.

Welfare Services for the Aged and the Infirm

(i) Homes, clubs and day care centres for the aged.

(ii) Infirmaries for the chronically ill.

Other Welfare Services for the Community

(i) Urban community centres, including, welfare aspects of slum improvement, clearance and prevention.

(ii) Short-term specialized courses of training for adult women seeking employment.

(iii) Other specialized courses of training for women as approved by the Board.

(iv) Dormitories and Night Shelters.

(v) Small production units set-up by voluntary welfare institutions, including co-operatives set-up for the welfare of women.

(vi) Holiday homes for children.

(vii) Community welfare services in rural areas.

(viii) Welfare services for the children of women who have formed themselves into a co-operative in the socio-economic programme.

Types of Grants

The CSWB provides grants for one or the other of the following purposes:

(a) Development and expansion (quantitatively, while also allowing for qualitative improvement); and
(b) Consolidation and improvement (continuance of an existing programme on a more systematic basis, and providing for qualitative improvement).

In addition to the general purpose grants, the Board gives grants for the following specific purposes:

(a) Buildings.
(b) Mobile vans.
(c) Hostels for working women.
(d) Hostels for the working blind and orthopaedically Handicapped.
(e) Condensed course of training for adult women.
(f) Welfare extension projects (Urban).
(g) Holiday homes for children.
(h) Night shelters.
(i) Welfare activities previously conducted in the welfare extension projects (Rural).

The Central Social Welfare Board functions through the State Social Welfare Advisory Boards. The Board helps and guides voluntary agencies for women welfare through financial assistance under certain conditions. A cadre of welfare and project officers of Board visit aided voluntary agencies in order to assess and evaluate their work and recommend financial assistance for the projects submitted by them. The programmes, which the Board assists, are working women hostels, condensed courses of education and training for women, homes for destitute women and those in moral danger or rescued from brothels, socio-economic programmes for women, creches for children of working women, public cooperation camps for women, etc.

The Central Board has a general body which comprises of all chairpersons of State and Union Territories Boards, five professionals, one each from the fields of law, medicine, nutrition, social work, education and social development, three eminent persons with extensive experience in social work, one representative each of Ministries of Welfare, Rural Development, Health, Education, Labour, Finance and the Planning Commission, two members of Lok Sabha and one member of Rajya Sabha. The Board has a Chairman. The Executive Director of the Board is the Member-Secretary. All of them are nominated by the Minister of Welfare. The administration of the Board is carried out by the Executive Committee, which comprises 15 members including the Chairman and the Executive Director. The Chairman of the Board is its Chief Executive. The Executive Director works under him. He is responsible for all aspects of the working of the Board and performs numerous functions. Every year a conference will be held at the national level, where the chairpersons of the state level boards and the central board members meet to discuss issues and future programmes.

The various schemes, which are funded by the Social Welfare Board, specifically deal with women, who are victims of social customs. The Board deal with groups such as widows and orphans. It seems to bring women dropouts into the fold of education. It deal with raising awareness for women on community activity and helping to organise very poor women to take up what today is called 'income generating activities'. In the old days these were called 'socio-economic-programmes'. It has been argued that the network of agencies that the Central Social Welfare Board was fostering and supporting, were dealing with welfare and not development. It has been argued that the concept of social welfare, being instrument of providing charitable services, which deal with women's gender specific problems like maternity, child health, leisure activities, etc., is not as pugnacious as what is called development, which hinges largely around women's productive role.

However, over the years, the Board has not only widened the scope of its programmes, but has also moved in policy approach from welfare to development to empowerment. Today, it is the pioneering national level organisation in the field of development and empowerment of women in the country. The CSWB was also envisaged as an interface between the Government and the voluntary sector for social development in the country. It has made a signal contribution in encouraging, assisting and promoting the growth of nearly twenty five thousand voluntary organisations for reaching the neglected women and children of the country.

The Union Ministry of Women and Child Development

Women as a target group were originally part of the Department of Social Welfare with a combination of programmes for reduction of physical disabilities, isolation and vulnerability such as old age and widow pension. The programmes like working women's hostels and vocational education for women were clubbed with the handicapped, children and other socially disadvantaged groups as targets. The Department of Social Welfare later became a ministry. In January, 1985, for the first time "Women" were emphasized as a special component of a newly formed department, i.e. the Department of Social and Women's Welfare. The women welfare programmes still were linked with disadvantaged and handicapped groups. In September, 1985 the pressure of the Nairobi closing decade conference (July 1985) and the awareness generated by it, led to the creation of a separate Department of Women and Children. The Department of Women and Child Development was the successor to the Department of Social Welfare, Ministry of Social Welfare and Ministry of Welfare. The Department has been upgraded to a ministry with effect from January 30, 2006. This Ministry represents the highest level of structure on women development in the country. The basic mandate to this newly created Ministry is to look into the issues concerning women. The Ministry is responsible for policy, planning guiding and monitoring programmes of women's development.

The Ministry of Women and Child Development deals with programmes and services concerned with the welfare of women. This is done in two ways:

(1) initiating programmes for women in the government sector; and

(2) assisting voluntary agencies engaged in welfare and development of women. Some of the schemes for which assistance is available are :

(i) Hostels for working women.
(ii) Employment and income generating projects.
(iii) Creches for children of working women.
(iv) Women development corporations.
(v) Support to Training and Employment of Women (STEP).
(vi) Setting up training centers for rehabilitation of women in distress.
(vii) Research on women's issues.
(viii) Training of personnel.

The Ministry implements certain innovative programmes in the areas of welfare and support services—employment and income generation, awareness generation and gender sensitization for women in particular. All these efforts are directed to ensure that women are empowered both economically and socially and thus, become equal partners in national development along with the men.

The Ministry establishes liaison with UN and international agencies, supports State Directorates dealing with women's programmes and provides assistance to the autonomous organisations like the Central Social Welfare Board, National Institute of Public Cooperation and Child Development and other national institutes and organisations concerned with human development. It brings about coordination with other Ministries and Departments of the Government of India concerned with women such as Ministries of Welfare, Rural Development, Agriculture Labour, Health and Family Welfare, Education, Planning Commission, University Grants Commission and various universities. The creation of the Department has given required impetus to the holistic development of women and children.

The Central Ministry of Women and Child Development has considerably strengthened the process of making prospective plans for women, children, the girl child and adolescent girls, as also set up the National Commission for Women, a National Creche Fund, a National Credit Fund, Mahila Samriddhi Yojana and Indira Mahila Vikas Yojana.[8] It has acted as an effective nodal unit for monitoring activities relating to women's development in various ministries of the government and taken them for review before the cabinet and its committees. Its work in preparing legal literacy manuals and gender sensitization of government personnel-administrative, police and judiciary as well as parliamentarians is commendable. The Minister is in-charge of the Ministry of Women and Child Development. There are one Secretary, two Additional Secretaries, three Joint Secretaries, one academic advisor and one Statistical Advisor who are assisted by Directors, Deputy Secretaries and Under Secretaries besides the office staff.

Organisational Structure of Ministry of Women and Child Development

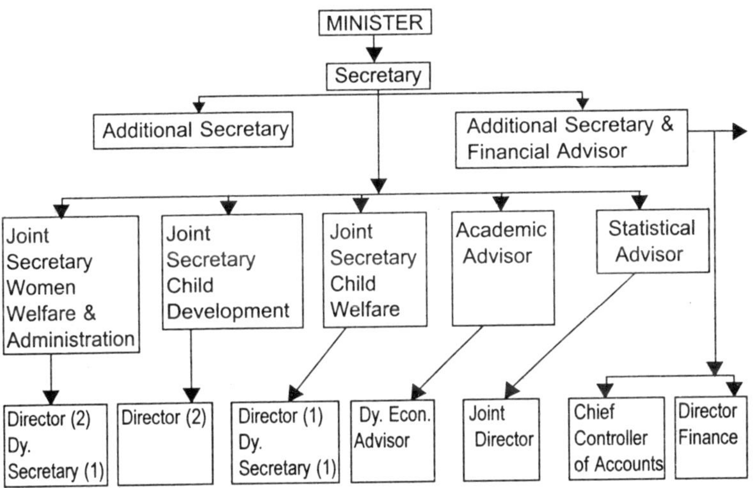

The activities of the Ministry are performed by the following bureaus:

(1) Bureau of Nutrition and Child Development (NCD).
(2) Bureau of Women's Welfare and Development (WWD).
(3) Bureau for Women's Programmes of Mahila Samriddhi Yojana, Indira Mahila Yojana and Rashtriya Mahila Kosh.
(4) Bureau of Child Welfare and Child Protection.
(5) Statistical Unit, Plan Research, Monitoring and Evaluation.

The Ministry has six autonomous organisations viz., National Institute of Public Cooperation and Child Development (NIPCCD), Rashtriya Mahila Kosh (RMK); Central Social Welfare Board (CSWB), Central Adoption Resource Agency (CARA), National Commission for Protection for Child Rights (NCPCR) and National Commission for Women (NCW). The first two—NIPCCD and RMK—are societies registered under the Societies Registration Act, 1860, while CSWB is a charitable company registered under the Indian Companies Act, 1956. The CARA is a central level institution for child welfare. The other two organisaitons are national level commissions. These organisations are funded by the Government of India and they assist the Ministry in its functions.

The Ministry has its own Research Division, which also sponsors research through Home Science Colleges, Schools of Social Work and University Departments of Sociology and Psychology and other institutions engaged in social science research. The research division of the department assisted by the National Institute of Public Cooperation and Child Development, sponsors and initiates research and evaluation studies and workshops on women related issues. The organisation and activities of the CSWB were already discussed. The objectives and schemes of RMK and the role of Women's Bureau are discussed in detail in the following pages.

Women's Welfare and Development Bureau

The Women's Welfare and Development Bureau is charged with the nodal responsibility of:

(a) coordination and collaborating with other central government Ministries;
(b) initiating policies, programmes and measures;
(c) collecting data and serves as a clearing house;
(d) monitoring programmes for women's welfare;
(e) coordinating the implementation of programmes at the State Government level;
(f) servicing the national committee, the steering committee, inter-departmental coordination committee, etc.;
(g) following up on the recommendations of the CSWI, the

Nairobi Forward Looking Strategies and other important reports;

(h) administration of legislative enactments;

(i) liaison with multilateral and UN agencies in the field of women's welfare; and

(j) monitoring beneficiary-oriented programmes for women.

The Bureau has also been realizing funds to the Central Social Welfare Board for the implementation of the following major schemes for the benefit of women:

(1) Socio-economic programmes with the objective of providing opportunities for employment to women who are economically backward, destitutes, widows, deserted and disabled.

(2) Development of a curriculum for education and vocational training programmes for adult women.

(3) Training of rural women in public corporation.

(4) Family Counselling centres.

(5) Creches for children of working and ailing mothers, supplementary nutrition programme and integrated pre-school projects.

The Bureau functions under a Joint Secretary in the Department of Women and Child Development of the Ministry of Human Resource Development. The Joint Secretary in-charge of the Bureau is designated as the Bureau Head, who reports to the Secretary in the Department of Women and Child Development and through the Secretary to the Ministry of State for Women and Child Development. To intensify efforts and measures needed for ensuring participation of women in national development, periodic coordination meetings are organised by the Bureau. These meetings are held with the representatives of women's voluntary organisations, ministries and departments concerned, Central Social Welfare Board, etc., to review the progress of women's welfare programmes and to discuss various issues related to exploitation of women and atrocities committed against them.

The Bureau also functions as a complaint cell, wherein complaints related to dowry demands, non-transfer of dowry to the bride on divorce or death, dowry deaths, etc., are being dealt with. As a nodal point, the WWD Bureau takes up various types of grievances. These include non-implementation of social legislations, non-compliance of policy decisions, guidelines or instructions relating to posting of husband and wife at the same station by government, public sector undertakings, retrenchment of *ad-hoc* female employees, provisions relating to maternity leave, bigamy committed by government employees violating the provisions of the conduct rules, cruelty towards the wife, desertion, unfair treatment or harassment of women employees, etc. The monitoring cell of the Women's Bureau set-up in 1985 has 27 programmes in 8-10 departments to monitor. The emphasis has been on reviewing targets and in a limited way assessing the quality of services.

Rashtriya Mahila Kosh

The Rashtriya Mahila Kosh (RMK) was set up on 30th March, 1993 as a registered society under the Societies Registration Act, 1860, under the auspices of the Union Department of Women and Child Development. RMK was given a one time corpus fund of Rs. 31 crore. The Kosh is administered by a Governing Board of 16 members consisting of senior officers of Central and State Governments and specialists and representatives of organisations active in the field of micro-credit for women. The Governing Board is chaired by Minister of State for Women and Child Development. Since its inception, the RMK has established itself as the premier micro-credit agency of the country, with its focus on women and their empowerment through the provision of credit for livelihood and related activities. Its success can be gauged by the geographical spread of its credit delivery system and its partnership with about 700 NGO partners.

The main objective of RMK is to facilitate credit support or micro-finance to poor women, as an instrument of socio-economic change and development. The RMK mainly channelises its support through non-governmental organisations, women development corporations, women cooperative societies, indira mahila block samities under the Indira Mahila Yojana and suitable state government agencies. The Kosh has taken a number of promotional measures for popularising the concept of micro-financing, thrift-credit, formation and stabilisation of Self Help

Groups and also enterprise development for poor women. Some of the promotional and other innovative schemes of RMK are explained below:

(a) Loan Promotion Scheme

The Loan Promotion Scheme (LPS) has been designed to promote the activities of thrift and credit among smaller but potentially capable NGOs which do not meet the requirement of 3 years experience in thrift and credit management. The requirement of experience under this scheme has been reduced to one year. In other words, the NGO must have at least 1 year's experience in thrift and credit. However, other eligibility norms are the same as in the case of RMK Main Loan Scheme. The maximum loan amount given to an NGO under this scheme is Rs. 5 lakhs.

(b) Self Help Group Development Scheme

Under the scheme of Self Help Group Development, financial assistance by way of interest-free loan convertible into grant on the fulfilment of specific conditions is given to the NGOs for formation, development and stabilisation of SHGs. The amount of assistance provided is Rs. 4,300 for one SHG or Rs. 1 lakh for 25 SHGs during the first year. The portion of interest-free loan which is not converted into grant at the end of 30 months is recoverable by RMK at 8 per cent rate of interest. Conversion into grant is contingent on the SHG or the NGO applying for substantive loans under the loan promotion scheme.

(c) Nodal Agency Scheme

The Nodal Agency Scheme of RMK has been introduced to utilise the services of experienced and reputed organisations to promote new potential NGOs through training, monitoring and to help these acquire necessary capability to avail credit facilities from RMK. The organisations with micro-credit experience, adequate infrastructure and training capabilities are eligible to take up Nodal Agency functions for RMK on entering into a Memorandum of Understanding with the RMK. The Nodal Agency will identify and prepare new NGOs to eventually link them with RMK for extending credit facilities to poor women for income generation activities. The Scheme has been revised and made target oriented where each Nodal Agency will link at least 12-15 new NGOs with Rashtriya Mahila Kosh under one stream.

(d) Marketing Finance Scheme

The scheme was introduced by RMK to help women beneficiaries to market their products.

Women Cells in Central Ministries

Besides the Union Department of Women and Child Development, there are other ministries and departments which provide funds for different aspects of women welfare and development programmes. They are:

1. Department of Education
2. Ministry of Welfare
3. Ministry of Health and Family Welfare
4. Ministry of Agriculture
5. Ministry of Rural Development
6. Ministry of Industry
7. Ministry of Textiles
8. Ministry of Science and Technology
9. Ministry of Environment and Forest
10. Ministry of Labour (Vocational Training and Employment)
11. Ministry of Food
12. Ministry of Energy

The schemes for women of the respective departments and ministries are being monitored by the Women Cells. The National Perspective Plan for Women had recommended that the Planning Commission and each ministry and department should have a women's cell. Pursuant thereto, women's cells were set-up in several ministries and departments. A special unit was also set-up in the Planning Commission.

National Commission for Women

In view of suggestions emerging at various forums and recommendations contained in reports of various committees and commissions, the Government of India realized the importance of various issues concerning women's status. Accordingly, it has set-up a statutory National Commission for Women, consisting of chairperson and six members representing trade unions, voluntary organisations, administration and social services. There is a member secretary, who may be an expert in management, or a member of civil service.

The main task of the Commission shall be to study and monitor all matters relating to the constitutional and legal safeguards provided for women, to review the existing legislations and suggest amendments, wherever necessary. It will also look into the complaints and take *suo moto* notice of the cases involving deprivation of the rights of women in order to provide support, legal or otherwise, to helpless women. The Commission shall monitor the proper implementation of all the legislations enacted to protect the rights of women, so as to enable them to achieve equality in all spheres of life and equal participation in the development of the nation.

Functions of the Commission

The Commission shall perform all or any of the following functions:

(a) investigate and examine all matters relating to the safeguards provided for women under the Constitution and other laws;

(b) present to the Central Government, annually and at such other times as the Commission may deem fit, reports upon the working of those safeguards;

(c) make such reports and recommendations for the effective implementation of those safeguards for improving the conditions of women by the Union or any State;

(d) review, from time to time, the existing provisions of the Constitution and other laws affecting women and recommend amendments thereto so as to suggest remedial legislative measures to meet any lacunae, inadequacies or shortcomings in such legislations;

(e) take up the cases of violation of the provisions of the Constitution and of other laws relating to women with the appropriate authorities;

(f) look into complaints and take *suo moto* notice of matters relating to —

(i) deprivation of women's rights;

(ii) non-implementation of laws enacted to provide protection to women and also to achieve the objective of equality and development; and

(iii) non-compliance of policy decisions, guidelines or instructions aimed at mitigating hardships and ensuring welfare and providing relief to women;

(g) call for special studies or investigations into specific problems or situations arising out of discrimination and atrocities against women and identify the constraints so as to recommend strategies for their removal;

(h) undertake promotional and educational research so as to suggest ways of ensuring due representation of women in all spheres and identify factors responsible for impeding their advancement, such as, lack of access to housing and basic services, inadequate support services and technologies for reducing drudgery and occupational health hazards and for increasing their productivity;

(i) Participate and advise on the planning process of socio-economic development of women;

(j) Evaluate the progress of the development of women under the Union and any State;

(k) Inspect or cause to be inspected a jail, remand home, women's institution or other place of custody where women are kept as prisoners or otherwise, and take up with the concerned authorities for remedial action, if found necessary;

(l) Fund litigation involving issues affecting a large body of women;

(m) Make periodical reports to the Government on any matter pertaining to women and in particular various difficulties under which women toil; and

(n) Any other matter which may be referred to it by the Central Government.

The Central Government shall cause all the reports to be laid before each House of Parliament along with a memorandum explaining the action taken or proposed to be taken on the recommendations relating to the Union and the reasons for the non-acceptance, if any, of any of such recommendations. Where any such report or any part thereof relates to any matter with which any State Government is concerned, the Commission shall forward a copy of such report or part to such State Government who shall cause it to be laid before the Legislature of the State along with a memorandum explaining the action taken or proposed to be taken on the recommendations relating to the State and reasons for the non-acceptance, if any, of any of such recommendations. The Commission shall, while investigating any matter, have all the powers of a civil court trying a suit and, in particular, in respect of the following matters, namely:

(a) summoning and enforcing the attendance of any person from any part of India and examining him on oath;
(b) requiring the discovery and production of any document;
(c) receiving evidence on affidavits;
(d) requisitioning any public record or copy thereof from any court or office;
(e) issuing commissions for the examination of witnesses and documents; and
(f) any other matter which may be prescribed.

Evaluation of the progress of the development of women under the union and any state is one of the statutory functions assigned to the Commission under Section 10(1) of the National Commission for Women Act, 1990. The task, obviously, is a stupendous one.[9] The Commission attempted to assess the progress of women's development in the following sectors:

1. Demography and Health,
2. Education, and
3. Employment.

The Commission called for information regarding the role and activities of Women's Cells since their setting up from all the concerned ministries and departments. The feedback indicated that most of the cells were dormant and many of them were not even aware of their scope and functions. Recognising the need to activate women's cells, to define their role and functions and to promote exchange of ideas and information among the cells, the Commission convened a meeting of senior officers of the concerned ministries and departments. Pursuant to the deliberations a sub-committee was set up to prepare guidelines for women's cells. The sub-committee consisted of representatives of the Commission as well as the Ministers of Finance, Rural Development and the Department of Women and Child Development. After considering the suggestions of the Sub-Committee, the Commission issued guidelines for women's cells, which included *inter alia* the following :

(a) The departments as well as public sector undertakings and autonomous bodies under their control, should set-up women cells in their organisations within a specific period.

(b) The women's cells should review the plan schemes and other programmes of the department or public enterprise concerned and ensure that wherever possible the aspect of women's development is promoted through these schemes.

(c) The programmes of their respective departments may be examined and wherever feasible, a component for women's development be introduced in the activity by getting the schemes amended suitably.

(d) The concerned department and public enterprise should collect basic information and data regarding employment of women in the organisation, their educational status and other relevant data.

Further, the guidelines indicated that these cells should promote:

(1) an all round development of women employees of the ministries, departments and other organisations; and

(2) the development of the male as well as female employees through non-formal and adult education, health care, family care assistance, training for skill formation, etc.

The Commission continued to pursue its mandated role and activities, the most prominent being the review of laws, looking into specific cases of complaints, atrocities, harassment, denial of rights and exploitation of women and taking remedial action to restore their legitimate rights. The Complaint and Counselling Cell is the core unit of the Commission. It processes complaints received by the Commission either orally or in writing or taken cognisance by the Commission *suo-moto* under Section 10 of the NCW Act, 1990.

Out of 41 legislations having direct bearing on women, the Commission reviewed and suggested remedial legislative measures in 32 Acts and forwarded the same to the Government for necessary action. These laws relate to sati, dowry, infant milk substitutes, maternity benefits, guardians and wards, indecent representation of women, immoral trafficking, medical termination of pregnancy, child marriage, family courts, married women's property, adoptions, pre-natal diagnostic techniques, factories, Hindu succession, minimum wages, ESI, bonded labour, etc. The Commission also recommended enhancement of maintenance allowance prescribed under Section 125 of Cr.P.C. and stringent punishment for outraging the modesty of women under Section 354 of the I.P.C.

State Level Institutions

Generally in States, Department of Social Welfare looks after the women development programmes. The Secretary of the Social Welfare in addition to his other welfare functions also looks after the welfare of women. In a combined department the work of women welfare is handled by a Deputy Secretary or a Special Secretary. At the Directorate level, the work is looked after by the Director of Social Welfare, who is Director of Social Welfare programmes in general.

On setting up the DWCD at the Centre instructions were issued to the States to set-up separate departments on this subject. Most of the State Governments have set-up directorates for Women and Child Development within the social welfare departments but separate independent departments headed by secretary level officials have come into existence in states like Haryana, Rajasthan, Maharashtra, Karnataka, Uttar Pradesh, Andhra Pradesh, Kerala and Tamil Nadu. The Rajastan Government created for instance a separate department of Women, Children and Nutrition in 1985, which was later named as the Department of Women and Child Development and various programmes running in different departments were placed under this Department. The other states have social and women's welfare departments or only a social welfare department. The other departments at the State level, which are concerned with women development are education, health and family welfare, labour, agriculture, etc. Each one of these are equally concerned about women development, particularly in relation to female education, family size, training and employment, role of women in agriculture development, etc.

The State Department or Directorate of Women and Child Development maintains liaison with other State level departments and with other bodies like the State Social Welfare Advisory Board, Women Development Cooperatives, Khadi and Village Industries Commission, etc. The Directorates implement various central and state schemes concerning women and child development. This is done through district level Social Welfare Officers and by the Block Development Officers at the block level.

Andhra Pradesh is one of the few states, which had created a separate ministry for women development and child welfare. The Ministry of Women Development and Child Welfare has been continuously working since 1976 in the State. The aim of this Ministry is to bring improvement in the living conditions of women and children and make them march ahead in the development path. According to an estimate 70 per cent of the state's population come under the umbrella of this Ministry.[10] The aims and objectives of the ministry include:

1. Establishment of Balwadis, Creches, Sisu Mandirs and Children Homes for child welfare,
2. Establishment of Short Stay Homes for destitute and affected women, who lost shelter and need protection,
3. Implementation of Integrated Child Development Service Scheme to provide nutritious food and education to children below 6 years,
4. Socio-educational and political development of women,
5. Implementation of Girl Child Protection Scheme,

6. Identification of orphan girls and initiating measures for their development, and
7. Undertaking various programmes like women economic empowerment and health awareness among women.

The women development and child welfare programmes are being undertaken throughout state under the guidance and control of a senior I.A.S. officer designated as Director. There are about 104 officers and employees in the Directorate. The state has been divided into six regions for administrative convenience and to administer the programmes of the Ministry. The Regional Deputy Director is the head of the regional office. On an average, 10 officers and employees are working in a regional office. The headquarters of the regional offices are located in Visakhapatnam, Eluru, Ongole, Kurnool, Warangal and Hyderabad. There are 3 to 6 districts under the jurisdiction of each regional office. There are district officers in all the 23 districts for the ministry. These officers designated as Project Directors organize and supervise ICDS centres and take necessary steps for women development and child welfare in the districts. A total of 345 officers and employees are working in the district offices.

The details on administrative set-up of the Ministry of Women Development and Child Welfare are given below:

(1)	**Office of the Director**:		
	Director	...	1
	Officers and employees	...	104
(2)	**Regional Offices**:		
	Deputy Directors	...	6
	Officers and employees	...	66
(3)	**District Offices**:		
	Project Directors	...	23
	Officers and employees	...	345
(4)	**ICDS Scheme**:		
	Child Development Programme Officers	...	251
	Supervisors	...	1,891
	Anganwadi Centres	...	37,303
	Mothers' Committees	...	36,436

There are modifications and changes in this machinery from time to time. There is budgetary allocation for the Ministry. The Government of Andhra Pradesh allocated an amount of Rs. 271,81,43,000 and Rs. 30,32,04,000 under plan and non-plan allocation, respectively to the Ministry for the year 2000-01. The allocation to the Ministry was increased by Rs. 100 crores in the 2002-03 Annual Budget. In addition to these allocations, the Central Government provides budgetary allocation to the State Ministry for the implementation of various programmes.

The Ministry has been undertaking its various programmes in order to fulfil its aims and objectives through different institutions and centres in the districts. There are about 251 ICDS projects covering 37,303 Anganwadi Centres in the State. Eighty one children homes are being maintained by the Ministry. There are six service homes, one each in Srikakulam, Krishna, Prakasam, Chittoor, Warangal and Hyderabad districts, which provide shelter to poor women. The Ministry is running nine State Homes for the girls, who are unable to protect themselves. At present there are 17 working women's hostels under the management of the Ministry of Women Development and Child Welfare. These hostels have been established to provide shelter to women employees from lower and middle income groups. One family counseling centre in each district is being run by the Ministry. There are two old age homes for women in the state-one in Chittoor and the other in Hyderabad—to provide shelter to old and orphan women. The details on district-wise institutions and centres are given in the Table 4.1.

A brief descriptions of the institutions, centres and services of the Ministry is given in the following pages.

Creches

The A.P. Ministry of Women Development and Child Welfare is maintaining 229 creches for the children in 23 districts. These creches are very useful to the children of SCs, STs and other weaker sections. There are 30 children in each creche. The creches are intended for children of below six years. Majority of the children benefited from these crèches are from the lower income families, particularly from agricultural labourers and labourers in unorganized sector. An amount of Rs. 373.03 lakhs was allocated

TABLE 4.1

District-wise Details of Schemes and Institutions

Sl. No.	Name of the District	ICDS		Institutions of the Ministry					
		No. of Projects	No. of Anganawadi Centres	Children Home	Collegiate Home	Service State Home	Working Women's Hostel	Old Age Home	Family Councelling Centres
1	2	3	4	5	6	7	8	9	10
1.	Srikakulam	10	1284	3	1	1	1		1
2.	Vizianagaram	9	1218	3			1		1
3.	Visakhapatnam	14	1621	5			2		1
4.	East Godavari	16	2058	4		1			1
5.	West Godavari	7	1064	3		1			1
6.	Krishna	13	2269	4	1		1		1
7.	Guntur	7	1025	3			1		1
8.	Prakasam	11	1559	3	1				1
9.	Nellore	12	1467	5		1	1		1
10.	Chittoor	16	2048	3	1		1	1	1
11.	Kadapa	11	1546	4					1
12.	Anantapuram	17	2316	3		1	1		1
13.	Kurnool	14	2042	3			1		1
14.	Warangal	12	2069	4	1	1	1		1

(Contd.)

TABLE 4.1 (*Contd.*)

1	*2*	*3*	*4*	*5*	*6*	*7*	*8*	*9*	*10*
15.	Khammam	13	2324	3			1		1
16.	Karimnagar	11	1702	3					1
17.	Adilabad	11	1846	4					1
18.	Hyderabad	5	646	2	1	1	1	1	1
19.	Rangareddy	7	1035	4					1
20.	Madick	7	1274	4					1
21.	Nizamabad	8	1254	3					1
22.	Nalgonda	9	1297	3					1
23.	Mahaboobnagar	11	2339	5		1			1
	Total	251	37303	81	6	9	17	2	23

for the maintenance of creches in the State during 1999-2000. A total of 6,568 children were benefited from these crèches.

Sisu Vihars

The Ministry is maintaining two Sisu Vihars, one in Chittoor and the other in Hyderabad for the welfare of orphan children. A total of 60 children can take shelter in these two Sisu Vihars. The parents, who are unable to take care of their children of below six years can admit them in these vihars. The couples, who do not have children can adopt the children from the Sisu Vihars according to law. The Government of Andhra Pradesh allocated an amount of Rs. 8.84 lakhs for the maintenance of the Sisu Vihars during 2001-02.

Balwadis

A total of 166 Balwadis are working at present in the State. In the last year 1918 children got shelter in these balwadies. The poor children in the age group of 3-5 years are eligible to get shelter in the balwadis. The children from the backward classes in rural areas and outskirts of cities are getting shelter in the balwadis. The mid-day meal scheme was implemented to the children in the balwadis. An amount of Rs. 241.78 lakhs was spent on the maintenance of balwadis in the year 2001-02.

Bal Vihars

The State Government is also maintaining Bal Vihars for the dropouts from the school. Shelter is provided to the children between 3 and 6 years to spend time happily in these Bal Vihars. There are 22 Bal Vihars in the State. The children from low income and backward classes can join these Bal Vihars, which facilitate physical and mental growth and creative capacity among the children. About 660 children joined Bal Vihars during the last year. An amount of Rs. 43.37 lakhs was allocated for the maintenance of Bal Vihars during 2001-02.

Sisu Sadans

A total of 81 Sisu Sadans are working in the State. The orphans, handicapped and the children of ex-servicemen will get entry into these sadans. The children between 6 and 10 years will get shelter here. The facilities like food, cloth and health protection are available to these children. There is a scope for studies upto 10th class here. During the year 2001-02, about 4,674 children were benefited from these sadans. In the same year, the State Government spent an amount of Rs. 453.27 lakhs for the benefit of children of these sisu sadans.

Balika Sadans

There are six Balika Sadans in the State. The women in the age group of 15-25 will get shelter in these sadans. Preference will be given to orphan and lower income group women. The women, who join these sadans can stay for a maximum period of 5 years. The staff of the sadan encourage the women to pursue their higher studies. They will be given training in nursing. They will be taught in typewriting, tailoring and embroidery. A total of 164 women stayed in all the six sadans during 2001-02. An amount of Rs. 31.01 lakhs provided for the management of these sadans during the same year.

Mother and Child Welfare Centres

The mothers will be given training on the health of children and their capacities will be increased in the mother and children welfare centres. The mid-day meal scheme will be implemented to the mothers. The mothers will also be given training on the importance of nutritious food, measures to be taken in child rearing and handicrafts. At present there are 42 centres in the State. The shelter is available to 30 mothers and 30 children in each centre. The children between 3 and 6 years and mothers between 15 and 45 years can stay in these centres. Two teachers and two ayahs are entrusted the job of maintaining these centres. For the maintenance of these centres, the State Government provided an allocation of Rs. 60.06 lakhs during 2001-02. About 2,520 mothers and children have been benefited from these centres.

Old Women Sadans

The aim of the old women sadans is to provide shelter for women above 60 years age and facilitate them to spend their remaining life peacefully. There are two old age homes for women in the state, one in Chittoor and the other in Hyderabad. The food, clothes and health of the old women will be taken care of in these homes. By the end of 2001-02, there were 34 old women in these two sadans. An amount of Rs. 8.77 lakhs was spent by the Government on the maintenance of these homes during the same year.

Rescue Home

A rescue home is working in Hyderabad under the management of Ministry of Women Development and Child Welfare. The women will be given shelter and protection here on court directions. In addition to shelter for a specific period, the food, clothes and medical facilities will be provided to them. At present 18 women are getting shelter in this home. The Government provide funds for the management of the rescue home.

Service Home

There are 5 service homes in the State, which benefit about 240 women belonging to poor families and in the age group of 18-25 years. The training programmes will be conducted for the benefit of women of these homes. The programmes on business techniques, work skills improvement, etc., will be conducted to them. The facilities of food, cloth, shelter and medicines will be provided to the women in the service homes.

State Home

The State Government has been running four state homes for the women, who cannot protect themselves. At present 210 women are sheltered in these homes, who have been provided training and education and encouraged self-employment. Free food and clothes will be provided to them during their stay in the homes. The State Government provides grants for the management of these homes.

Working Women's Hostels

The working women's hostels have been established to provide accommodation to women employees belonging to lower and middle income groups. At present there are 17 hostels under the management of Ministry of Women Development and Child

Welfare. The women employees will be charged nominal fee for their stay and food in the hostels.

In addition to the maintenance of above mentioned institutions, the Ministry of Women Development and Child Welfare conducts programmes which facilitate employment to women. The training will be provided to the women between 15 and 45 years of age on tailoring, handicrafts, computers and electronics. The exhibitions will be conducted for the marketing of goods made by the women. The women welfare organizers of the Ministry will visit the houses and explain about the income generating works to the women.

State Social Welfare Advisory Boards

In order to achieve decentralization, the CSWB had set-up its counterparts in the States. By August, 1954 Social Welfare Advisory Boards had been set-up by all State Governments, with the following functions:

(a) to act as media for exchange of information between the field and the centre and *vice versa;*

(b) to invite, receive, examine and recommend to the Central Social Welfare Board applications for grants-in-aid from voluntary welfare institutions;

(c) to supervise generally and report on the working of the aided institutions;

(d) to advise and assist the Central Board in sponsoring new welfare programmes and activities wherever they were needed within their States;

(e) to co-ordinate the welfare and development activities undertaken by the various Departments of the State Government with a view to avoiding duplication;

(f) to undertake such other activities as might be conducive to the fulfilment of these objectives;

(g) to promote the growth of voluntary social welfare agencies, with special reference to development of welfare services in areas not covered at present;

(h) to assist the Central Social Welfare Board in the provision of a field counselling service for aided agencies;

(i) to administer the programmes of rural welfare projects;

(j) to stimulate effective co-ordination among voluntary welfare agencies at the State and local levels; and

(k) to assist the Central Social Welfare Board and the State Governments in the further development of welfare service.

Women Development Corporations

The Women Development Corporations are the newly created state level autonomous organisations set-up at the initiative of the Government of India. The scheme to set-up Women's Development Corporations (WDCs) in all the states and union territories was formulated in 1985-86. The outlay for the plan was Rs. 16 crores and the annual plan in 1985-86, was Rs. 50 lakhs.

According to the scheme, the Central Government was to assist the State Governments by providing upto 49 per cent of the total capital cost of each corporation. Fifteen WDCs have been set-up so far in different states and union territories. Some of the corporations were established much before the announcement by the Centre to set-up WDCs.[11] These include the Maharashtra Mahila Arthik Vikas Maha Mandal Ltd. (1975), Punjab Women and Children Development and Welfare Corporation (1979), Chandigarh Children and Women Development Corporation (1982), Gujarat Women Economic Development Corporation (1981), Tamil Nadu Development Corporation (1983) and Andhra Pradesh Women's Cooperative Finance Corporation Limited (1975). The rest of the WDCs were set-up under the scheme in the states of Bihar, Himachal Pradesh, Manipur, Orissa, Uttar Pradesh, Kerala among others.

The objectives of the WDCs, as outlined in the guidelines, emphasized the need for providing employment to women from the rural sector and poverty households, so that they may become economically independent and self-reliant. The other important objective was to identify women entrepreneurs, provide technical consultancy services and facilitate availability of credit through banks and other financial institutions. The profiles of some women development corporations are described briefly.

Andhra Pradesh Women's Co-operative Finance Corporation

The Andhra Pradesh Women's Co-operative Finance Corporation (APWCFC) is a Government of Andhra Pradesh undertaking. It was established in the year 1975 with the aim of empowerment of women on the eve of International Women's year. The Corporation was registered under the Provision of Section 7 of Andhra Pradesh Cooperative Societies Act, 1964. The head office is located at headquarters the State Capital city. The corporation is one of the front runners in promotion of economic activities among the rural women in Andhra Pradesh. The Corporation is promoting different traditional and non-traditional economic activities among the poor and deprived by providing skill development training in marketable trades with the support of AP State Government, National Bank for Agriculture and Rural Development (NABARD), Small Industries Development Bank of India (SIDBI) and Government o India through the Women and Child Development Department under different schemes. The core activities of the corporation are:

1. Management of Mahila Sisu Kendrams in the State.
2. Working Women's Hostels.
3. Coordination of Programmes of Non-Governmental Organisations (NGOs).
4. Marketing.
5. Micro Finance Programme.
6. Running Training-*cum*-Production Units.

The management of the Corporation is vested with the Board of Directors. The Board consists of eighteen persons of whom six are elected by the General Body from among the delegates of affiliated 'A' class share holders and the rest shall be nominated by the Government from various government departments. An eminent person is appointed as Chairperson by the state government. The structure of the organisation is extended to the different levels such as district, mandal and village levels. The officers of the Corporation at headquarters are:

(1) Chairperson	1
(2) Directors	4
(3) Managing Director	1
(4) Marketing Manager	1
(5) Development Officer	1
(6) Administrative Officer	1
(7) Monitoring Officer	1
(8) Liaison Officers	3

Mahila Sisu Vikasa Kendrams have been created during 1987-88 as an extended activity of the Corporation in all the districts in the State.[12] These Vikasa Kendrams are nucleus women resource centres with

1. 10-12 acre area
2. Training classrooms
3. Training-*cum*-production equipment
4. Dormitories and Hostels
5. Creches
6. Capacity to house 200 women

APWCFC is running 23 District Kendrams for promotion of different traditional and non-traditional economic activities among the poor and deprived women. All the Mahila Kendrams are in rural areas in each of the 23 districts of Andhra Pradesh and are well equipped with training equipment, stay and boarding facilities, and administrative set-up. These Kendrams are Resource Centres for the overall development of women in the district. It may not be exaggerated to say that these Kendrams, besides training a large number of women in income generating activities, are also the source of confidence for women in the districts, when they feel helpless to survive. Most of the women trained in the Kendrams belong to deprived sections.

To facilitate the stakeholders for having more access to information about the multi-faceted activities of the Corporation and to spell out its mission and vision for better understanding and utilization, the Corporation is launching its monthly magazine Taruni, which provides complete information about the core activities of the Corporation at the state level, and the activities undertaken through the Mahila Vikasa Kendrams at the district level, with the objective of empowering women of different groups (NGOs, Women Entrepreneurs, Self Help Groups, etc.) by providing access to the latest information on women related issues. The corporation undertakes the following activities in the state.

Vocational Training Programmes

The APWCFC is conducting various skill development training programmes through the Durgabai Mahila Sisu Vikasa Kendrams. Training is given in a variety of vocational programmes for the benefit of the target women under various schemes. The programmes include courses and trades such as computer training, pre-primary teachers training, community health workers, multi-purpose health workers, food processing, designing and manufacturing of garments, embroidery, screen printing, lace making, block printing, manufacture of jute articles and other courses like personal secretary, health workers, lab technician, etc. These programmes are progressing with the assistance of Government of India and other agencies like District Rural Development Agency (DRDA), SC Co-operative Finance Corporation, Integrated Tribal Development Agency (ITDA), Municipalities, etc.

Residential training is imparted in specific trades with market oriented course contents using wide variety of training methodologies such as group discussions, role plays, panel discussions, interactive session, field visits, exposure tours, guest lectures, personality development and spoken English courses linked up with employment placement through self employment and wage employment.

Construction and Management of Working Women's Hostels

With an intension of creating a safe and secured living accommodation for working women the Corporation had with the assistance of Government of India constructed 14 WWHs and out of which 10 WWHs are managed by Women Development and Child Welfare Department and 4 are managed by APWCFC. Constructions of 4 WWHs buildings are in progress.

Entrepreneurship Development Programmes

Entrepreneurial, managerial and accounting skills are imparted to the women trained in various vocational training programmes. Some of these programmes are conducted with assistance from NABARD and other line departments dealing with various schemes like Prime Minister Rozgar Yojana (PMRY), Chief Minister Empowerment for Youth (CMEY), Swarnayanthi Gram Swarozgar Yojana (SGSY), Sampurna Grameena Swarozgar Yojana (SGSRY), etc.

Sensitization Programmes

Sensitization programme to tackle the issue of gender discrimination and insensitivity towards women is conducted to field functionaries of various departments and women groups involving the line departments in the district such as Women Development Department, Health and Family Welfare Department, Rural Development Department, etc.

Production Units

The production units have been set with a vision that they provide gainful employment to ex-trainees. The painting, screen painting, bakery, dress-making, leather articles, soap making, units are functioning in the premises of the Kendrams. Two major units—off-set printing and screen printing units are functioning in the premises of Head Office. The production units are contributing for the self-sustainability of the Kendrams.

Demonstration Programmes

Demonstration programmes are being conducted to provide exposure-*cum*-training in some trades like floral arrangements, embroidery, saree rolling, bakery, fabric painting, pot painting, fast food, preparation of jam jellies, squashes, etc. for the house wives, school and college dropouts.

Residential Bridge School for School Dropouts

This programme is undertaken to mainstream the girl child labour working with hazardous and non-hazardous industries and school dropout through the bridge school. Bridge course is conducted for 100 children per annum through each district centre.

These programmes are conducted with assistance from International Labour Organisation (ILO) and District Primary Education Programme (DPEP).

Anganwadi Training Centers

These training centers are imparting training to Anganwadi Supervisors, workers and helpers of ICDS Projects.

Incubators

Incubators have been set-up with the equipment available in the Mahila Vikas Kendrams to facilitate those women who have entrepreneurial skills but lack of finance to set-up their own units. It is available on nominal rent basis to encourage women entrepreneurs and women groups for starting their production prior to establishing their own units.

Mother Units

Mother units have been set-up to facilitate those women who have the skill but lack entrepreneurial skills. These centers provide transfer of technologies, training to women, quality control and production techniques. Women manufacture the products in their households with semi-finished raw materials given through these centers, and send them back for ultimate packing, pricing, branding and marketing.

Land Utilization

Every Mahila Vikasa Kendram has 4 to 6 acres of land vacant for development. For optimum utilization of vacant land medicinal plants, fruit gardens, flower orchids, aqua-culture, nursery, kitchen garden, etc. are grown depending on the suitability of the soil.

Marketing—Taruni Resource Center

Taruni Resource Center has been set-up with a vision to create marketing platform to the products produced by rural women. The resource center provides continuous skill up gradation and guidance to the women producers. This would eliminate middlemen and improve bargaining power. Through this center, facility for design development and brand management, exposure to modern marketing and sales techniques would be provided through exclusive workshops, seminars, buyer and seller meets and exposure to social development aspects are also provided.

Micro Finance Programme

Keeping in view the recent trends in micro finances, a need was felt to develop a easy friendly non-cumbersome micro finance programme to facilitate women to encourage to take up income generation activities and also to encourage to establish their own micro enterprises. Loans are sanctioned to individuals up to Rs. 50,000 for taking up their vocational activity. The criteria for availing the loan is that the women have not received any other loans from any other organisations and are not a part of DWCRA group. Preference is given to beneficiary who is linked to Vana Samrakshana Samithi, Sainik Welfare, Police Welfare, etc., so that the loan amount is recovered with least difficulty. The easy monthly installment is also flexible so that the repayment is regular in monthly instalments.

Training Programme of Family Welfare Department

The Corporation is providing training to women health volunteers under the Training Programme of Department of Family Welfare through Mahila Sisu Vikasa Kendrams in the State. This training is aimed at providing training to the women health volunteers to build awareness among rural women about institutional deliveries safe motherhood and child care through the primary health centers and district hospitals.

The Gujarat Women's Development Corporation

The Gujarat Women's Development Corporation was set-up as a registered society in March 1981. The Corporation became a company in August 1988 under the Companies Act, 1956, and started functioning effectively since January 1989. The Corporation has a total share capital of Rs. 10 crores from the Central and the State Government at the rate of 49.51, respectively, of which it has received an amount of Rs. 277 lakhs from the State and Rs. 170.05 lakh from the Central Government. Like other women's development corporations, it is not getting any more assistance from Central Government since 1992. It has no individual shareholder to contribute in the share capital. The entire fund comes from the State Government for the annual budget. The proposal prepared by the Corporation is sent to the Commissioner, Cottage Industries, the controlling authority for any grant from state government.

The Corporation is managed by a Board of Directors which consists of official and non-official members. The non-official members and Chairperson are nominated by the state government. The Managing Director is an IAS officer who looks after the overall activities of the Corporation, below him is the General Manager. In order to achieve the objectives of economic development of women, the Corporation has taken up schemes for income and employment generation. For social justice and women's equality, schemes for awareness generation, holding of workshops and seminars, etc., are being implemented.

Haryana Women and Weaker Sections Development Corporation

The Haryana Economically Weaker Sections Development Corporation was established in 1982. In 1987 it was decided by the State Government that a women wing would be created in the existing Corporation, and it was renamed HWWSDC. The Corporation has a non-official as the Chairperson, a full time Managing Director and a Board of Directors comprising officials, and the regular administrative infrastructure at the head office in Chandigarh. The Corporation reaches out to the districts through District Project Officers who work in close liaison with the DRDA. The district managers of the Corporation are ex-officio Assistant Project Officers of the DRDA. The Corporation provides financial assistance to economically weaker sections under the following sectors:

(i) Agriculture and allied sectors,
(ii) Industry sector,
(iii) Business sector, and
(iv) Professional and self-employment sector.

Training courses are offered in motor car driving and for laboratory technicians jobs.

Mahila Vikas Nigam, Himachal Pradesh

It was established in 1989 under Section 25 of the Companies Act, 1956. The main aim of the Corporation is to promote socio-economic development of the women of Himachal Pradesh. The Nigam is headed by a Chairman. The Board of Directors of the Nigam consists of the Managing Director, an IAS Officer and a few ex-officio members. The Managing Director also looks after the day to day activities of the Himachal Pradesh Scheduled Castes and Scheduled Tribes Corporation (HPSC/STDC). However, the Board of Directors of Nigam passed a resolution in 1991 transferring all its activities and functions along with funds and staff to the HPSC/STDC. Since then the Nigam has been functioning as a special wing of HPSC/STDC. The Nigam helps women to procure loans from the bank at a low rate of interest, for self-employment. Under the Women Development Programme, women are eligible for loans upto Rs. 50,000 with interest subsidy. Preference is given to widows, destitutes and educated unemployed women.

Karnataka State Women's Development Corporation

The Karnataka Corporation was incorporated under the Companies Act, 1956, with an authorized share capital of Rs. 5 crores, of which 51 per cent was to be held by the Government of Karnataka and 49 per cent by the Government of India. Recently, the Corporation got permission to convert itself into a non-profit co-operative society. This exempts it from paying income tax. The net profit earned will not be distributed to shareholders. In a way the profit earned is a source of income and same can be invested in such a way that it will generate interest. This will help the organisation to become self-reliant. The Corporation directly comes under the control of the Department of Women and Child Development. The Board of Directors of the Corporation consists of the Chairperson, Managing Director and other members. A brief description of the various activities of the Corporation is given below:

1. As ordered by the Government 75 per cent of the work of stitching of uniforms in all districts shall be entrusted to the KSWDC Ltd. Through this scheme, the Corporation

helps women tailors by providing them an opportunity to earn about Rs. 20 to Rs. 30 per day for a period of about 3 months.

2. The Grihakalyana Scheme is intended to enable women to take up income-generating activities, such as purchase of sewing machine, petty business, dairy, readymade garments, preparation and selling sweets, tea stall, fish business, and kerosene oil business, etc.
3. The skills of SC women to take up income-generating activities or jobs, have been enhanced through a skill development programme of the Corporation
4. The programme for the all round development of devadasis in the districts of Belgaum and Bijapur has been entrusted to KSWDC. The Corporation has undertaken schemes to impart skills for income generation to devadasis and their families.
5. A training-*cum* production centre scheme was envisaged by the Corporation to help women to acquire necessary skills through training and later engage themselves in production, is envisaged.
6. The Corporation has taken up training programmes to promote skill development of the women belonging to lower income groups in order to take up income generating activities for supplementing family income or to improve their economic status.
7. The Corporation has organised publicity campaigns at the district level to give wide publicity to the schemes approved. To identify suitable beneficiaries, voluntary organisations and Mahila Samajams have been encouraged to take up the awareness campaigns. The Corporation has provided an about of Rs. 1000 for each district for conducting these publicity campaigns. During the awareness programme, the concept of overall development in respect of food, nutrition, family planning, sanitation, health, hygiene, legal support, status of women, assistance from various departments, schemes available for women, etc., are covered to up-date the information on both rural and urban women.
8. The Training of women entrepreneurs through Women

Development Corporation is a new scheme launched by State Government to provide basic inputs on need and awareness of self-employment opportunities suitable for women below the poverty line or marginally above the poverty line, slum-dwellers, etc. This programme motivates, assists, identifies potential entrepreneurs by extending financial support to take up income generating activities.

Kerala State Women's Development Corporation

Kerala State Women's Development Corporation was set-up in 1988 under the Companies Act 1956 with an aim to formulate, promote and implement any scheme for the welfare of the women from the poverty household and enable them to earn their livelihood. It receives funds from both the State and Centre on a 51:49 ratio. It has a Board of Directors comprising Chairman, Managing Director and six other members. The six members of the Board are nominated by the State Government. The Secretary, Social Welfare to Government of Kerala is the part-time Chairman of the Corporation and Director Welfare Department is the part-time Managing Director of the Corporation. The Corporation is located at Trivandrum.

The Corporation conducts workshops, seminar and awareness building programmes. It undertakes research on women's issues. On the basis of the recommendations, development programmes are designed and implemented. The Corporation runs a training-*cum*-production centre. The women have been provided training and are employed in the trades like manufacturing envelopes, file boards, book-binding, etc. The products are supplied to the stationery department of the State Government.

Madhya Pradesh Women's Economic Development Corporation

Madhya Pradesh Women's Economic Development Corporation was established as registered society in 1988. The main aim of the Corporation is to uplift the economic status of the poor and needy women. The Corporation consists of a 11-member board, out of which one is the chairman and five are ex-officio members, and the rest are officials. The Corporation provides loans to women to start petty business. To start with, the women are given a loan of Rs. 500 and a very small amount towards repayment of loan. It organises entrepreneurship development programmes and provides marketing facilities to the producers group.

Mahila Arthik Vikas Maha Mandal, Maharashtra

This was established in 1975. The MAVIM was established to facilitate the economic advancement of the poor women of Maharashtra. The MAVIM has an ex-officio Chairman. The Managing Director, a senior IAS Officer appointed by the state government, looks after its overall management. The head office is located in Bombay but has district level offices, which are looked after by the regional managers. The Maharashtra Mandal:

(1) explores avenues for generating employment for women;
(2) undertakes different types of surveys in the consumer market to identify types of services and commodities that are in great demand;
(3) develops projects for income generating activities for women. Acts as a facilitator to develop entrepreneurship among women by providing various support seminar's such as vocational consulting, financial assistance through banks marketing linkages, etc.;
(4) implements various development programmes sponsored by government of India for women; and
(5) organises women into cooperative societies or registered groups.

Mahila Vikas Samabaya Nigam, Orissa

This Nigam was established in 1991. The Nigam is headed by its Chairman. The Managing Director, an IAS Officer, looks after overall management of the Corporation. The Corporation has nearly 20 staff at the headquarters. At the district level, the Corporation is managed by the District Rural Development Agency and the District Manager. At the block level it is managed by the Block Development Officer and at the village level by women's societies.

The Corporation conducts training programmes for women in

various trades, such as manufacturing of electronic items, food processing, carpet-weaving, the management of fast food units, auto rickshaw driving, gem cutting, leather bag manufacturing, etc. It organises training programmes for the elected women representatives of the panchayat to make them aware of constitutional provisions, various administrative procedure, etc. It is also engaged in gender sensitization programmes for the elected representatives and in developing leadership qualities among them. The Corporation provides marketing support to women's organisations involved in production. It provides facilities or working capital to the producers if the product is of light quality. It participates in tenders on behalf of women's organisation. It facilitates the participation of the producers in different exhibitions to promote sales.

The Punjab Women and Children Development and Welfare Corporation

This was established in the year 1979. The Board of Directors of the Corporation consists of Chairman, Managing Director and five ex-officio directors. The Corporation has a complete staff at the district level with project officers and field staff who are responsible for identification of beneficiaries and provide them training for self-employment.

The Corporation has undertaken a number of schemes for encouraging prospective entrepreneurship amongst women and creating employment for them in diversified sectors and fields. The Corporation runs training centres in various trades so that women could take up self-employment on completion of training. The training is given on handicrafts, knitting and in tailoring. Also, it runs an Anganwadi Training Centre under the ICDS programme of Government of India. The curriculum includes training in health, nutrition, child-care, social work, art and craft for the benefit of expectant mothers and children under the age group of 0-6 years.

The Tamil Nadu Corporation for Development of Women

The Tamil Nadu Corporation for Development of Women Limited became a company in December 1983, under the Companies Act, 1956 with an authorized share capital of Rs. 100

lakh. The Corporation directly comes under the control of the Directorate of Social Welfare. The Board of Directors consists of the Chairperson, the Managing Director and a few ex-officio members. Since its inception, this Corporation has taken up a wide range of activities for providing various income-generating activities for women. This Corporation has formulated these schemes and has also mobilized the resources from the various financial agencies such as Norwegian Agency for International Development (NORAD), Support to Employment Programme (STEP), Special Central Assistance (SCA), Special Programme Funds, International Fund for Agricultural Development (IFAD), etc.

Uttar Pradesh Mahila Kalyan Nigam

The Uttar Pradesh Mahila Kalyana Nigam was established in March 1988 under the Companies Act, 1956. It comes under the Department of Women and Child Development, Directorate of Human Resource Development of the state government. The objectives of the Corporation are :

1. To enhance economic development of women.
2. To impart training for income generating activities.
3. To promote setting up of cottage industries by providing financial support.

The Corporation has a total share capital of Rs. 5 cores, of which it has got Rs. 1.09 crores till date from the Central and State Governments, at the ratio of 49:51, respectively. The Board of Directors of the Corporation consists of official and ex-officio members. The Chairperson is an ex-officio member, the Managing Director is an IAS officer, and below him there is a General Manager. The Corporation has undertaken the following programmes in order to achieve its objectives:

(1) Under the Kaushal Sudhar Yojana programme, Training-*cum*-Production Centres are being established for the products of Chikan, Leaf Plates, Readymade Garments, Cotton Carpets, Applique Work, Artificial Gem Cutting, and Fibre Glass Moulding

(2) The Margin Money Loan Yojana Scheme is implemented jointly by the Corporation and the bank. The beneficiaries receive the loan from the bank.
(3) The Corporation had undertaken the construction of Elak Shramajivi Mahila Chhatravas (Working Women's Hostels) in the state.
(4) The scheme of Vipanan Sahayata Yojana takes care of the marketing of products. Centres located in the hills and interior areas do not have facilities to sell their products. The Corporation helps the producer by selling their products through its sales counters.
(5) The Corporation organises fairs, exhibitions-*cum*-sale, etc., with a view to increase outlay, publicise itself and to build awareness amongst other women's groups.

Mahila Mandals

Mahila Mandals or women's forums were set-up as the instruments to bring women into the institutional framework of rural development. There is a great deal of variation in the substance and performance of these "Women's Clubs". Some were registered, federated, some informal, most of them became part of the rural elite organisations with very few representatives of the working classes. According to an estimate, there were more than 50,000 Mahila Mandals reported to be working in rural areas. The Mahila Mandals became the focal points for providing services to and participation of women in social welfare and community development programmes.

The Mahila Mandals work under the supervision and guidance of the village level official functionaries. In the rural areas, besides ten Gram Sevakas (village level workers) supported by Agriculture Extension Officers, two posts of Gram Sevikas (lady village level workers) per community development block supervised by Mukhya Sevika (Lady Social Education Organiser) were created to look after rural women's programmes in the community development blocks. These functionaries organised Mahila Mandals who set-up Balwadis (Pre-school centres), undertook tasks such as health and nutrition education, better home management facilities, literacy, sanitation, family welfare, food preservation, storage and agriculture demonstration including poultry, calf and goat rearing, social forestry, etc.

Since the fifties, national development strategies have promoted women's grassroots organisations (Mahila Mandals) for the delivery of services or for income generating activities under India's Community Development Programme. The structure, effectiveness and perspectives of these organisations varied from state to state. Several reviews and evaluations of mahila mandals have commented on the content, non-representative character, vagueness of objectives, lack of resources and poor performance of these organisations. The Report of the Committee on the Status of Women in India observed that though some members of the mahila mandals have acquired both interests and experience in developmental activities, their purely voluntary and non-representative status denied them recognition from local statutory self-governing institutions. Instead, the CSWI recommended the setting up of statutory women's panchayats at the village level as a 'transitional measure' to ensure 'greater participation by women in the political process'. The Committee on the Panchayati Raj Structure (1977) also emphasized the need for village level women's organisations to influence both the directional and implementation levels of development planning.

Voluntary Organisations

Voluntary organisations in India have undertaken several programmes for the development of women. In fact, voluntary action has been throughout a prominently visible strain of our cultural milieu. It is well-known that almost as a sequel to the reform movement of the nineteenth century, a number of voluntary organisations, especially for the welfare of women and children were organised. The tempo generated during that period continued in the days of freedom struggle and even gained momentum after independence as a result of government's policy commitment to support and strengthen voluntary organisations.

The major problem in development programmes of the government is that women beneficiaries are rarely involved in the process of planning and implementation. Conscious efforts were not made to identify women beneficiars and when they were identified they have not been supported sincerely. Various factors such as low literacy, the restrictive social structure, predominance of patriarchical society, lack of decision making opportunity and ability and low exposure to growth opportunities are also responsible for the lack of development impetus among women. In view of these difficulties being noticed in the governmental effort, the voluntary organisations are considered as more appropriate instruments to carry out the task of women's development because of their attributes of flexibility, quickness, innovativeness and human touch. In fact, successive plan documents and reports of official commissions and committees have acclaimed positive dimensions of functioning of voluntary organisations and their increasing relevance. It was stated, for instance, in the Third Five Year Plan document itself, that 'properly organised voluntary effort may go far towards augmenting the facilities available to the community for helping the weakest and the most needy to a somewhat better way.[13] Voluntary organisations can also go in search of new needs, work in new areas, unveil social evils and give attention to hitherto unattended and unmet needs. Due to encouraging policy of the government and the initiative of the people themselves, the voluntary sector has borne rich fruit in the sense that there has been a profusion of voluntary organisations working for women. It is important to put their services on record as they have been the greatest and most effective instruments for spreading awareness about their rights among women and rousing their level of expectation from society and government.[14] It may also be mentioned that the government has provided a forum to voluntary organisations to meet and promote voluntary action. Advisory councils have been set-up by the Departments of Family Welfare, Education and Rural Development. The Planning Commission too consults them not only through its various subject committees on plan making but also whenever any important new schemes have to be formulated. The Department of Women and Child Development works for most of its schemes for women through the voluntary organisations who are funded for implementing those schemes.

At present it is estimated that there are about 10,000 voluntary organisations in the country engaged in welfare and developmental work. These organisations have introduced development schemes affecting lives of rural and urban women.[15]

While some organisations like Akhil Hind Mahila Parishad (All India Women's Conference), Bharatiya Grameena Mahila Sangh (National Association for Rural Women in India) and Andhra Mahila Sabha are working exclusively for the benefit of women, other organisations are working for the development of women as one of their programmes.

The educational programmes—both formal and non-formal, provide opportunities to women for their upward social and economic mobility. The programmes of health are intended to make women healthy and fit for production work. The encouragement of NGOs to take up economic activities enable the women to improve their living conditions and supplement their family income. Some voluntary organisations organise women for the successful implementation of development programmes. Some other programmes like relief and rehabilitation have also been undertaken exclusively for destitute women by some organisations. The Young Women's Christian Association (YWCA), The Kusturba Gandhi National Memorial Trust and the Bharatiya Grameena Mahila Sangha have taken up several programmes both in rural and urban areas. The other known women's organisations are Jagori, Saheli, Manushi, Stree Seva Mandir, SEWA, Working Women's Forum, Centre for Women Development Studies, etc. All these and other national level organisations for the welfare and development of women and children function through their state and district units which are in the nature of their affiliations. At the village level, all these national level women's voluntary organisations function through Mahila Mandals.

Notes and References

1. Institute of Social Studies Trust, *Institutional Mechanism for Women's Advancement*, Women Studies Resource Centre, New Delhi, 1995, p. 5.
2. See Government of India, *Towards Equality: Report of the Committee on the Status of Women in India*, Ministry of Education and Social Welfare, New Delhi, 1975.
3. N.J. Usha Rao, *Women in a Development Society*, Ashish Publishing House, New Delhi, 1983, p. 23.
4. Paul D. Chowdhry, *Women Welfare and Development*, Inter-India Publications, New Delhi, 1992, p. 275.

5. Sudhir Varma, "Women in Development: Need for a Strong National Machinery", *Administrative Change*, Vol. XIX, Nos. 1-2, July 1991; June 1992, p. 17.
6. Government of India, *First Five Year Plan (1951-56)*, Planning Commission, New Delhi, 1951,
7. For a detailed discussion on the Functions of Central Social Welfare Board see P.M. Parwar, *Social Work and Social Welfare in India*, Sublime Publications, Jaipur, 2007, pp. 231-47.
8. Mira Seth, *Women and Development: The Indian Experience*, Sage Publications, New Delhi, 2001, p. 68.
9. S.K. Khanna, *Women and Human Rights*, Commonwealth Publishers, New Delhi, 1998, p. 68.
10. B. Chandrasekhar, *Women Development and Welfare Schemes*, Lakshmi Publications, Hyderabad, October, 2002, p. 11.
11. Institute of Social Studies Trust, *A Study of Women Development Corporations in India*, Women's Studies Resource Centre, New Delhi, 1995, p. 4.
12. Andhra Pradesh Women Cooperative Finance Corporation, *Taruni-Educating, Enlightening, Enriching and Empowering*, Hyderabad, 2006, p. 2.
13. Mira Seth, *op. cit.*, p. 70.
14. Government of India, *Third Five Year Plan (1961-66)*, Planning Commission, New Delhi, 1961, pp. 292-93.
15. Neera Desai and Vibhuti Patel, *op. cit.*, p. 52.

Organisational Structure, Functions and Programmes of Women Development Organisations

The Constitution of India stresses the need for promoting the educational and economic interests of the weaker sections of the people; and as women are handicapped by social customs and traditions, they need special attention to help them to play their full and proper role in national life. The Planning Commission had, therefore, identified major areas for women's development and designed programmes in those areas.[1] These programmes may be broadly classified as follows:

1. Programmes under statutory obligations such as the Suppression of Immoral Traffic Act, 1956 or the Maternity Benefit Act, 1961, etc.
2. Development programmes which provide essential services and opportunities such as education, health, nutrition, family planning and training.
3. Programmes for special groups of women such as assistance to widows, aged and destitute women and rural, SC, ST, BC women.

There is a three-tier structure for planning and administering women's welfare and development programmes with agencies at the central, state, and local levels. The organisations at all the three levels are recognized as the ideal types for successful implementation of women's development programmes. Each of them has, however, a definite role. The central level organisations and their administrators are given planning and supervisory responsibility of women development programmes. They are responsible for establishing a women development project and for recommending its organizational structure, its functional definition and the terms of its functioning. They can influence only at the outset, when a programme is being funded or set into operation or during the process of review and evaluation leading to refunding decisions. They participate in decisions about procedures, personnel and procurement policies and relationships to other agencies.

The state level organisations operating from the capital city involved in administering women development programmes on a more continuous basis than that of central level organisations. Their responsibilities include supervision of technical and administrative operations as well as backup support. They are also concerned with establishing routines for linking field operations with the central office, supplies, communications, guidance feedback and procedures.

The local organisations and their administrators are in charge of operations of the programmes in the district. The role of these organisations in women's development is decisive sometimes. Very often, the successes and failures of the programme are attributed to the efficiency of local organisation. In other words, the major responsibility for implementing programmes lies on various departments and agencies of Government at local level. So for a better understanding of the administration of women development programmes, the study of role and functions of local organisations is more useful. The local analysis is a better reflection of reality than that of the organisations at the other two levels, i.e. central and state level.

The organizational structure, functions, programmes and other related aspects of central and state level institutions responsible for administration of women's development programmes are examined in Chapter 4. An attempt is made in this chapter to examine the organizational structure, functions and programmes of local organisations administering women's welfare and development programmes in Visakhapatnam district.

Profile of Visakhapatnam District

Visakhapatnam District is one of the three north coastal districts of Andhra Pradesh having as per 2001 census a population of 37.89 lakhs spread in an area of 11,161s kms. It lies between 17°–15° and 18°–32° northern latitude and 80°–54° and 83°–30° in eastern latitude. It is bounded on the north partly by the State of Orissa and partly by Vizianagaram District, on the south by the East Godavari District, on the west by the State of Orissa and on the east by the Bay of Bengal. The district is characterized by two distinct geographical divisions viz. the plains and hilly regions, i.e. the strip of land along the 132 kms. The plains region includes coast line and the interior area. The hilly region of the eastern ghats flanking it on the north and west is said to be agency area.[2]

Most part of the district is hilly and picturesque especially in the north and the agency tract is all hilly regions of eastern ghats running parallel to the coast from the north east to the south-west comprising Paderu, G. Madugula, Pedabayalu, Munchingput, Hukumpet, Drumbriguda, Araku Valley, Anantagiri Chintapali, G.K. Veedhi. The highest peak in the district is Sankaram in S. Kota which is about 1,615 meters while the average height of the hills is 914 meters. The plains division is an agricultural and mineral belt watered and drained by many rivers, i.e. Sarada, Champavati, Gasthani, Varaha and Tandava and Rivulets, viz. Meghadrigedda and Gambheermgedda. Along the sea shore, lies salt and sandy swamps.

The total area of district is 11.34 lakh hectares of which 35.1 per cent alone is arable area while 42.1 per cent is forest area. The rest is baren and uncultivable land. More than one-third of the district is covered by forests which are of moist and dry deciduous. The species available in the forests include Guggilam, Tangedu, Chiriman, Kamba, Yegiri, Nallamaddi, Somida and Bomboo shrubs. The district has a livestock of 13.03 lakhs of which cattle form 35 per cent, buffaloes 29 per cent, sheep 14 per cent and goats 18 per cent. Bears, Bisons, Cheetahs and Tigers, among other wild animals are found.

Almost 70 per cent of the villages have red loamy soils while sandy loam soils come next with around 20 per cent of the villages. Black cotton soils are also found at K. Kotapadu, Devarapalli, Cheedikada and Paderu. The district receives annual rainfall of 1202 mm of which south-west monsoons accounted for almost 71 per cent of the normal rain fall while north-east monsoon constituted almost 9 per cent of the normal rainfall (2000-01). The rest is shared by summer showers and winter rains.

The district administration in Visakhapatnam has taken up varied measures for the overall development of the district keeping in view the requirements of all sections of the people especially the weaker sections. The government has brought in need based welfare measures such as total literacy, avoiding child labour, subsidies to peasants in the drought affected mandals, Neeru-meeru (rain and ground water preservation) programme, food for work programme, housing to the economically backward classes, family planning programme, velugu programme to provide employment to weaker sections. Adarana Programme especially intended for the backward classes, youth societies for providing loans to youth so that they would take self-help programmes, mother and child welfare programmes through Anganavadis, DWACRA scheme, which is said to be the finest for women to come out economically, programmes for environmental protection and social forestry, providing industrial infrastructure facilities, plans to establish Aparal Park, Leather Park and Pharmacity in the vicinity of Parawada village. Several hundred, thousand crores of rupees have been spent for the implementation of these programmes in the district.

In Visakhapatnam district, the organisations involved in women welfare and development are not many. On thorough examination of various departments and organisations engaged in developmental activities, it is observed that the following organisations are undertaking various programmes beneficial to women:

1. District Women and Child Development Agency.
2. District Rural Development Agency.

3. District Scheduled Castes Cooperative Service Society.
4. District Backward Classes Cooperative Service Society.

The objectives, organizational structure, functions and programmes of all the district level organizing are discussed in this chapter.

District Women and Child Development Agency

As part of women empowerment policy of Government of Andhra Pradesh, the Programme Office of District ICDS Cell and District Women and Child Welfare Office were merged into one agency called as District Women and Child Development Agency (DWCDA). The Visakhapatnam District Agency started functioning from 6th October, 1997. The State Government had ordered that all women and child welfare activities in the district should be undertaken by this agency. The District Agency is headed by an officer called Project Director, drawn from Group-I Services of the State. He is assisted by the Assistant Project Officer and other staff in the office. The details of the officials of the DWCDA office are given below:

Project Director	...	1
Assistant Project Officer	...	1
Executive Officer	...	1
Assistant Manager	...	1
Superintendent	...	1
Senior Assistants	...	5
Junior Assistants	...	2
Typists	...	3
Driver	...	1
Attenders	...	4
Watchman	...	1

The above officials have been posted both under plan and non-plan expenditure. It is interesting to note that the appointment of majority of the officials is temporary. The posts of Assistant Project Officer, Superintendent, one typist and two drivers only are permanent. The remaining posts including the Project Director are temporary. There are some important institutions, which are working for the welfare of women and children in the district. All these institutions are functioning under the District Agency. The name and number of these institutions are given below:

Children Homes	...	5
Working Women Hostels	...	2
Sishi Gruha	...	1
Creches	...	8
Balwadies	...	6
Bala Vihar	...	1
District Craft Training Centre	...	1
Women & Child Welfare Centres	...	2
Durgabai Mahila Sisu Vikasa Kendram	...	1

The services provided by each of the above institutions are described briefly.

Children Homes

Out of the five children homes, the homes in Bhimunipatnam and Narsipatnam are intended for scheduled castes children. The homes in Paderu and Chintapalli are for scheduled tribe children. The remaining home in Kasimkota is open for all categories of children. The sanctioned and present strength of each children home is 60. Each children home has sanctioned posts of Superintendent, Matron, Cook, Sevika, Attender and Watchman. The posts of Superintendent, Matron and Sevika are permanent and the remaining posts of cook, attender and watchman are temporary. At present, most of the posts are vacant. There are no matrons and superintendents, who are important officials to run the children homes, for two children homes. We can imagine the maintenance of the children homes which have no superintendents and matrons.

Working Women's Hostels

There are two working women hostels in the city of Visakhapatnam under the management of District Women and Child Development Agency. The intake of one hostel is 75 and of the other is 50. The staff of each hostel includes superintendent, matron, cook, helper and watchman. An attender was also posted in the hostel, which has a total strength of 75. The posts of superintendent, matron and attender are permanent and the other posts are temporary.

Creches

The District Women and Child Development Agency runs 8 creches, out of which 2 are mobile creches. Each creche is managed by a teacher and 2 ayahs. All the posts of creches, i.e. 8 teachers and 16 ayahs are temporary. Some of these posts are at present vacant. In each creche about 30 children below the age of 6 years of taken care of.

Balwadies

There are 6 balwadies in the district managed by the District Agency. For the management of each balwadi there is a teacher and one ayah. All the posts are temporary. Each balwadi caters to the needs of about 30 children in the age group of 3-5 years.

Bala Vihar

There is a bala vihar in the district, which is being run by a teacher and a sevika. These two posts are plan posts and are permanent.

Sishu Gruha

A Sishu Gruha was sanctioned for Visakhapatnam district during 2006-07 by Central Adoption Resource Agency. The institution is located at Marripalem area of Visakhapatnam city. The strength of the Sishu Gruha is 8 children. A Child Welfare Committee was formed to look after the Sishu Gruha. The Committee meets and takes steps for adoption of children.

District Craft Training Centre

The District Craft Training Centre is established in the year 1998 in Visakhapatnam to give training to the women in handicrafts. The posts of instructress and watchman sanctioned under non-plan to this centre are temporary.

Women and Child Welfare Centres

The District Agency also runs two women and child welfare

centres at Narsipatnam and Bheemunipatnam. Each centre is being run by a teacher and an ayah. Both the posts are temporary and the posts of ayahs are vacant.

Durgabai Mahila Sisu Vikasa Kendram

Durgabai Mahila Sisu Vikasa Kendram (DMSVK) in Visakhapatnam, former Telugu Bala Mahila Pragathi Pranganam, is situated in Pine Apple Colony of Visakhapatnam city in 10 acres land and it is functioning from 28.03.1992. The main aim of this Institution is to impart training in vocational programmes to poor, destitute, deserted, orphans and widow women candidates between age group of 16-35 years[3]. The Pranganam was well-established with equipment for imparting training in Computer, Beautician, DTP, Embroidery, Pre-School, Book Binding and Printing, Handycraft, Type, Soft Toys, Zaricraft, Community Health Workers Course, Screen Printing, Lace Making, Jute Bag Making, Rexene Wear, House Keeping, Hosiery, etc. The Visakhapatnam Kendram has the infrastructure facilities like 7 computers with one printer, 2 embroidery machines and 10 sewing machines. The beautician infrastructure is also available in the Kendram.

The District Manager is the head of the DMSVK. She is also the head of the AWTC and the Hostel located in the premises of the Kendram. The employees of the DMSVK are under the control of the District Manager. The District Manager is under the administrative control of the Project Director of DWCDA. The designations of the staff of the DMSVK are given below:

1. Manager
2. Asst. Manager
3. Upper Division Accountant
4. Co-ordinator
5. Instructor
6. Lower Division Clerk
7. Matron
8. ANM
9. Attender
10. Cook
11. Helper

12. Sweeper
13. Day Watchman
14. Night Watchman

The details of the programmes and the women benefited from these training programmes are given in the Table 5.1.

TABLE 5.1

Programme-wise Beneficiaries

S. No.	*Name of the course*	*No. of beneficiaries*	*No. of rehabilitated*
1.	Bakery	21	19
2.	Tailoring	27	21
3.	Book binding and printing	15	10
4.	Beautician	129	94
5.	Soft toys	49	35
6.	OMC Office Management Course	18	13
7.	Computer Training	75	58
8.	DTP	101	69
9.	Pre-School	10	05
10.	Dress-making Garments	30	18
11.	Leather bags	22	14
12.	Personal Secretary	20	11
13.	Leather & Rexine	25	18
	Total	542	385

A total of 542 women were benefited from the various training programmes undertaken by the kendram during the last 5 years. About 385 women were rehabilitated in different activities. There is an Anganwadi Workers Training Center (AWTC) in the Pranganam. The Anganwadi Training Centre was started working in Mahila Pranganam from 1994. Anganwadi workers were trained in Job Course, Refreshment, Sandwich and Orientation Courses. The DMSVK had also undertaken the training programmes sponsored by Family Welfare Department to women candidates for controlling and maternal and child deaths. Target for the district is 2,254. Till now 1,846 completed training. For Rehabilitation of Girl Child Labour the Bridge Course was started in this Pranganam in 1997 with the assistance of National Child

Labour Project (NCLP) and District Primary Education Programme (DPEP). After completion of course, the trainees were joined in the hostels of Social Welfare Department, Backward Classes Welfare Department and Children Homes of Women Development and Child Welfare Department. Under production activities this pranganam has been taking up departmental work orders of Printing and Book Binding and Tailoring. This pranganam is also participating in every exhibition by displaying all varieties of Hand Embroidery Works, Jute Products and Printing and Book Binding works. There is a hostel in the premises of the pranganm. The trainees are accommodated in this hostel during the training period.

The above institutions of District Agency cater to the needs of women and children in the district. The District Agency also has been implementing the following programmes:

1. Integrated Child Development Services Scheme (ICDS)
2. National Nutrition Programme
3. Girl Child Protection Scheme
4. Swayam Siddha Scheme
5. Badi Bata Scheme
6. Balika Mandal Scheme

Twenty two I.C.D.S. projects were sanctioned to Visakhapatnam district so far.[4] The first project was started in 1980. The last project was sanctioned in 2006. Out of 22 projects, four are urban projects, 10 are rural projects and the remaining 8 are tribal projects. A total of 3,121 Anganwadi Centers are working under these projects. The number of Anganwadi Centers varies from project to project. There are as many as 237 Anganwadi Centers under Pendurthi Rural ICDS Project. The lowest number of Anganwadi Centers, i.e. 74 are under the Koyyuru Tribal ICDS Project. The details of ICDS projects are given in the Table 5.2.

The total coverage of population in the district by ICDS is 25,76,530.[5] The Mothers' Committees have been formed in all 3,121 Anganwadi Centers. About 20,640 mothers are involved in the Mothers' Committees. About 1,30,840 children in the age group of 0-6 years and 34,000 pregnant and lacting mothers are covered under the ICDS Scheme in the district. For the management of

TABLE 5.2

Integrated Child Development Service

S.No.	*Name of the Project*	*Year of starting*	*No. of AWCs in the project*	*Nature of project*
1.	Visakhapatnam-I	1980	100	Urban
2.	Paderu	1980	192	Tribal
3.	Koyyuru	1981	74	Tribal
4.	Araku	1982	171	Tribal
5.	Ananthagiri	1982	96	Tribal
6.	Munchinput	1983	87	Tribal
7.	Pedabayalu	1983	76	Tribal
8.	Chintapalli	1992	174	Tribal
9.	G. Madugula	1984	96	Tribal
10.	V. Madugula	1981	109	Rural
11.	Kotaurtla	1990	188	Rural
12.	Bheemunipatnam	1996	177	Urban
13.	Narsipatnam	1998	177	Rural
14.	Ravikamatam	1998	198	Rural
15.	Kasimkota	2002	172	Rural
16.	K. Kotapadu	2002	133	Rural
17.	Nakkapalli	2002	208	Rural
18.	Pendurthi	2002	237	Rural
19.	Sabbavaram	2002	130	Rural
20.	Yalamanchili	2002	150	Rural
21.	Visakhapatnam-II	2006	102	Urban
22.	Anakapalli	2006	74	Urban

ICDS scheme, the posts of Child Development Project Officer (CDPO), Assistant Child Development Project Officer (ACDPO), Supervisor, Senior Assistant, Junior Assistant, Typist, Driver, Attender and Watchman were sanctioned. The number and status of their functioning are given in the Table 5.3.

The Table 5.3 indicates that some of the posts are not filled. All the 12 posts of ACDPOs are vacant at present. There are no full time CDPOs for 10 ICDS projects. More than half of the typist posts are vacant. There are also vacancies in other categories of employees. This analysis makes its clear that there are vacancies in each category of officials. Each Anganwadi Center is being managed by a teacher and an ayah, who are part-time workers of the ICDS projects.

TABLE 5.3

Details of ICDS Staff

S. No.	*Name of the Post*	*Sanctioned posts*	*Functioning*	*Vacant*
1.	CDPO	22	12	10
2.	ACDPO	12	—	12
3.	Supervisor	129	71	58
4.	Senior Assistant	15	13	2
5.	Junior Assistant	17	12	5
6.	Junior Assistant-*cum*-Typist	3	—	3
7.	Typist	14	8	6
8.	Drivers	14	12	2
9.	Attenders	21	14	7
10.	Watchman	10	9	1

The Visakhapatnam District Women and Child Development Agency has been implementing the other important programmes like Girl Child Protection Scheme, Balika Mandal Scheme and Swayam Siddah Scheme. A total of 2,099 children of 0-7 age groups have been benefited from the Girl Child Protection Scheme implemented by the District Agency during the last three years. Under the Balika Mandal Sceme, 187 Balika Mandals were formed from the 17 ICDS Projects. From each mandal, three members had been selected as change agents and given training in 5 batches. The civil works like laying c.c. roads in the villages, construction of community halls, bus shelters, etc. have been undertaken by the District Agency with the cooperation of Swayam Siddha SHGs in the areas of Narsipatnam and Ravikamatham ICDS Projects.

District Rural Development Agency

In India 75 per cent of the population lives in rural areas and nearly 70 per cent of the workforce depends upon agriculture and allied activities. The contribution of the rural sector to national income is substantial. Such an important sector will naturally draw the attention of the people and the Government for its reconstruction.[6] After Independence, considerable efforts have been made towards improving the quality of life of our rural poor. Various programmes have been taken up in successive five year plans to provide to the villages certain economic and social infrastructure, ensuring facilities like roads, electricity, road transport, drinking water, medical care, primary schools, etc. These programmes are also expected to increase income of the individual rural poor families. Thus, the trust for rural development has been two-pronged one, providing certain social goods and services in terms of social and economic infrastructure and the other, increasing income of individual rural people.

India has had executed more than 40 programmes of rural development since independence beginning with the Community Development Programme of 1952. These programmes are designed for the benefit of rural poor including rural women. The successful implementation of rural development programmes hinges directly the destiny of as much as 75 per cent of the country's population.

Both the Central Government and the states are deeply involved in rural developmental programmes, but the role of the Centre, primarily, is one of policy-making, determination of priorities, monitoring and evaluation, and provision of financial assistance. The Ministry of Rural Development is the nodal agency for rural development in the Government of India, but also involved are various other departments and ministries which, too, have their own programmes and schemes for people in rural areas. The Ministry of Rural Development is presently administering the various anti-poverty programmes, and its bureaucracy advises the states on all conceivable matters.

The Ministry of Rural Development is administratively headed by a Secretary to the Government of India, assisted by an Additional Secretary, seven Joint Secretaries and other supporting staff of Directors, Deputy Secretaries, Under Secretaries, Deputy Commissioners, and Assistant Commissioners. Broadly, the Ministry is divided into seven wings, each headed by a Joint Secretary. These wings are: administration, finance, IRD, L.R., monitoring, RE and TM. The Joint Secretary (Administration) is assisted by four Under Secretaries, one Deputy Director and one Director (Media).

The Joint Secretary (Finance) is assisted by one Director, two Under Secretaries, Deputy Controller (Accounts) and Senior Assistant, and other usual supporting officers. The Joint Secretary

(IRD) is supported by one Director and two Deputy Commissioners and two Deputy Secretaries, one for IRD and, three Assistant Commissioners. The Joint Secretary (LR) exercises administrative control over two Advisers, one Director, two Deputy Secretaries, one Joint Director, one Assistant Commissioner, one Deputy Commissioner, one Deputy Adviser, one Under Secretary, one Assistant Commissioner, and one Deputy Adviser. The Joint Secretary (Monitoring) gets the monitoring work done through two Advisers, one Joint Director, one Deputy Secretary, one Deputy Commissioner, two Deputy Directors. The Joint Secretary (RE) is assisted by three Directors, two Deputy Secretaries, two Under Secretaries and one Deputy Director. The Joint Secretary (TM) is assisted by two Advisers, one Additional Adviser, two Deputy Secretaries, one SE, two Deputy Advisers, one Under Secretary, one SSA, one Deputy Director, eight Assistant Advisers, one Deputy Director and one Under Secretary. These officers are assisted by a number of supportive staff. Thus, there are a large number of officers at the central level to deal with the rural development programmes.

The Ministry has also the following organisations under its administrative control:

- (i) Directorate of Marketing and Inspection, Jaipur.
- (ii) The National Institute of Rural Development (NIRD), Hyderabad.
- (iii) The Council for Advancement of People's Action and Rural Technology (CAPART).

The Ministry of Rural Development looks after all such matters as are related to panchayati raj, land reforms, land tenure, land records, consolidation of holdings, acquisition of land for purposes of the Union, recovery of land revenue, land improvement and agricultural loans, collection and assessment of land revenue, duties in respect of succession to agricultural land, matters relating to Minimum Needs Programme, water supply, sewage, drainage and sanitation relating to rural areas, working out of strategies and programmes for rural employment, implementation of specific programmes of rural employment such as National Rural Employment Programme (NREP), Rural Landless Employment

Guarantee Programme (RLEGP), IRDP, DPAP, DDP, public cooperation, warehousing and godowns in rural areas, rural housing, establishment of rural agricultural markets, cooperatives, rural roads, rural infrastructure facilities, and extending cooperation to international organisations meant for rural development such as Centre for Integrated Rural Development for Asia and Pacific (CIRDAP) and the Afro-Asian Rural Reconstruction Organisation (AARRO).

To assist the Department of Rural Development, there is a Central Committee on Integrated Rural Development Programme (IRDP) and the allied programmes of TRYSEM and DWCRA. The Secretary, Department of Rural Development, acts as the Chairman of this Committee. The other members of the Committee are: Secretary, Department of Agriculture and Cooperation or his nominee; and Adviser (Rural Development), Planning Commission or his nominee; Secretary, Department of Women and Child Development or his nominee; Secretary, Expenditure or his nominee; Secretary, Industries Ministry or his nominee; Secretary, Ministry of Welfare or his nominee; a Representative from P.M. Office; Resident Representative, KVIC, New Delhi; Joint Chief Officer RPCD, RBI, Bombay; Additional Secretary, Department of Rural Development; Joint Secretary, Finance, Department of Rural Development; Joint Secretary, IRD, Department of Rural Development and Joint Secretary, Banking Division, Ministry of Finance. In all, 17 persons plus State Secretaries of Rural Development are invited in groups of 5-6 States.

The functions of the Committee are to:

(a) frame and revise guidelines for the IRDP and allied programmes of TRYSEM and DWCRA;
(b) ensure effective implementation of the framed guidelines;
(c) review preparation of district plans, etc.;
(d) review the linkages for the supporting services for the IRDP beneficiaries;
(e) consider changes in the administrative set-up under IRDP and other rural development programmes;
(f) review the progress of these programmes in physical, financial and qualitative terms;

(g) consider concurrent evaluation report;

(h) provide a forum for a continuous dialogue with the State Governments; and

(i) consider proposals for strengthening the infrastructure of training institutions; establishment of new training institutions; modifications in the norms prescribed for grant of stipend; and pattern of training institutions under TRYSEM.

There is another High Level Committee on Credit Support for IRDP at the Central level headed by the Secretary, Department of Rural Development. This Committee includes senior officials of the Government of India, state governments, Commercial Banks; NABARD, and RBI. It has to consider the problems that arise at the time of implementation of the programmes and review the credit arrangements to recommend remedial measures for improving the implementation process.

Rural development is the direct responsibility of the state governments, and to this end each state has created an administrative machinery at the headquarters which is expected to lay down policies in the field of rural development to oversee their implementation, provide finances and act as trouble-shooter. As regards the organizational set-up at the state headquarters for the administration and execution of the rural development programmes, there was a rural development department headed by an officer of the rank of a full-fledged Commissioner in Andhra Pradesh. Both the Forests and Rural Development Departments were placed under the administrative control of the Principal Secretary assisted by a full-time Commissioner for Rural Development. The subjects of Forests and Rural Development were separated in 1999. The subject of Panchayati Raj was added to the Ministry of Rural Development. Now there is a separate Ministry of Rural Development in the State. To assist the Department of Rural Development a State Level Coordination Committee has been provided. The State Level Coordination Committee provides leadership and guidance to the DRDAs in the planning, implementation and monitoring of the programme, secures inter-departmental coordination between various implementing agencies of development programmes.

The body responsible for implementation of schemes and plans in rural development in the district is the District Rural Development Agency (DRDA). Despite the existence of panchayati raj institutions, which were created to carry out rural development programmes, having the necessary experience and expertise, separate institution like DRDA has been constituted at the district level, additionally for the purpose. It is in this perspective that DRDA of Visakhapatnam district has been chosen to examine its role in the development of rural women. The aim was to see that rural development takes place by seeking cooperation of various governmental agencies, local bodies and also financial institutions, like grameen banks, commercial banks, nationalized banks and rural cooperative and agricultural banks. The institution of District Rural Development Agency was entrusted with the responsibility of dealing with various agencies mentioned above in the implementing process of the programmes which aimed at providing benefit to various sections of people like small farmers, rural artisan, and landless agricultural labourers, apart from unemployed youth. Thus, the entire rural manpower and woman power was to be motivated to participate in such programmes to help them emerge above the poverty line.

Organisational Structure of DRDA

The DRDA of Visakhapatnam came into existence in 1980 by integrating the schemes of Small Farmers Development Agency, Integrated Rural Development Programme, Training of Rural Youth for Self-Employment and Antyodaya Programme. The DRDA was registered under the Societies Act of Government of Andhra Pradesh. It is a body corporate with all characteristic features. It comprises a Governing Body, Chairman, Executive Chairman, Executive Committee and the Project Director. The Zilla Parishad Chairman is the Chairman and the District Collector is the Executive Chairman of the Governing Body. The Project Director acts as the Member-Secretary of the Society's Governing Body. The Governing Body of DRDA of Visakhapatnam consists of the following as members:

1. All Members of Legislative Assembly of the District.
2. All Members of Parliament of the District.

3. One-fifth of Mandal Parishad Presidents of the District by rotation.
4. Chief Executive Officer, Zilla Parishad.
5. Project Officer, Integrated Tribal Development Agency.
6. Chairman, District Cooperative Central Bank.
7. Chairman, Andhra Pradesh Grameen Vikas Bank.
8. Manager, Lead Bank.
9. Additional General Manager, NABARD.
10. General Manager, District Industries Centre.
11. Development Officer, Khadi and Village Industries Commission.
12. District Medical and Health Officer.
13. District Employment Officer.
14. Executive Director, District SC Cooperative Service Society.
15. Executive Director, District BC Cooperative Service Society.
16. Project Director, District Women and Child Development Agency.
17. Chairman, Visakha Cooperative Dairy.
18. Two Representatives of the Beneficiaries.
19. Two Representatives of Non-Governmental Organisations.

Broadly, the membership of Governing Body of DRDA includes all MLAs and MPs of the district, some Mandal Parishad Presidents, the Heads of financial institutions in the district, district level officers of the Government and development organisations and representatives of non-government organisations and beneficiaries. The Governing Body provides guidance and direction to the DRDA. An Executive Committee is formed to assist the Agency. The Committee consists of all the district level officers. The meetings of the Governing Body and the Executive Committee are held once a quarter and once a month, respectively.

Functions of DRDA

The DRDA has been made the overall in-charge of the planning, implementation, monitoring and evaluation of the rural development programmes in the district. The functions of the

DRDA are:

(i) Identification of families below the poverty line;
(ii) Preparation of Action Plans and Schemes for assisting these families to improve their economic conditions in order to come above the poverty line;
(iii) Arrangement of institutional credit support to the identified beneficiaries to be assisted;
(iv) Overall charge of planning, implementation, monitoring and evaluation of the IRDP throughout the district;
(v) To keep the district level and mandal level agencies informed of the basic parameters, the requirements of the programme and the tasks assigned to them;
(vi) To coordinate and oversee the surveys conducted, preparation of the perspective plans, annual plans of the blocks and finally, to prepare a district plan;
(vii) To evaluate and monitor the programmes so as to ensure its effectiveness;
(viii) To secure inter-sectoral and inter-departmental coordination and cooperation;
(ix) To give publicity to the achievements made under the programme and disseminate knowledge and build up awareness about the programme undertaken; and
(x) To send periodical returns to the state governments in the prescribed manner.

Staff of DRDA

The DRDA is headed by a full-time Project Director, a senior scale officer from Group-I Service of Government of Andhra Pradesh. He is assisted by the Additional Project Director and other officers and office staff. The staff of DRDA is broadly categorized into the Executive, Office and Supporting staff. The officers and officials under each category are given below:

Executive Staff	
Project Director	1
Additional Project Director	1
Assistant Project Officers	6
Administrative Officer	1

Assistant Project Manager	1
Accounts Officer	1
District Project Managers	3
Deputy Statistical Officer	1
Office Staff	
Assistant Registrar	1
Office Superintendent	1
Upper Division Steno	1
Senior Assistants	3
Junior Assistants	10
Typist	1
Drivers	3
Attenders	7
Sweeper	1
Supporting Staff	
Office Assistants	3
Group Assistants	5
Receptionist	1
Driver	1
Attenders	3

The designations of the officials have been given in hierarchical order in each category. Out of six Assistant Project Officers, one is incharge of marketing and evaluation and is working from the District Office. The Assistant Project Officers are also called Area Coordinators, who are ordered to coordinate the programmes of the DRDA from different areas in the district. The District Project Managers assist the administration of DRDA and one of them is exclusively appointed to look after the financial matters of the Agency. Generally, the DRDAs in India are equipped with a planning team consisting of an economist, a credit planning officer and a rural industries officer to undertake preparation of the plan, project formulation and implementation in respect of different sectors. The officers for various fields like agriculture, animal husbandry, women welfare, etc. may also be appointed or deputed to DRDAs. There is, however, no such planning team or field-wise officers in the Visakhapatnam DRDA.

Programmes of DRDA

The DRDA had undertaken many rural programmes since its inception.[7] The following programmes have been undertaken in recent years by the DRDA:

1. Organisation of Self-Help Groups, Organisation of Village Organisations, Mandal Mahila Samakhyas and Zilla Mahila Samakhyas
2. Swarnajayanthi Gram Swarozgar Yojana Scheme
3. Pavala Vaddi (Interest subsidy) Scheme
4. Pension Scheme
5. National Family Benefit Scheme
6. Deepam Scheme
7. Establishment of Rajiv Internet Village Centers
8. Establishment of Bulk Milk Cooling Centers
9. Indira Parspara Hami Pathakam
10. Padi Pasuvula Appu Hami Pathakam
11. Training in Fashion Technology
12. Etikoppaka Toys Project (SGSY)

Most of these programmes are implemented under the DWACRA and SGSY. Out of the 12 above programmes, seven programmes are exclusively intended for women. The members of all the self-help groups are women. There are 31041 SHGs in the District. The total members of these groups are 3,76,812. The mandal-wise SHGs organised during 2004-05 are given in the following table.

TABLE 5.4

Mandal-wise SHGs

Name of the Mandal	*Total SHGs*
Anakapalli	1331
Kasimkota	1154
Yelamanchili	1045
Rambilli	788
Atchutapuram	930
Payakaraopeta	908
Nakkapalli	1065

S. Rayavaram	1106
Paravada	607
Sabbavaram	888
Munagapaka	892
K. Kotapadu	901
Chodavaram	1055
Butchayyapeta	724
Ravikamatham	756
Rolugunta	615
Madugula	840
Cheedikada	768
Devarapalli	815
Pendurthi	356
Bheemunipatnam	616
Anandapuram	720
Padmanabham	617
Narsipatnam	881
Makavarapalem	722
Kotavuratla	660
Nathavaram	746
Chintapalli	868
Golugonda	663
G.K. Veedhi	812
Koyyuru	809
Paderu	731
G. Madugula	702
Hukumpeta	840
Pedabayalu	820
Munchingiputtu	702
Araku	674
Dumbriguda	638
Ananthagiri	636
Total SHGs	31,401

In addition to the Government grants under various schemes, the SHGs in the district received an amount of Rs. 120.26 crores from the banks during 2005-06 under the SHG-Bank Linkage Programme. During the same year an amount of Rs. 17.24 crores was released to SHGs in the district as interest subsidy under Paval Vaddi Scheme. Under Deepam Scheme, a total of 23,121 gas connections were given to the women in the district during 2004-05. Dairy activity is being encouraged in big way since 2004-05 among SHG members as income generating activities. Tie-up arrangements have been made with the private diaries for marketing the milk produced by the SHG members. Four Bulk Milk Cooling Centers have been established in the district to enable SHG members to get a substainable regular income. These cooling centers are under the management of Mandal Samakyas. The DRDA sanctioned an amount of Rs. 10 lakhs for each cooling center.

The DRDA had taken up Human Insurance from 2005-06 through Zilla Samakhya under Indira Paraspara Hami Pathakam. Memorandum of Understanding was signed with the TATA-AIG and New India Assurance Company to provide insurance facility to the SHG members at low premium of Rs. 100 with the coverage of Rs. 25,000 for natural death of the insurer as well as her spouse and Rs. 50,000 for accidental death of the insurer. Another insurance scheme namely Milch Cattle Insurance was taken up during the same year under Padi Pasuvula Appu Hami Pathakam. The DRDA had entered into MoU with the New India Assurance Company to provide insurance to the milch cattle purchased by the SHG Women at low premium of Rs. 200 with coverage of Rs. 10,000. The total milch animals covered under the insurance during 2005-06 are 10320.

The State Government released an amount of Rs. 29.67 crores during 2004-05, Rs. 30.82 crores during 2005-06 and Rs. 21.22 crores during 206-07 under Swarnajayanthi Gram Swarozgar Yojana Scheme to Visakhapatnam DRDA. The funds available with the DRDA under SGSY is being untilised on subsidy to rural poor (including women) to undertake income generating activities and training to improve the skills of the beneficiaries. The funds are also being utilized as revolving fund and for infrastructure development. The total expenditure incurred by the DRDA during 2004-05 is under different heads of expenditure is given below:

Revolving Fund	: Rs. 20.70 crores
Training Fund	: Rs. 1.09 crores
Infrastructure Fund	: Rs. 8.83 crores
Subsidy Fund	: Rs. 0.47 crores

The revolving fund was released to SHGs, Mandal Offices, Village Organisations and RIV-e Seva centers. The training is being given to SHG women in tailoring, embroidery, dress-making, toys-making, coir mat weaving, fish breeding, etc., with the funds available under SGSY scheme.

The funds under this scheme are also utilized to give orientation training to SHG members. Under SGSY infrastructure, funds were released for construction and repairs of DWCRA buildings, training centres, RIV-e-Seva centers. The funds were also used for purchase of equipment for training and e-seva and bulk milk centers. Expenditure of DRDA, Visakhapatnam, under subsidy of SGSY during 2004-05 include funds released to SHGs and individual members for undertaking income-generating activities like dairying.

The two important projects undertaken by the Visakhapatnam DRDA under SGSY scheme are Fashion Technology Project and Etikoppaka Toys Project. The total cost of Fashion Technology Project is Rs. 12.16 out of which the Central and State Government subsidy (grant) is Rs. 8.16 crores. The balance amount of Rs. 4 crores was taken as loan from banks. Under this project about 15,500 women were trained in Garment Construction, Surface Ornamentation and Machine Embroidery. About 5,280 women were shown employment so far in garment construction and Surface Ornamentation.

The total cost of Etikoppaka Toys Project is Rs. 1.42 crores. The Government of India and Government of Andhra Pradesh provided an amount of Rs. 1.12 crores as grant (subsidy). The remaining amount of Rs. 30 lakhs was taken as loan from the bank. Under this project about 300 artisans in Etikoppaka Cluster have been organised into SHGs. A common facility centre was constructed in Etikoppaka and un-interrupted power supply was provided to it. The artisans have been linked with the bank for capital investment required for toys making.

District Scheduled Castes Cooperative Service Society

The State of Andhra Pradesh has 1,23,39,496 SC population (2001 census) which forms nearly 16.2 per cent of the total population. Among the 23 Districts, Nellore has the highest SC population (22%) followed by Prakasam (21.29%), West Godavari (19.17%), Chittoor (18.75%), Karimnagar (18.62%), Adilabad (18.54%) and Guntur (18.32%). Out of 59 sub-castes, Madigas and Malas are the two prominent sub-castes among Scheduled Castes in Andhra Pradesh. The literacy rate among the Scheduled Castes is 53.52 per cent as against the overall literacy rate of 60.47 per cent in Andhra Pradesh.

A vast majority of the SC families earn their livelihoods from agriculture—mostly as agricultural labourers, and some from farming operations. Allied occupations like dairy, piggery, sheep and goat rearing, poultry, etc., also provide livelihood to a substantial number of scheduled castes. Many landless scheduled castes have migrated to urban and semi-urban areas finding jobs as construction labourers and in the tertiary sector. As per the agricultural census, there are 115.32 lakh holders covering 359.98 lakh acres in the State against which the 13.67 lakh SC farmers hold 28.33 lakh acres. The percentage of the SC farmers who have land is 11.85%, while the extent held by them is a meager 7.87% of the total extent.[8] Majority of bonded labour belong to Scheduled Castes. Most of the persons engaged in sweeping, scavenging, flaying and tanning are Scheduled Castes. Majority of Scheduled Castes people are still below the poverty line. They are not only economically backward but are also victims of social exploitation. Considerable efforts have been made to extend the benefits of development programmes for them and also to ensure their upward mobility.

The Special Component Plans of Central Ministries and of States and Union Territories (UTs) are partly envisaged to help the poor Scheduled Castes families through composite income generating programmes such family-oriented programmes as to cover all the major occupational groups amongst them such as share croppers, fishermen, sweepers and scavengers and unorganised urban labour below poverty line. The Special Central Assistance is an additionality to the Special Component Plans of States and UTs. It is intended to encourage higher investments in various sectors in the States and UTs towards economic development of targeted Scheduled Caste population. The strategy of development of Scheduled Castes include the arrangement of Scheduled Caste Development Corporations. Recognizing the need for flow of adequate fund for the economic development of the SCs, Scheduled Caste Development Corporations were first set-up in the States of Andhra Pradesh, Gujarat, Haryana, Kerala, Punjab and Tamil Nadu as early as in the Fourth Five Year Plan.

Today as many as 18 states and 3 UTs covering 99.9 per cent of the Total SC population in the country have these Corporations and these corporations are functioning as one of the most important instruments for the economic development of the target groups.

The Corporations in the states of Himachal Pradesh, Kerala, Karnataka, Orissa, Madhya Pradesh and West Bengal cater to the STs also while the Jammu and Kashmir Corporation covers the Backward Classes too. Maharashtra Corporation covers neo-Budhists in addition to SCs. Most of the SCDCs came up during late seventies and early years of the Sixth Plan period, when Government of India, considering the utility of the SC Corporations, started assisting them by contributing to their share capital on a matching basis with the State Governments in the ratio of 49:51. From Sixth Plan onward, the scheme of Scheduled Caste Development Corporations has been the most important centrally sponsored scheme for the economic development of the Scheduled Castes. A brief description of Andhra Pradesh Scheduled Caste Cooperative Finance Corporation and the detailed discussion on Visakhapatnam District S.C. Cooperative Service Society are given in this part.

Andhra Pradesh Scheduled Caste Cooperative Finance Corporation was set-up in the year 1974 with a view to take up programmes for the economic development of Scheduled Caste families in the State. The Corporation is registered under the AP Cooperative Societies Act with a share holding pattern of 51:49 per cent between the State Government and Government of India, respectively. The Corporation has been established with the following main objectives:

- (i) To provide financial assistance for creation of income generating assets;
- (ii) To offer training programmes for skill up-gradation leading to self and wage employment;
- (iii) To empower women self-help groups for taking up economic support activity; and
- (iv) To plug critical gaps of finance in economic support schemes.

The Head Office of the Corporation formulates policy, in terms of preparation of annual action plans, monitors implementation of schemes by way of conducting review meeting and securing progress reports on monthly basis. The Corporation mobilizes resources from Government of India, State Government and other financial institutions and in turn releases to District Societies for implementation of schemes.

The Corporation is provided with necessary funds by the State Government and Government of India to carry out its activities. The pattern of funding is as follows:

(i) Share capital: Proportionate share by State Government and Government of India in the ratio of 51:49 respectively.

(ii) Special Central Assistance for filling the infrastructural and viability gaps.

(iii) Matching Assistance:

  (a) For promotional activities and surveys and studies—1% of cumulative share capital contribution of the Government of India;

  (b) Setting up monitoring, evaluation, recovery and technical wings—3% of cumulative share capital contribution of the Government of India; and

  (c) Managerial support;

(iv) Grant from State Government.

The Vice-Chairman and Managing Director, manages the affairs of the Corporation, under the guidance of a Committee. The Vice-Chairman and Managing Director is assisted by General Managers, subject specialists (Special Officers) and other supporting staff.

During the last 33 years of its existence, the Corporation has provided assistance of Rs. 3025.1919 crores for the benefit of 41,57,625 SCs in the State.[9] While the per capita investment during 1974-75 was only Rs. 730, it has increased gradually to Rs. 18,000 in recent years. The coverage provided during 1974-75 was Rs. 25.64 lakh and 3495 beneficiaries in terms of financial and physical achievements. This has increased multi-fold during the past 32 years.

The Visakhapatnam District Scheduled Castes Cooperative service Society (DSCCSS) was established in 1974 and registered under Andhra Pradesh Cooperative Societies Act 1964. The District Society receives grants from the Andhra Pradesh Scheduled Caste Cooperative Finance Corporation and implements schemes for the welfare and development of Scheduled Castes in the district. The District Society also mobilizes local resources in terms of SGSY subsidy, subsidy from DRDA, SCSP from line departments, loans from banks and 15 per cent earmarked funds from the local bodies. The task of monitoring Scheduled Caste Sub-plan allocations and expenditure is entrusted to the society.

Functions of DSCCSS

The main functions of the society are indicated below:

(i) Identification of eligible SC families and SC clusters through special surveys and motivating them to undertake suitable economic development schemes;

(ii) Sponsoring these schemes to financial institutions for credit support;

(iii) Providing financial assistance in the form of margin money or direct loan on low rate of interest and subsidy in order to reduce their repayment liability;

(iv) Providing credit and subsidy support to other agencies and institutions like KVIC, Department of Handlooms and Textiles and Department of Sericulture, etc;

(v) Providing necessary link or tie-up with other poverty alleviation programmes, viz., IRDP through credit and subsidies support;

(vi) Providing infrastructure to enable the group of beneficiaries to take up their own ventures in a common work place;

(vii) Imparting training in different skills to the target group includes coordination with the help of local agencies, departments, training institutions and voluntary organisations; and

(viii) Evaluation and monitoring of the schemes and providing missing critical inputs as and when necessary, including arrangement for supply of raw-materials, marketing of finished goods, etc.

Organisational Structure of DSCCSS

The District Society functions under the guidance of a committee under the Chairmanship of the District Collector. The following are the members of the Committee:

1. Project Director,
   District Rural Development Agency
2. Project Director,
   District Women and Child Development Agency
3. Joint Director, Agriculture
4. General Manager, District Industries Center
5. Chief Executive Officer, Zilla Parishad, Visakhapatnam
6. Deputy Director, Social Welfare, Visakhapatnam
7. District Cooperative Officer, Visakhapatnam
8. Executive Director, District Society of S.C. Corporation
9. Manager, Lead Bank
10. District Employment Officer

The day-to-day affairs of the society are managed by the Executive Director, a senior officer from Group-I Service of the State. He is assisted by subject specialists and other subordinate staff in the implementation of the schemes. The following are the officers and staff of the society.

Executive Director	1
Executive Officers	2
Assistant Executive Officer	1
Assistant Section Officer	1
Superintendent	1
Senior Assistant	2
Junior Assistant	6
Attenders	6
Drivers	4
Ayahs	2
NMRs	3

Programmes of DSCCSS

The Visakhapatnam District Society of SC Corporation has been implementing SC welfare programmes in the District. A brief description of the schemes implemented by the society during the last five years is given in the following pages.

Land Purchase Scheme

The Land Purchase Scheme is one of the priority schemes implemented by the SC Corporation and its subsidiary agencies namely District Societies. The main objective of this scheme is to provide a valuable and durable asset to Scheduled Castes, so that there is upliftment of not only their economic status but also the social status. From 1982 till 2006-07, an extent of 73,936.57 acres of land has been purchased and allotted to 62,967 beneficiaries at a cost of Rs. 185.57 crores. The Visakhapatnam District Society purchased 165 acres of land at a cost of Rs. 134.26 lakhs and allotted to 264 beneficiaries. About 30 per cent of the beneficiaries are landless agricultural women labourers. The details of beneficiaries, land purchased and amount spent during the last 5 years are given in the following table.

TABLE 5.5

Land Purchase Scheme

Year	*Land purchased (Acres)*	*Amount spent (Rs. lakhs)*	*No. of Beneficiaries*
2002-03	50	61.50	15
2003-04	80	40.81	196
2005-06	35	31.95	53
Total	165	134.26	264

Land Development

Under the land development programme, the Government assigned lands and ceiling lands are developed. The details of this programme of Visakhapatnam District Society are given in the following table.

TABLE 5.6

Land Development Programme

Year	*Extent of land (Acres)*	*Amount spent (Rs.lakhs)*	*No. of Beneficiaries*
2002-03	111.49	3.75	150
2003-04	700.45	23.56	419
2006-07	1,098.17	121.72	822
Total	1,910.11	149.03	1,391

An extent of 111.49 acres of land was developed by the District Society at a cost of Rs. 3.75 lakhs during 2002-03.[10] From this a total of 150 scheduled caste people were benefited. During 2003-04 an amount of Rs. 23.56 was spend to develop 700.45 acres of land for the benefit of 419 landless agricultural labour.[11] The land development programme was not, however, undertaken during 2004-05 and 2005-06. Again in the year 2006-07, the Society developed 1098.17 acres of land by spending an amount of Rs. 121.72 lakhs. The total beneficiaries of this programme is 822.

Minor Irrigation

The Minor irrigation programme is being taken up by the District Society in assigned lands, ceiling lands, purchased lands, developed lands and patta lands. Schemes like Borewells, Lift Irrigation Energisation, etc. are incorporated in the minor irrigation programme. While taking up minor irrigation sources, preference will be given to such scheduled castes who have compact blocks of land at one place. In case the compact blocks are not available, individual cases can be taken up on merits such as fulfilment of distance norms and pre-feasibility of electricity. The bore wells schemes are taken up in the lands of small and marginal scheduled caste farmers with electricity feasibility. The minimum extent to be considered under each bore well is 5 acres and above and a minimum number of beneficiaries are 3 and above.

The Lift Irrigation schemes are taken up in the lands of Scheduled Caste farmers. The scheme comprises of identification of Scheduled Caste beneficiaries with lands in compact blocks near perennial source of water like rivers, streams, etc. conducting surveys, preparation of estimates and execution of work and development of ayacut by way of laying pipelines upto the ridge point of the ayacut. The beneficiaries dig field channels from the ridge points. The minimum extent to be considered under each Lift Irrigation Scheme is 50 acres and above and the number of beneficiaries is 10. The expenditure for energisation of Minor Irrigation Programmes is also being met by the District Society. The service connection charges and line laying charges are being paid by the Society. The details of the Minor Irrigation Programmes undertaken by the Visakhapatnam District Society are given in the following table.

TABLE 5.7

Minor Irrigation Programme

Year	*Extent of land (Acres)*	*Amount spent (Rs. lakhs)*	*No. of Beneficiaries*
2002-03	150	37.08	201
2003-04	160	30.25	171
2004-05	340	74.14	948
2005-06	578	27.96	923
2006-07	515	50.33	374
Total	1743	219.76	2617

In a period of 5 years from 2002-03 the District Society had implemented various minor irrigation programmes to provide irrigation facility to 1743 acres benefiting 2617 Scheduled Caste farmers (both men and women) with an outlay of Rs. 219.76 lakhs.

Horticulture

The farmers in India find it profitable to diversify into horticulture crops. But the Scheduled Caste farmers are not coming forward for taking horticulture plantations due to poverty and long gestation period. The Department of Horticulture is promoting area expansion of fruits and vegetables coupled with drip and sprinkler irrigation system by providing subsidy. However, the SC farmers are unable to pay the non-subsidy portion and make use of the subsidy. In view of this, the SC Corporation provides loan to meet the non-subsidy component of the horticulture plantation. Normally the SC families possessing light to marginal soils with water source are identified for cultivation of horticulture crops. The corporation tries to take maximum support from the regular Horticulture Department and RLEGP to secure full coverage of Scheduled Castes. The farmers with requisite zeal, aptitude and commitment to the programme are selected. The District Society undertake the task of identification of beneficiaries, procurement of plant material, securing subsidy, etc. The SC farmers in the district are encouraged to take up horticultural crops like mango, guava, ber, citrus, coconut, causurina, oil palm, cashew, sapota, etc. The farmers are also encouraged for taking up inter crops such as vegetables and pulse crops to generate income during gestation period. The District Society had provided horticulture implements to SC horticulture farmers. The details of horticulture programme of the Society are given in the Table 5.8.

TABLE 5.8

Amount Spent on Horticulture Crops

Year	*Extent of land (Acres)*	*Amount spent (Rs. lakhs)*	*No. of Beneficiaries*
2002-03	136.71	10.90	821
2003-04	175.92	19.15	196
2005-06	439.04	22.95	433
2006-07	205.60	7.95	210
Total	957.27	60.95	1660

The Society encouraged 1660 SC farmers to take up horticultural crops in an extent of 957.27 acres during the last 5 years. Most of the beneficiaries are woman. For instance, during 2006-07, out of 210 beneficiaries 185 are women. Some of the SC farmers are benefited from inter crops such as vegetables and pulses. Out of 821 SC farmers, who benefited from the horticulture crops during 2002-03, 642 had taken up the inter crops.

Animal Husbandry

The animal husbandry sector is the most feasible and viable scheme among development activities for the upliftment of the below poverty line people. It provides sustainable income and meaningful livelihood with minimum skills and available resources with them. The animal husbandry programme is, therefore, one of the important programmes of the SC Corporation. The schemes under this programme include dairying, milk vending, sheep rearing, ramlamb rearing, etc.

The dairying is the major activity which provides daily regular income through vending milk. The dairy scheme requires green fodder cultivation with minimum of ¼acre per unit with irrigation facility. The 1/4 acre with perennial fodder can yield the required green fodder for 2 milch animals. Therefore, the people who have land with irrigation facility or the people who are included under Land Purchase Scheme or Minor Irrigation Scheme are considered for the selection and implementation of the dairy scheme. An amount of Rs. 185.45 lakhs was spent by Visakhapatnam District Society during 2006-07 for purchase of Cross Breed Cows and Graded Murrah Buffaloes and for fodder development.[12] The total number of beneficiaries of dairy scheme is 672 out of which 660 beneficiaries are SC women (98 per cent).

The sheep rearing is the other important adaptable sector under the animal husbandry programme of the SC Corporation and the District Society. The sheep rearing requires minimum inputs and skills and resources like land, etc. It provides regular income through sale of ramlambs. The Society provides margin money, arranges margin money and bank loan for purchase of sheep. The Society had provided an amount of Rs. 5.89 lakhs for the benefit of 97 SC people during 2006-07. Out of the 97 beneficiaries women beneficiaries are 11.

Self-Employment Schemes

The SC Corporation had encouraged the SC candidates who studied upto 10th class to establish industry, service and business sector schemes. The broad objective is to enable easy access to credit for poor educated unemployed SC youth at a cheaper rate of interest for self-employment units and to identify entrepreneurial capabilities among SC youth and facilitate them to emerge as successful entrepreneurs in the society. Under the Self-Employment Schemes, the educated unemployed SC youth are provided margin money with back end subsidy from various institutions like KVIB, Industries Department, National Scheduled Caste Finance Development Corporation (NSCFDC), National Safai Karmachari Finance Development Corporation (NSKFDC), etc.

In Visakhapatnam District, the unemployed SC youth had undertaken many self employment units with the support of SC Corporation and assistance of financial institutions. For example, the cobbler bunks had been set up by the traditional cobblers with a unit cost of Rs. 50,000 with subsidy from the Government, margin money from the Corporation and loan from the banks. The cement hallow bricks and other building material units had been started with the assistance from NSFDC and NSKFDC.

The NSCFDC had provided micro credit assistance to SC Women Self Help Groups. The micro credit assistance enabled the SC women to undertake income generating activities. The Pavala Vaddi Scheme had also been extended to these SHGs. The Corporation had come to the rescue of the SC beneficiaries who are in need of immediate financial assistance due to distress.

Term loans had been arranged for rehabilitation of scavengers and bonded labour. The financial assistance had also been provided to poor educated unemployed Karamchari youth at a cheaper interest rate for undertaking self-employment units. The flayers and tanners who are engaged in unhygienic occupation of handling skins or raw hides had been provided revolving fund though Mandal Mahila Samakhyas. The details of amount spent by the Society on different self-employment schemes are given in the Table 5.9.

TABLE 5.9

Amount Spent on Self-employment Schemes

Year	*Amount Spent (Rs. in lakhs)*	*No. of Beneficiaries*
2002-03	703.23	2554
2003-04	814.47	4515
2004-05	424.37	2289
2005-06	449.65	2415
2006-07	609.92	568
Total	3001.64	12341

The Visakhapatnam District Society had spent an amount of Rs. 3001.64 benefiting 12,341 SC candidates on different self-employment schemes, during a period of five year plans from 2002-03 to 2006-07.

The beneficiaries under different self-employment schemes are:

1. Unemployed educated SC youth; and
2. Vulnerable groups like Bonded Labour, Jogins, Scavengers, Safai Karamcharies, Flayers, Tanners, Cobblers, Atrocity Victims, etc.

Training and Awareness Programmes

The SC youth from rural areas, who could not pursue their higher education are neither becoming fit for wage earning nor securing gainful employment. As such there is discontentment, which lead to social tensions. While the job opportunities are shrinking in the public sector, the employment opportunities are getting widened in the private sector, especially in urban-based service sector. To compete in the open job market, the additional inputs are required for SC youth for developing their skills, as they come from poor social and economic background. This has prompted the SC Corporation to focus on organizing skill development programmes for SC youth. The Corporation had also taken up training and awareness programmes for the beneficiaries of its different programmes. The financial allocation of SC Corporation for these programmes in the Visakhapatnam District is presented in the Table 5.10.

TABLE 5.10

Amount Spent on Training and Awareness Programmes

Year	*Amount Spent (Rs. in lakhs)*	*No. of Beneficiaries*
2002-03	29.37	982
2003-04	71.35	587
2004-05	13.62	150
2005-06	21.73	757
2006-07	24.41	483
Total	160.48	2959

The Visakhapatnam District SC Cooperative Service Society spent an amount of Rs. 160.48 lakhs on training and beneficiary awareness programmes from 2002-03 to 2006-07. The total number of beneficiaries under different training programmes is 2959. The number of beneficiaries does not include the beneficiaries who were benefited from different awareness programmes of the Society. The beneficiaries of various programmes will be given training before taking up the unit. They will also be made aware of various aspects of the unit or scheme. For instance, the beneficiaries selected under Land Purchase Scheme had been given training by the District Society. Similarly Animal Husbandry and Horticulture training was arranged for all the beneficiaries selected.

District Backward Classes Cooperative Service Society

The backward classes constitute half of the total population of Andhra Pradesh. Among the BCs half of them are women. According to an estimation there are 2.50 crores backward class women.[13] About 80 per cent of the BC people are artisans who are living below the poverty line. The Government of Andhra Pradesh initiated several measures and have implementing many programmes to improve the living standards of BCs in the state and make them lead a good life.

The State Government has reserved 25 per cent seats in educational institutions and posts in government offices. The State Government had also reserved 25 per cent of house sites and 15 per cent of the houses constructed by the Housing Board for BCs.[14] The BC students, whose family income is Rs. 44,000 and below per annum are exempted from payment of tuition fees and are eligible for award of scholarships, hostel facilities, etc. The text books are provided to the BC students upto 10th class. Sixty-one Ashram Schools are being run by the State Government for the children of fishermen community. Similarly, there are 22 Ashram Schools for the children belonging to Vaddera and Shepherd communities. At present, there are 1150 hostels for BC boys and 277 hostels for BC girls. The study circles have been established to give coaching to BCs for civil services examinations. Recently, the role of study circles have been expanded by introducing coaching for entrance examination to professional and technical courses. All these programmes are being implemented and overseen by the Backward Classes Welfare Department of the Government of Andhra Pradesh.

While the educational programmes are being implemented by the Backward Classes Welfare Department, the responsibility to ensure livelihoods to the disadvantaged groups of BCs and to promote entrepreneurship among these groups has been given to the Andhra Pradesh Backward Classes Cooperative Finance Corporation.[15] The BC Corporation was established in 1976 with its headquarters at Hyderabad. The Chairman of the Corporation is a person nominated by the State Government. The executive head of the Corporation is the Vice-Chairman and Managing Director who is a senior I.A.S. Officer. He is assisted by the following officers and office staff:

General Manager	1
Development Officer	1
Assistant Development Officer	1
Office Superintendent	1
Senior Assistants	4
Junior Assistants	4
Typists	3
Attenders	5

Organisational Structure of DBCCSS

The Corporation undertakes various BC welfare and development programmes through its District Societies. The Visakhapatnam District Backward Classes Cooperative Service Society (DBCCSS) is one such organisation. The Visakhapatnam District Society started its activities from the year 1976, the year of its as well as the Corporation's establishment. There is a governing body for the society for which the District Collector is the Chairman. The other numbers of the Governing Body are:

1. Project Director, District Rural Development Agency.
2. Chief Executive Officer, Zilla Parishad, Visakhapatnam.
3. District Cooperative Officer.
4. District B.C. Welfare Officer.
5. Municipal Commissioner, Visakhapatnam Municipal Corporation.

6. Executive Director, DBCCSS.
7. General Manager, District Industries Centre.
8. Manager, Lead Bank.
9. Joint Director, Agriculture
10. Project Director, DWCDA.

The administrative head of the society is the Executive Director, a Group-I Service Officer. He is assisted with following officers and staff:

Executive Officer
Assistant Executive Officer
Loan Inspectors
Superintendent
Senior Assistant
Accountant
Junior Assistant
Typists
Record Keepers
Attenders
Drivers

The post of Executive Officer and one post of Loan Inspector are vacant, at present.

Objectives of DBCCSS

The main objective of the Society is to sanction the financial assistance to the BCs who are below poverty line. The other important objectives of the society are to:

1. eradicate poverty and eliminate current inequalities that prevent the members of BCs from realising their full potential;
2. establish a just and egalitarian society;
3. provide access to opportunities for employment;
4. helping BCs to establish secure livelihoods;
5. upgrade the skills of BCs to capture economic opportunities; and
6. promote entrepreneurship among BCs.

Functions of DBCCSS

The main function of the Society is to implement the development programmes meant for the BCs in the district. In this direction the following functions are being performed by the Society:

1. Providing assistance to individuals and groups of BCs;
2. Involving banks with certain component of loan;
3. Securing assistance from the financial institutions like National Backward Classes Finance Development Corporation;
4. Imparting pre-grounding training for beneficiaries;
5. Selection of beneficiaries;
6. Fixation of unit cost;
7. Focusing on recovery of loans to ensure use and sustainability; and
8. providing improved tools, small technological equipment.

Programmes of DBCCSS

The Visakhapatnam District Backward Classes Service Cooperative Society had undertaken the following schemes for the benefit of BCs in the district:

1. Margin Money
2. National Backward Classes Finance Development Corporation (NBCFDC) Term loan
3. Micro Credit
4. Education Loan
5. Swarnima
6. Adarna
7. Dhobighats
8. Special Packages

The scheme-wise achievements are discussed hereunder. The financial allocation for each scheme and the number of BC people benefited from these schemes during the last five years, i.e. from 2002-03 to 2006-07 are given in the Table 5.11.

TABLE 5.11

Financial Allocation on Various Schemes

(*Rs. in Lakhs*)

Sl. No.	*Name of the Scheme*	*2002-03*		*2003-04*		*2004-05*		*2005-06*		*2006-07*	
		No. of Beneficiaries	*Amount Spent*	*No. of Beneficiaries*	*Amount Spent*	*No. of Beneficiaries*	*Amount Spent*	*No. of Beneficiaries*	*Amount Spent*	*No. of Beneficiaries*	*Amount Spent*
1.	Margin Money	2224	46.80	936	15.86	1027	18.60	1065	18.86	693	23.71
2.	NBCFDC	1036	17.68	105	1.74	—	—	—	—	—	—
3.	Micro Crdit Finance	2652	39.78	1155	17.40	—	—	—	—	510	7.43
4.	Education Loan	58	20.50	41	10.00	25	9.26	44	17.11	23	8.83
5.	Swarnima	1100	17.68	285	4.35	—	—	—	—	—	—
6.	Adarana	—	—	2878	329.00	—	—	—	—	—	—
7.	Dhobhighats	—	—	950	28.00	—	—	—	—	112	8.00
8.	Special Package	—	—	4394	216.00	—	—	—	—	—	—
	Total	7280	142.44	10704	622.35	1052	27.86	1109	35.97	1338	47.97

1. Margin Money

This Scheme is started to assist the beneficiaries to establish the small business units upto Rs. 50,000 for purchase of autos, etc. for income generation activity. Under this scheme, the Society shall finance 20 per cent of the units cost and remaining 80 per cent to be financed by the bank for establishing of the units. The District Society had financed 160 SHGs at Rs. 22,500 covering 2,424 beneficiaries with an outlay of Rs. 46.86 lakhs during 2002-03 and 58 SHGs covering 936 beneficiaries with an outlay of Rs. 15.86 lakhs during 2003-04. The Margin Money Scheme was continued in the years 2004-05, 2005-06 and 2006-07. During the period of 5 years the Society had financed a total of 410 SHGs covering 6,145 beneficiaries with an outlay of Rs. 123.89 lakhs as margin money.[16]

2. NBCFDC. Term Loan

This Scheme was started during the year 2000 with an aim to give financial assistance to educated unemployed youth to establish units worth upto one lakh without bank finance. Under this scheme 85 per cent of the unit cost will be sanctioned as term loan and remaining 15 per cent have to borne by the beneficiary towards contribution. Under this scheme the units like, autos, cars, xerox units, boats, etc. were sanctioned to the beneficiary. The Society secured an amount of Rs. 17.68 lakhs during 2002-03 and Rs. 1.74 lakhs during 2003-04 as term loan from NBCFDC. About 1,141 unemployed youth were benefited from this scheme.

3. Micro Credit

Under this scheme the SHGs consisting of poor BC women will be given initially Rs. 25,000 as loan and after repayment of the same within 18 instalments, another Rs. 75,000 will be given as loan in 3 instalments. The groups in turn will lend the money to the group members for interest at 12 per cent to 24 per cent per annum. Under this scheme the Society had provided financial assistance to 176 SHGs during 2002-03, 79 SHGs during 2003-04 and 34 SHGs during 2006-07. The poor BC women benefited from this scheme during the above three years were 4317.

4. Education Loan

Education Loan Scheme was introduced with a purpose to

give education loans to the BC students upto Rs. 3.00 lakhs in four instalments for those who are studying professional courses like IIT, MBBS, Engineering, Hotel Management, etc. In a period of 5 years starting with the financial year 2002-03, the Society had given educational loan to 191 students with a total outlay of Rs. 65.70 lakhs.

5. Swarnima

This scheme is started with a motive to give direct financial assistance to the B.C. women to establish small business units. Under this scheme 85 per cent of the unit cost will be sanctioned as term loan and remain 15 per cent shall be borne by the beneficiary. The term loan is to be repaid in 10 years with a interest of 4 per cent. Under this scheme, the Society sanctioned an amount of Rs. 17.68 lakhs during 2002-03 and Rs. 4.35 lakhs during 2003-04. A total of 1385 B.C. women were benefited by this scheme.

6. Adarana

Adarana Scheme was introduced with a motive to give tool kits to the BC occupational groups and artisans. The funding pattern under this scheme is 15:35:50 being the beneficiary contribution, subsidy and bank loan respectively. During the year 2003-04 the District Society had given tool kits to 4345 artisans with an outlay of Rs. 331 lakhs.[17]

7. Dhobhighats

During the year 2003-04, the Government have sanctioned Rs. 30.00 lakhs for construction of 30 Dhobhighats (Rs.1.00 lakh per Dhobhighat) and Rs. 16.00 lakhs for repairs to 40 existing Dhobhighats (Rs. 0.40 lakhs each). The Government sanctioned Rs. 8 lakhs for construction of another 8 Dhobhighats in the year 2006-07 in the District. About 1022 washermen communities were benefited from this scheme.

8. Special Packages

During the year 2003-04, the Government have introduced special package for accelerated development of BCs who are below poverty line. Under this scheme, weavers, barbers, tailors, blacksmith, rajakas and toddy tapers were given financial assistance. During the year 2003-04, the District Society had given financial assistance to 4396 beneficiaries with an outlay of Rs. 216.00 lakhs.

Notes and References

1. S.R. Bakshi and Kiran Bala, *Welfare and Development of Women*, New Delhi, Deep and Deep Publications, 1999, p. 160.
2. T. Appa Rao, *North Andhra, Industries, Institutions and Cultural Heritage*, Sarvani Printers, Visakhaptnam, 2004, p. 30.
3. *Note on DMSVK*, Visakhapatnam, 2007, p. 1.
4. Project Director, District Women and Child Development Agency, *Department Note*, Visakhapatnam, 2006, p. 1.
5. *Ibid.*, p. 3.
6. Hoshiar Singh, *Administration of Rural Development*, Sterling Publishers, New Delhi, 1995, p. 13.
7. Project Director, District Rural Development Agency, *Brief Note on DRDA Activities*, Visakhapatnam, 2007, pp. 1-13
8. A.P. S.C. Cooperative Finance Corporation, *Marching Towards Economic Upliftment of Scheduled Castes*, Hyderabad, 2007, p. 2.
9. A.P.S.C. Cooperative Finance Corporation, *Action Plan 2007-08*, Hyderabad, 2007, p. 3.
10. District S.C. Cooperative Service Society, *Brief Note on S.C. Action Plan 2002-03*, Visakhapatnam, p. 1.
11. District S.C. Cooperative Service Society, *Performance under S.C. Action Plan 2003-04*, Visakhapatnam, p. 1.
12. District S.C. Cooperative Service Society, *Progress Report under S.C. Action Plan 2006-07*, Visakhapatnam, p. 1.
13. B. Chandrasekhar, *Women Development and Welfare Schemes*, Lakshmi Publications, Hyderabad, October 2002, p. 128.
14. K. Asaiah, "Status of Backward Classes" in R.S. Rao *et. al.* (eds.), *Fifty Years of Andhra Pradesh, 1956-2006*, Centre for Documentation, Research and Communication, Hyderabad, 2007, p. 455.
15. Government of Andhra Pradesh, *Strategy Paper on Backward Classes Welfare in Andhra Pradesh*, Department of B.C. Welfare, Hyderabad, February 2001, p. 3.
16. District B.C. Cooperative Service Society, *Targets and Achievements on Various Schemes from 2002-03 to 2006-07*, Visakhapatnam, p. 1.
17. District B.C. Cooperative Service Society, *Note on Developmental Activities*, Visakhapatnam 2004, p. 4.

Perceptions on Women Development Organisations

Local organisations are central actors in development strategies. They got prominence in recent years. The concerns for efficiency and effectiveness led to the development practitioners, government and donor agencies rely on local organisations. They have become popular as mechanisms for local management of development resources and benefits. However, many of these local organisations do not perform as expected, and development practitioners are uncertain about their effectiveness, fairness and sustainability. Given the prevalence of local organisations and their high profile in contemporary development programmes, these uncertainties need to be address. An attempt is made in the present study to meet this need. As a part of it, the perceptions of the officers and beneficiaries of the women development organisations are sought to assess the effectiveness and efficiency of the organisations in implementing the programmes.

Analysis of performance tells us what different organisations do and how well they do it. Studies undertaken in recent years demonstrate that four factors play significant roles in shaping an organisation's performance: assets, processes, linkages, and context. The first three of these are attributes particular to an organisation, while the last relates to the environment in which the organisation and its members operate.

Assets include human, material and financial assets. The human assets include the quantity and quality of human resources, while material assets include physical resources. Financial assets refer to the monetary resources of an organisation. The knowledge of organisational rules, transparency of operation and decision-making process are the three key process variables. The form of linkages with line agencies, panchayati raj institutions and other organisations working in a study sector also shapes an organization's performance. The context variables include the physiographic, social, infrastructural and state context of the location in which an organisation operates. The opinions of officials and beneficiaries, elicited in this study, on most of these variables have been analysed in this chapter.

Officials Perceptions

The opinion of 52 officers of 4 women development organisations in Visakhapatnam District were elicited on various aspects of their respective organisations. The break-up of these officers is as follows:

DWCDA	32
DRDA	10
DSCCSS	05
DBCCSS	05

The officers have different designations and authority at different levels—they are higher level, middle level and lower level officers. These officers include Project Director, Additional Project Director, Executive Director, Executive Officer, District Manager, Assistant Executive Officer, Assistant Project Officer, Assistant Project Manager, Child Development Officer, Loan Inspector, ICDS Supervisor, Superintendent, Matron and Anganwadi Teacher, etc. These officers have major role in the implementation of development programmes and hence, the study confined to ascertain their opinion.

An organisation's performance is contingent on its personnel.

The quantity (number), quality, qualification and perceptions of officials have greater importance for performance of local organisations. The number of employees including the officers was already given in the Chapter 5. Their nature of employment, age, educational qualifications, and training received by them, have been examined in this chapter, for a better understanding of their perceptions on various aspects of women development organizations.

Nature of Employment

TABLE 6.1

Nature of Employment

S.No.	Nature of Employment	Number	Percent
1.	Recruited	36	69.23
2.	Deputed	16	30.77
	Total	52	100.00

Out of 52 sample officials nearly 70 percent of them have been recruited for their respective women development organisations. The remain 16(30.77 percent) officials have been deputed to the women development organisations from the other governmental departments like Revenue and Panchayati Raj.

Age of the Officials

TABLE 6.2

Age of the Officials

S.No.	Age Group	Number	Percent
1.	20-30	4	7.69
2.	31-40	15	28.85
3.	41-50	22	42.31
4.	51-60	11	21.15
	Total	52	100.00

The officials spread over different age groups. There are only

4 officials under 20-30 years age-group. The official respondents in the age-group of 31-40 years constitute 28.85 percentage. More than 40 percent of the officials are in the age group of 41-50 years. The remaining 11(21.15 percent) officials are in the age-group of 51-60 years.

Education of Officials

TABLE 6.3

Education of the Officials

S. No.	Qualification	Number	Percent
1.	S.S.C.	5	9.62
2.	Intermediate	6	11.54
3.	Graduates	22	42.31
4.	Post Graduate	19	36.53
	Total	52	100.00

More than 80 percent of the officials are graduates and postgraduates. Out of 52 official respondents more than one-third of them are postgraduates. The officials whose education is SSC and Intermediate constitute only 21.16 percent. It is clear from the above data that the overwhelming majority of officials have higher educational qualifications.

Service of Officials

TABLE 6.4

Number of Years of Service

S.No.	Years of Service	Number	Percent
1.	1-5 years	9	17.31
2.	6-10 Years	11	21.15
3.	11-15 years	30	77.16
4.	16-20 years	10	19.23
5.	Above 20 years	6	11.54
	Total	52	100.00

The number of years of service of about 30 percent of respondents is between 11 and 15 years. The service of more than one-fifth of the officials ranges from 6 to 10 years. The officials whose service ranges from 1 to 5 years constitute 17.31 percent and whose service ranges from 16 to 20 years constitute 19.23 percent. Six officials have been in the service for more than 20 years. It is clear from the above table that the majority of the officials have more than 10 years service in their respective agencies.

Training

The officials of any organisation receive training both pre-entry and in-serving training. The officials working in the women development organisations are to be trained in or oriented towards the implementation of the programmes of their respective organisations. The researcher had attempted to get the information from the officials themselves on the training they received. About 75 percent of them reported that they received training. They were requested to give the details of the training and the number of times they received training. Their replies have been presented in the following table.

TABLE 6.5

Training

S. No.	*No. of Times*	*Number*	*Percent*
1.	Once	16	30.77
2.	Twice	23	44.23
3.	No Training	13	25.00
	Total	52	100.00

Sixteen official respondents received training only once during their service period in their respective agencies. The officials who received training twice constitute 44-23 percent. The remaining 13(25 percent) officials had not attended any type of training. It is clear from that three-fourths of officials got trained during their tenure in their respective agencies.

In the present study, the opinion of the officials was ascertained regarding the organisational structure, infrastructural facilities (physical resources), personnel (human resources), financial resources, process of implementation of programmes and linkages with other organisations. The officers were requested to give their opinion on the adequacy of the machinery for women development. They were also asked about the problems or challenges encountered by them or by their organisations. Finally, they were requested to suggest measures for effective implementation of women development programmes.

Organisational Structure

The performance of an organisation depends upon its structural arrangements. Hence, the officials were asked whether the present organisational structure of their agencies were effective, and whether they were satisfied with it. Their replies have been presented in the following table.

TABLE 6.6

Satisfaction about the Organisational Structure

S. No.	*Satisfaction*	*Number*	*Percent*
1.	Satisfied	39	75.00
2.	Not satisfied	13	25.00
	Total	52	100.00

Three-fourths of the officials respondents said 'yes' and they were satisfied with their present organisational structure of their respective agencies. Only 25 percent of respondents responded negatively on this aspect. The respondent officials were also asked whether they would like to suggest any alternative organizational structure or change in the existing structure. Their responses have been presented in the following table.

TABLE 6.7

Alternative Organisational Structure

S.No.	*Opinion*	*Number*	*Percent*
1.	Yes	31	59.61
2.	No	21	40.39
	Total	52	100.00

Nearly 60 percent of the respondents preferred to suggest alternative structure to the existing organisational structure. They were, however, not in a position spell out about the alternative or new structure. Though majority of the officials were happy with the existing organisational structure they wanted some changes in the structure.

Infrastructural Facilities

The women development organisations need infrastructural facilities like accommodation, vehicles, modern facilities like computers, etc., and the other required facilities for imparting training to the officials as well as beneficiaries. All the four organisations have been housed in pucca and own buildings. They have computing facilities. The field officials have been given vehicles to make trips to their respective areas of operation. The ICDS project office and DMSVK of DWCDA have been equipped with required additional facilities. For instance, the DMSVK, an institution to impart training to women was well-established equipment for imparting training in computer, beautician, embroidery, book-binding and printing, handicrafts, etc. The officials were requested to respond on the adequacy of the existing infrastructural facilities in their respective organisations. Their observations have been presented in the Table 6.8.

TABL 6.8

Infrastructural Facilities

S.No.	*Opinion*	*Number*	*Percent*
1.	Adequate	27	51.92
2.	Not Adequate	25	48.08
	Total	52	100.00

Only a little more than half of the respondents reported that the infrastructural facilities were adequate. The official respondents who were not satisfied with the infrastructural facilities constitute 48 percent. When the respondents were also asked whether they need any more facilities, they said yes. They did not, however, give any particular facility required by them.

Even the respondents, who were not satisfied with the facilities currently available in their organisation or to them, have no idea about the facilities required by them.

Staff Position

The official respondents were requested to give their opinion on the adequacy of the existing staff of their agencies. Their replies have been presented in the following table.

TABLE 6.9

Staff Position

S. No.	*Staff Position*	*Number*	*Percent*
1.	Adequate	21	40.38
2.	Not Adequate	31	59.62
	Total	52	100.00

Sixty percent of the official respondents had reported that the present staff strength was not adequate. Only 21(40 percent) respondents replied positively about the sufficiency of staff position of their organisations. The officials were asked to give their requirement for additional staff. All the respondents were unanimous in demanding for more staff. They were, however, not sure about the number of employees they required further. Hence, they did not give any number as their requirement.

Financial Resources

We very often hear that many governmental organisations are starved of funds. The officers of these organisations complain that there are severe financial constraints on their work. The officials were requested to respond on the adequacy of funds, regularity in releasing the funds, requirement for additional funds, etc. Their responses have been presented in the Tables from 6.10 to 6.12.

Only a little more than one-third of the respondents agreed that the funds allocated to their organisations were adequate. In other words, two-thirds of the respondents reported that the funds allocated to their organisations were not adequate.

TABLE 6.10

Funds are not Adequate

S.No.	Opinion	Number	Percent
1.	Agree	18	34.62
2.	Disagree	34	65.38
	Total	52	100.00

TABLE 6.11

The Allocated Funds Released Regularly

S. No.	Opinion	Number	Percent
1.	Yes	27	51.92
2.	No	25	48.08
	Total	52	100.00

More than half of the respondents (27) reported that the funds were released regularly. The opinion on this aspect has been evenly divided as the remaining 25 respondents responded negatively on this issue.

TABLE 6.12

Some More Funds Required

S. No.	Opinion	Number	Percent
1.	Yes	36	69.23
2.	No	16	30.77
	Total	52	100.00

More than two-third of the respondents reported that some more funds were required by their organisation for successful implementation of the programmes. The remaining respondents said no when they were asked about the requirement for additional funds. Those who reported requirement of some more funds were requested to specify the purpose. But they did not reveal any purpose.

Cooperation from other Organisations

The cooperation of other organisations influence the performance of organisations at the local level and development outcomes. There are many organisations in the district which influence the women development organisations. The Panchayati Raj Institution undertake activities like identification of beneficiaries on behalf of the DRDA. The Revenue Department allocates land to the DSCCSS and DBCCSS. Like wise some other government departments and agencies provide facilities to the various schemes of women development organisations. Similarly, there are many non-governmental organisations working in the district for the welfare and development of women. The cooperation of higher level authorities of the respective local level or field level organisations is also crucial in their successful functioning and implementation of development programmes. More important is the cooperation of beneficiaries with the development organisations. The official respondents were requested to give their opinion on the cooperation they received from their respective officials or higher level offices, other governmental organisations, non-governmental organisations and beneficiaries. Their responses have been presented in the Tables 6.13 to 6.16.

TABLE 6.13

Cooperation from the Head Office

S.No.	*Opinion*	*Number*	*Percent*
1.	Yes	45	86.54
2.	No	7	13.46
	Total	52	100.00

TABLE 6.14

Cooperation from the other Governmental Organisations

S.No.	*Opinion*	*Number*	*Percent*
1.	Yes	42	80.77
2.	No	10	19.23
	Total	52	100.00

TABLE 6.15

Cooperation from the Non-Governmental Organizations

S.No.	Opinion	Number	Percent
1.	Yes	40	76.92
2.	No	12	23.08
	Total	52	100.00

TABLE 6.16

Cooperation from the Beneficiaries

S. No.	Opinion	Number	Percent
1.	Yes	36	69.23
2.	No	16	30.77
	Total	52	100.00

Without full cooperation from the head office, the local organisation can not function to its full capacity. In the present study, the 100 per cent cooperation was not reported. However, an overwhelming majority (86.54 per cent) of the official respondents reported that the head office is very cooperative. The official respondents who reported that the other governmental organisation were cooperating in their endeavour to uplift women constitute 80.77 per cent. More than three-fourth of respondents said 'yes', when the attention of the respondents was drawn about the cooperation from non-governmental organisations. About 69 per cent of the respondents gave positive reply about the cooperation from the beneficiaries. The data on cooperation from different agencies and beneficiaries indicate that the women development organisations are in a better environment and the significant positive association with their respective head offices, other organisations (both governmental and non-governmental) and beneficiaries.

Factors Influencing Efficiency of the Organisation

The opinion of the officials was ascertained about the factors that influence most of the efficiency of their respective organisations. Their responses have been presented in the Table 6.17.

TABLE 6.17

Most Influencing Factors

S.No.	*Factors*	*Number*	*Percent*
1.	Infrastructural Facilities	8	15.38
2.	Personnel	12	23.08
3.	Funds	15	28.85
4.	Cooperation from other Organisations	17	32.69
	Total	52	100.00

The organisational and administrative structure, infrastructural facilities, personnel, funds, cooperation from other organisations are some of the factors that influence the efficiency of any governmental or developmental organisation. One-third of the respondents, i.e., 17 (32.69 per cent) reported that the cooperation from higher level or head office, other governmental organisations, non-governmental organisations and beneficiaries was the most influencing factor for the efficiency of their respective organisations. The next highest number of officials, i.e. 15 (28.85 per cent) reported that availability of funds was an important influencing factor. Nearly one-fourth of the respondents, i.e. 12 (23 per cent) felt that the availability of adequate staff was the most influencing factor. The remaining 8 officials felt that the infrastructural facilities were the most influencing factor. None of the respondents considered the existing organisational and administrative structure as the most influencing factor.

Institutional Adequacy

The officials were further requested to give their opinion on the adequacy of existing institutions for women development. Their responses have been presented in the Table 6.18.

TABLE 6.18

Institutional Adequacy

S.No.	*Opinion*	*Number*	*Percent*
1.	Yes	37	71.15
2.	No	15	28.85
	Total	52	100.00

About 71 per cent of the respondents said 'yes' when their attention was drawn to the issue of adequacy of existing or present institutions working for the development of women. The remaining 29 per cent of the respondents said no on this issue. This percentage was, however, increased when the officials were asked whether they wanted the government to create some more institutions for women development. Forty per cent of the officials said yes on this aspect. Their responses have been presented in Table 6.19.

TABLE 6.19

More Institutions for Undertaking Women Development Programmes

S.No.	*Opinion*	*Number*	*Percent*
1.	Yes	21	40.38
2.	No	31	59.62
	Total	52	100.00

Problems Encountered

The officials were asked to give their observations on the problems encountered by their respective organisations. Their response have been presented in the Table 6.20.

Nearly one-third of the officials observed that non-availability of funds was the most serious problem faced by their respective organisations. One-fourth of the respondents reported that their organisations were facing the problem of shortage of staff. The officials who reported inadequate infrastructural facilities constitute 15.38 per cent. The selection of beneficiaries (9.62 per cent), cooperation from other organisations (7.69 per cent) and political interference (11.54 per cent) are some other problems reported by the officials.

TABLE 6.20

Problems Encountered by the Organisations

S.No.	*Problem*	*Number*	*Percent*
1.	Inadequate infrastructural Facilities	8	15.38
2.	Inadequate Staff	13	25.00
3.	Non-Availability of Funds	16	30.77
4.	Selection of Beneficiaries	5	9.62
5.	Cooperation from other organizations	4	7.69
6.	Political Interference	6	11.54
	Total	52	100.00

Suggestions for Effective Implementation of Programmes

As a remedy to solve or meet the problems faced by the women development organisations and improve their efficiency in the implementation of the programmes, the officials were requested to give their suggestions. Their responses have been presented in the Table 6.21.

TABLE 6.21

Suggestions

S. No.	*Suggestions*	*Number*	*Percent*
1.	More staff	13	25.00
2.	More funds	14	26.92
3.	Cooperation from other organizations	5	9.62
4.	No political interference	12	23.00
5.	Other Suggestions	8	15.38
	Total	52	100.00

The officials gave many suggestions. Their number varies from one suggestion to the other. Those who suggested more funds constitute 26.92 per cent. The suggestion of one-fourth of the officials is more staff. Nearly one-fourth of the officials suggested that there should not be any political interference in the selection of beneficiaries and implementation of programmes. The officials who suggested the cooperation from other organisations constitute only 9.62 per cent. The officials who suggested measures like conduct of awareness, counseling, motivation and education, programmes for women constitute 15.38 per cent.

Perceptions of Beneficiaries

The institutions of government implement various development programmes in order to generate employment as well as income for the poor people in general and women in particular. The present inquiry is confined to the analysis of administration of women development programmes. A sample of 425 women beneficiaries were selected to analyze the administration of women development programmes. The sample women beneficiaries are the beneficiaries of the 4 agencies in Visakhapatnam district. The details of agency-wise beneficiaries are given below.

District Women and Child Development Agency	130
District Rural Development Agency	120
District Scheduled Castes Cooperative Service Society	95
District Backward Classes Cooperative Service Society	80

It is essential to have an idea about the socio-economic conditions of the beneficiaries as a part of ascertaining their views on administration of women development programmes. Therefore, the socio-economic conditions and political background of the beneficiaries were also ascertained in this study. This part is devoted to the examination of the socio-economic conditions and political background of the beneficiaries and analysis of their opinion on various aspects of women development programmes including the benefit utilization.

Social Background of Beneficiaries

In a heterogeneous, complex and stratified society like India, the position, the dependence and disabilities of women are results of a variety of social and economic factors. Therefore, it is necessary to examine their socio-economic conditions. The social background of the beneficiaries has been examined in terms of age, education, caste, religion, place of birth, place of residence, marital status, nature of family, family size, head of the household, etc.

Age

TABLE 6.22

Age of the Beneficiaries

Age/Years	*DWCDA*	*DRDA*	*DSCCSS*	*DBCCSS*	*Total*
Below 20	18 (13.85)	08 (6.67)	05 (5.26)	09 (11.25)	40 (9.41)
21–30	71 (54.62)	66 (55.00)	36 (37.90)	31 (38.75)	204 (48.00)
31–40	24 (18.46)	31 (25.83)	31 (32.63)	28 (35.00)	114 (26.82)
41–50	10 (7.69)	12 (10.00)	18 (18.95)	8 (10.00)	48 (11.29)
Above 50	07 (5.38)	03 (2.50)	05 (5.26)	04 (5.00)	19 (4.48)
Total	130 (100.00)	120 (100.00)	95 (100.00)	80 (100.00)	425 (100.00)

It can be seen from the above table that nearly half of the beneficiaries, i.e. 204 out of 425 are in the age group of 21-30 years. The beneficiaries under this age group of DWCDA and DRDA are more than 50 per cent and that of DSCCSS and DBCCSS are more than one-third. The next highest number of beneficiaries is in the age group of 31-40, i.e. 24 (18.46 per cent) of DWCDA, 31 (25.83 per cent) of DRDA, 31 (32.63 per cent) of DSCCSS and 28 (35 per cent) of DBCCSS. The total beneficiaries under other age groups, i.e. below 20 years, 41-50 and above 50 years are 40 (9.41 per cent), 48 (11.29 per cent and 19 (4.48 per cent) respectively. It is clear from the data that the majority of beneficiaries are young in age. A very negligible number of beneficiaries are aged above 50 years. A close observation of the above table also reveals that from the age group of 21-30 years a fall in the number of beneficiaries of all the organisations can be seen as age increases.

Education

TABLE 6.23

Education of Beneficiaries

Education	*DWCDA*	*DRDA*	*DSCCSS*	*DBCCSS*	*Total*
Illiterate	13 (10.00)	46 (38.33)	59 (62.11)	27 (33.75)	145 (34.12)
Primary Education	11 (8.46)	35 (29.17)	09 (9.47)	31 (38.75)	86 (20.24)
Secondary Education	36 (27.69)	33 (27.50)	22 (23.16)	14 (17.50)	105 (24.71)
Intermediate	48 (36.93)	06 (5.00)	05 (5.26)	08 (10.00)	67 (15.76)
Degree & above	22 (16.92)	—	—	—	22 (5.18)
Total	130 (100.00)	120 (100.00)	95 (100.00)	80 (100.00)	425 (100.00)

In the sample, 145 beneficiaries accounting to 34.12 per cent are illiterate and only 22 had access to college level education. Out of 425 beneficiaries, the beneficiaries who received primary education, secondary education and intermediate education are 86 (20.24 per cent), 105 (24.71 per cent) and 67 (15.76 per cent) respectively. There is wide variation in the educational levels of beneficiaries of different organisations. About 59 (62.11 per cent) beneficiaries of DSCCSS are illiterates while their number is 46 (38.33 per cent) in the case of DRDA and 27 (33.75 per cent) in the case of DBCCSS. Only 13 (10 per cent) of beneficiaries of DWCDA are illiterate. The highest number of beneficiaries of DWCDA (i.e. 48 out of 130) received primary education. The next highest number is 36 who received secondary education. All the 22 respondents who are graduates are beneficiaries of DWCDA. The number of beneficiaries of DRDA who received primary education are 35 (29.17 per cent), secondary education 33 (27.50 per cent) and 6 (5 per cent). In the case of DSCCSS, the number of beneficiaries who received primary, secondary and intermediate education are 9 (9.47 per cent), 22 (23.16 per cent) and 5 (5.26 per cent) respectively. The highest number of beneficiaries of DBCCSS, i.e. 31 (38.75 per cent) received primary education. The secondary and intermediate education was received by 14 and 18 beneficiaries respectively. It is clear by the above table and its explanation the educational levels of the beneficiaries of DWCDA are high while these levels are poor in the case of beneficiaries of DSCCSS.

Caste

TABLE 6.24

Caste of the Beneficiaries

Caste	*DWCDA*	*DRDA*	*DSCCSS*	*DBCCSS*	*Total*
S.C.	24 (18.46)	07 (5.83)	95 (100.00)	—	126 (29.65)
S.T.	11 (8.46)	05 (4.17)	—	—	16 (3.76)
B.C.	72 (55.39)	90 (75.00)	—	80 (100.00)	242 (56.94)
O.C.	23 (17.69)	18 (15.00)	—	—	41 (9.65)
Total	130 (100.00)	120 (100.00)	95 (100.00)	80 (100.00)	425 (100.00)

The above table indicates that out of the total sample beneficiaries the backward classes women are more in number, i.e. 242 accounting 56.94 per cent followed by Scheduled Castes, who are 126 and they are accounted for 29.65 per cent. Only 41 (9.65 per cent) belong to open category (other castes/forward castes). The remaining 16 beneficiaries belong to Scheduled Tribes. The main reason for the highest number of beneficiaries from Backward Classes and the next highest number from Scheduled Castes is that all the beneficiaries of DBCCSS are the Backward classes women and that of DBCCSS are Scheduled Castes women. The women from the Scheduled Castes, Scheduled Tribes and Backward classes are also benefited from the DWCDA and DRDA. For instance, 72 per cent of the beneficiaries of DWCDA and 75 per cent of beneficiaries of DRDA belong to Backward Classes. The number of Scheduled Caste beneficiaries of DWCDA and DRDA is, of course, small when compared with the Backward Classes.

Religion

TABLE 6.25

Religion of Beneficiaries

Religion	*DWCDA*	*DRDA*	*DSCCSS*	*DBCCSS*	*Total*
Hindu	117 (90.00)	97 (80.83)	80 (84.21)	68 (85.00)	362 (85.18)
Muslim	06 (4.62)	11 (9.17)	—	—	17 (4.00)
Christian	07 (5.38)	12 (10.00)	15 (15.79)	12 (15.00)	46 (10.82)
Total	130 (100.00)	120 (100.00)	95 (100.00)	80 (100.00)	425 (100.00)

Table 6.25 reveals that out of 425 sample beneficiaries 362 i.e. 85 per cent are Hindus, 46 are Christians and the remaining 17 are Muslims. There is no much difference in the percentage of beneficiaries of each organisation. Out of 130 beneficiaries of DWCDA 117 (90 per cent) are Hindus. Out of the remaining 13 beneficiaries 7 are Christians and 6 are Muslims. Out of 120 beneficiaries of DRDA 97 (80 per cent) are Hindus and the remaining are Christians (19) and Muslims (11). There are no Muslims among the beneficiaries of DSCCSS and DBCCSS. Eighty five per cent of beneficiaries of DSCCSS are Hindus and the remaining 15 per cent are Christian. Similarly 80 (84.21 per cent) beneficiaries of DSCCSS are Hindus and 15 (15.79 per cent) are Christians.

Marital Status

TABLE 6.26

Marital Status of Beneficiaries

Marital Status	*DWCDA*	*DRDA*	*DSCCSS*	*DBCCSS*	*Total*
Married	59 (45.38)	104 (86.67)	80 (84.21)	62 (77.50)	305 (71.76)
Unmarried	63 (48.46)	09 (7.50)	05 (5.26)	12 (15.00)	89 (20.94)
Widowed	08 (6.16)	07 (5.83)	10 (10.53)	06 (7.50)	31 (7.30)
Total	130 (100.00)	120 (100.00)	95 (100.00)	80 (100.00)	425 (100.00)

Table 6.26 denotes that out of 425 sample beneficiaries 305 are married, 89 unmarried and 31 are widowed. Out of 305 married

women 104 received loan from DRDA, 80 from DSCCSS and 62 from DBCCSS and 59 received benefit from DWCDA. Among the unmarried women the number of beneficiaries of DWCDA are the highest, i.e. 63 (48 per cent). The percentage of widowed women ranges from 10.53 per cent (DSCCSS) to 5.83 per cent (DRDA). There are no divorced women among the beneficiaries of either organisation.

Nature of Family

The nature of family also play an important role in the development of women. The family determines the autonomy and independence of women. The need of family may compel women to get some benefit from the governmental organisations. Therefore, data are collected on this aspect and has been presented in Table 6.27.

TABLE 6.27

Nature of Family

Nature of Family	*DWCDA*	*DRDA*	*DSCCSS*	*DBCCSS*	*Total*
Joint Family	53 (40.77)	47 (39.17)	24 (25.26)	10 (12.50)	134 (31.53)
Nuclear Family	71 (54.62)	66 (55.00)	67 (70.53)	65 (81.25)	269 (63.29)
Women Headed Family	06 (4.61)	07 (5.83)	04 (4.21)	05 (6.25)	22 (5.18)
Total	130 (100.00)	120 (100.00)	95 (100.00)	80 (100.00)	425 (100.00)

The Table 6.27 reveals that out of 425 selected beneficiaries 269 belong to nuclear families, while 134 belong to joint families and remaining 22 are from women headed families. The beneficiaries belonging to all three categories of families can be found in the selected beneficiaries of all the four organisations. There is, however, variation in number and percentage of beneficiaries of one organisation to that of another organisation. For instance, the beneficiaries belonging to nuclear families varies from 55 per cent (DWCDA and DRDA) to 81 per cent (DBCCSS). Similarly, the percentage of beneficiaries belonging to joint families varies from

12.50 per cent (DBCCSS) to 40.77 per cent (DWCDA). The difference between the percentage of beneficiaries of different organisations under the category of women headed family is, however, marginal.

Size of the Family

The Table 6.28 indicates the data pertaining to the aspect of size of the family of the sample beneficiaries.

TABLE 6.28

Size of the Family

No. of Family Members	*DWCDA*	*DRDA*	*DSCCSS*	*DBCCSS*	*Total*
1–2	16 (12.31)	15 (12.50)	16 (16.84)	24 (30.00)	71 (16.71)
3–4	57 (43.85)	69 (57.50)	60 (63.16)	44 (55.00)	230 (54.11)
5–6	52 (40.00)	30 (25.00)	17 (17.89)	10 (12.50)	109 (25.65)
7–8	05 (3.84)	06 (5.00)	02 (2.11)	02 (2.50)	15 (3.53)
Total	130 (100.00)	120 (100.00)	95 (100.00)	80 (100.00)	425 (100.00)

It can be observed from the Table 6.28 that the size of the family of the majority of the beneficiaries, i.e. for 230 (54 per cent) beneficiaries is 3-4 members. The family size of about one-fourth of the beneficiaries is 5-6 members. The family size of 71 beneficiaries is 1-2 members. The size of the family of 15 beneficiaries is 7-8 members. The percentage of beneficiaries under each size of family varies from organisation to organisation. The percentage of beneficiaries, whose family size is 1-2 members ranges from 12 per cent (DWCDA) to 30 per cent (DBCCSS). Similarly, the percentage of beneficiaries, whose family size is 3-4 members ranges from 63 per cent (DSCCSS) to 44 per cent (DWCDA). The percentage of beneficiaries whose family size is 5-6 members ranges from 18 (DSCCSS) to 40 per cent (DWCDA). There is, however, no significant variation in the number and percentage of beneficiaries whose family size is 7-8 members.

Head of the Family

In order to understand the position of women beneficiaries in the family, the information is collected as to their relationship with the head of the family. Relevant information can be seen in Table 6.29.

TABLE 6.29

Head of the Family

Head of the Household	*DWCDA*	*DRDA*	*DSCCSS*	*DBCCSS*	Total
Father	67 (51.54)	09 (7.50)	05 (5.26)	08 (10.00)	89 (20.94)
Mother	15 (11.54)	05 (4.17)	03 (3.16)	05 (6.25)	28 (6.59)
Husband	48 (36.92)	91 (75.83)	76 (80.00)	59 (73.75)	274 (64.47)
Beneficiaries	—	11 (9.17)	08 (8.42)	05 (6.25)	24 (5.65)
Others	—	04 (33.33)	03 (3.16)	03 (3.75)	10 (2.35)
Total	130 (100.00)	120 (100.00)	95 (100.00)	80 (100.00)	425 (100.00)

A close examination of Table 6.29 indicates that the husbands of 274 beneficiaries are the heads of their respective families. A small number of beneficiaries, i.e. 24 are themselves heads of their respective families. Father is the head of the family of about one-fifth of the beneficiaries and mother for 28 beneficiaries' families. The sons of four beneficiaries are heads of their respective families. The father-in-laws are heads of the families of 3 beneficiaries and mother-in-law for another three beneficiaries. It is clear from the data that at least a small number of beneficiaries are heading their families. There is, however, wide variation in the number as well as percentage of the beneficiaries whose head of the family is father or husband. The father is the head of the family of more than half of the beneficiaries of DWCDA. The husband is the head of the family of the 80 per cent of the beneficiaries of DSCCSS.

Economic Background of Beneficiaries

The economic background of the sample beneficiaries of the four governmental organizations has been analysed in terms of their category, income, occupation and assets. The data on economic background of the beneficiaries have been presented in Tables 6.30 to 6.33.

Category of the Family

TABLE 6.30

Category of the Family

Category of Beneficiary	*DWCDA*	*DRDA*	*DSCCSS*	*DBCCSS*	*Total*
Marginal Farmers	10 (7.69)	12 (10.00)	06 (6.32)	08 (10.00)	36 (8.47)
Small Farmers	08 (6.15)	07 (5.83)	02 (2.11)	03 (3.75)	20 (4.70)
Agricultural Labourers	23 (17.69)	59 (49.17)	46 (48.42)	26 (32.50)	154 (36.24)
Non-Agricultural Labourers	82 (63.08)	38 (31.67)	41 (43.15)	39 (48.75)	200 (47.06)
Rural Artisans	07 (5.39)	04 (3.33)	—	04 (2.50)	15 (3.53)
Total	130 (100.00)	120 (100.00)	95 (100.00)	80 (100.00)	425 (100.00)

The Table 6.30 reveals that 200 beneficiaries (nearly half of the total) belong to the non-agricultural labour families followed by 154 beneficiaries, who belong to the families of agricultural labour families. The Table 6.30 also indicates that 36 beneficiaries can be found in the category of marginal farmers and 20 in the category of small farmers. Out of 425 sample beneficiaries only 15 are rural artisans. The number of beneficiaries in each of these categories varies from organisation to organisation. While the beneficiaries of DWCDA under the category of non-agriculture labour account for 63 per cent of its total beneficiaries selected (130), the beneficiaries of DRDA under this category constitute only 31 per cent of its total beneficiaries (120). Similarly, the beneficiaries of DRDA under the category of agricultural labourers constitute 49 per cent, while the per cent of beneficiaries of DWCDA under the same category constitute only 17.69 per cent.

Occupation of the Beneficiaries

Occupation is the major factor that reflects the living conditions of the people. Occupational status has been a major criteria in socially differentiating individuals and groups. It can influence roles, pattern of interaction, life style and habits. It also gives an understanding about the economic viability of the people. The data relating to the occupation of the beneficiaries of women development organisations are presented in the Table 6.31.

TABLE 6.31

Occupation of Beneficiaries

Occupation	*DWCDA*	*DRDA*	*DSCCSS*	*DBCCSS*	*Total*
Agriculture	12 (9.23)	18 (15.00)	08 (8.42)	10 (12.50)	48 (11.29)
Business	24 (18.46)	17 (14.17)	06 (6.32)	06 (7.50)	53 (12.47)
Agricultural Labour	20 (15.38)	29 (21.17)	28 (29.47)	19 (23.75)	96 (22.59)
Non-Agricultural Labour	33 (25.39)	25 (20.83)	30 (31.58)	20 (25.00)	108 (25.41)
Other Occupations	41 (31.54)	31 (25.83)	23 (24.21)	25 (31.25)	120 (28.24)
Total	130 (100.00)	120 (100.00)	95 (100.00)	80 (100.00)	425 (100.00)

On the whole, nearly half of the sample beneficiaries are labourers, both agricultural (96) and non-agricultural (108) labourers. Out of 425 sample beneficiaries only 48 (11 per cent) are cultivators. More than one-fourth of the sample beneficiaries engaged in other occupations like, tailoring, embroidery work, carpentry, cigar making, sweet cover making, pickle making, etc., which are also called self-employment schemes. About 53 (12.47 per cent) of the sample beneficiaries had undertaken petty business like kirana shop, pan shop, fancy shop, etc. The analysis of the data presented through the Table 6.31 gives a clear indication that there is a shift from the category and occupation of the family, particularly from the occupation categories of agricultural labour and non-agricultural labour. For instance, according to the data presented in the Table 6.30, the beneficiaries, who belong to the category of agricultural labour families constitute 36 per cent of the sample beneficiaries, whereas the beneficiaries whose occupation is agricultural labour constitute only 22.59 per cent, which means one-third of the beneficiaries had shifted to other occupations from that of the occupation of their families. Similarly, the beneficiaries from the non-agricultural labour families had preferred other occupations like petty business and self-employment works. This is true in the case of the beneficiaries of all the women development organisations.

Income of the Beneficiaries

Individual income represents not only purchasing capacity but also indicates economic status. Income of the beneficiaries becomes a major factor on judging their economic status, and their behavioural pattern. It is an important economic criterion to assess the quality of life. For better understanding of the programme implementation, income of the beneficiaries is a pre-requisite. Hence, an attempt has been made to find out the income status of the beneficiaries. The range of annual income of the beneficiaries of all women development organisations, under study, has been given in Table 6.32.

TABLE 6.32

Annual Income of Beneficiaries

Income Rs.	*DWCDA*	*DRDA*	*DSCCSS*	*DBCCSS*	*Total*
Below 5,000	19 (14.62)	31 (25.83)	21 (22.11)	08 (10.00)	79 (18.59)
5000–10000	45 (34.62)	65 (54.17)	65 (68.42)	36 (45.00)	211 (49.65)
10000–15000	34 (26.15)	14 (11.67)	07 (7.37)	19 (23.75)	74 (17.41)
15000–20000	11 (8.46)	04 (3.33)	02 (2.10)	15 (18.75)	32 (7.53)
Above 20000	21 (16.15)	06 (5.00)	—	02 (2.50)	29 (6.82)
Total	130 (100.00)	120 (100.00)	95 (100.00)	80 (100.00)	425 (100.00)

Nearly half of the total sample beneficiaries, i.e. 211 (49.65 per cent) are earning between Rs. 5001 to Rs. 10,000 per annum, 79 (18.65 per cent) beneficiaries are earning below Rs. 5,000, 74 (17.41 per cent) beneficiaries are earning between Rs. 10,001 to Rs. 15,000, 32 (7.53 per cent) beneficiaries are earning between Rs. 15,000 to Rs. 20,000 and only 29 (6.82 per cent) beneficiaries are earning above Rs. 20,000 per annum. Among the beneficiaries of DSCCSS as high as 68 per cent of the beneficiaries are earning between Rs. 5001 and Rs. 10,000.

The above table makes it clear that the annual income of 68 per cent of total beneficiaries is Rs. 10,000 and less than Rs. 10,000.

This percentage is higher in the case of beneficiaries of DSCCSS and DRDA. For example, the beneficiaries of DSCCSS constitute 90.50 per cent and the beneficiaries of DRDA constitute 86 per cent under the income category of between Rs. 10,000 and less. There are only six beneficiaries of DRDA and two beneficiaries of DBCCSS, whose annual income is above Rs. 20,000. There is no single individual among the beneficiaries of DSCCSS, who has the annual income of above Rs. 20,000.

Assets of the Beneficiaries

The selected beneficiaries of all the organisations under study were asked to give details about their assets. Their responses on this aspect of research have been shown in Table 6.33.

TABLE 6.33

Assets Particulars of Respondents

Assets of the Family	*DWCDA*	*DRDA*	*DSCCSS*	*DBCCSS*	*Total*
No assets	60 (46.15)	64 (53.34)	80 (84.21)	35 (43.75)	239 (56.24)
House	35 (26.92)	18 (15.00)	10 (10.53)	16 (20.00)	79 (18.59)
Land	17 (13.08)	21 (17.50)	03 (3.16)	18 (22.50)	59 (13.88)
Milch Cattle	18 (13.85)	17 (14.16)	02 (2.10)	11 (13.75)	48 (11.29)
Total	130 (100.00)	120 (100.00)	95 (100.00)	80 (100.00)	425 (100.00)

The Table 6.33 denotes that 56.00 per cent of sample beneficiaries do not possess any asset. This percentage is as much as 84 per cent in the case of beneficiaries of DSCCSS. Out of 425 selected beneficiaries, 59 beneficiaries own land, 79 beneficiaries have houses and 48 beneficiaries have milch cattle. The number of beneficiaries of each category of asset holding varies from the organisation to organisation. The asset holding of the beneficiaries of DSCCSS is very poor when compared with the asset holding of the beneficiaries of other three organisations. Among the beneficiaries of DSCCSS, only 10 beneficiaries own house, 3 hold land and 2 have milch cattle. Among the beneficiaries of other three organisations, 54 per cent of DBCCSS own either house or land or milch cattle.

Political Background of the Beneficiaries

We very often hear that there are politics in distribution of benefits to the people. Only the people who are close to a party particularly the ruling party get the benefits of the government. In view of these observations, it is felt necessary to examine the political background of the beneficiaries of women development organisations. The data on political affiliation, participation in politics, etc., have been presented in Tables 6.34 to 6.37.

Political Affiliation

The political affiliation of the beneficiaries has been examined in terms of their membership and leadership in the political parties and their inclination towards a particular party as follower or sympathizer. The data on these aspects have been presented in the following Table 6.34.

TABLE 6.34

Political Affiliation of Beneficiaries

Membership	*DWCDA*	*DRDA*	*DSCCSS*	*DBCCSS*	*Total*
Members	10 (7.69)	13 (1083)	9 (9.47)	7 (8.75)	39 (9.18)
Followers	16 (12.31)	9 (7.50)	11 (11.58)	8 (10.00)	44 (10.36)
Sympathisers	41 (31.54)	54 (45.00)	46 (48.42)	9 (11.25)	150 (35.29)
Leaders	10 (7.69)	9 (7.50)	6 (6.32)	8 (10.00)	33 (7.76)
No Affiliation	53 (40.77)	35 (29.17)	23 (24.21)	48 (60.00)	159 (37.41)
Total	130 (100.00)	120 (100.00)	95 (100.00)	80 (100.00)	425 (100.00)

It is interesting to note from the above table that on the whole more than one-third of the beneficiaries (159) have no affiliation to any political parties. Another one-third of the beneficiaries (150) are the sympathizers and one-tenth of the beneficiaries are followers of different political parties. The remaining 72 beneficiaries are affiliated to political parties. Among these 72 beneficiaries, 39 are only members and 33 are also leaders in their respective parties. The above table also give organisation-wise break-up of beneficiaries, who have no political affiliation. For instance, 60 per cent of DCCSS, 40.77 per cent of DWCDA, 29 per cent of DRDA and 24 per cent of DSCCSS beneficiaries have no affiliation with either of the parties. The percentage of beneficiaries, who are sympathizers of different political parties range from as low as 11.25 per cent (DBCCSS) to as high as 48.42 per cent (DSCCSS).

Party Affiliation

The party affiliation of beneficiaries, who are members and leaders of different political parties has been presented in Table 6.35.

TABLE 6.35

Party Affiliation of Beneficiaries

Assets of the Family	*DWCDA*	*DRDA*	*DSCCSS*	*DBCCSS*	*Total*
Congress	12 (9.23)	11 (9.17)	12 (12.63)	09 (11.25)	44 (10.35)
T.D.P.	06 (4.62)	08 (6.67)	03 (3.16)	05 (6.25)	22 (5.18)
B.J.P.	02 (1.54)	—	—	—	02 (0.47)
C.P.M.	—	02 (1.66)	—	01 (1.25)	03 (0.71)
C.P.I.	—	01 (0.83)	—	—	01 (0.23)
None	110 (84.61)	98 (81.67)	80 (84.21)	65 (81.25)	353 (83.06)
Total	130 (100.00)	120 (100.00)	95 (100.00)	80 (100.00)	425 (100.00)

As already stated out of 425 sample beneficiaries only 72 beneficiaries are members of the political parties. Out of these 72 beneficiaries, 44 beneficiaries are Congress Party members, 22 beneficiaries are the members of the Telugu Desam Party. Only a small single digit number of beneficiaries (6) are members of CPI (M) (3), BJP (2) and CPI (1). The data from the above table make it clear that more than four-fifths of the beneficiaries did not claim membership of any political party including the ruling Congress Party.

Participation in Politics

The participation of sample beneficiaries have been examined in terms of their participation in elections. The data regarding their contest in elections have been presented in Table 6.36.

TABLE 6.36

Contests in Election

Whether contested	*DWCDA*	*DRDA*	*DSCCSS*	*DBCCSS*	*Total*
Yes	26 (20.00)	27 (22.50)	12 (12.63)	19 (23.75)	84 (19.76)
No	104 (80.00)	93 (77.50)	83 (87.37)	61 (76.25)	341 (80.24)
Total	130 (100.00)	120 (100.00)	95 (100.00)	80 (100.00)	425 (100.00)

Out of 425 sample beneficiaries, 84 beneficiaries had contested in elections. The percentage of beneficiaries of DBCCSS who contested election is more, i.e. 23.75, while it is half, i.e. 12.63 per cent in the case of beneficiaries of DSCCSS. The nature or position to which the beneficiaries contested in the elections is given in the following Table 6.37.

TABLE 6.37

Nature of Elections

Nature of Election	*DWCDA*	*DRDA*	*DBCCSS*	*DSCCSS*	*Total*
Ward Member	15 (76.19)	19 (60.00)	10 (83.34)	10 (76.93)	54 (73.77)
Village President	06 (19.05)	05 (20.00)	01 (8.33)	07 (15.38)	19 (16.39)
M.P.T.C.	05 (4.76)	03 (20.00)	01 (8.33)	02 (7.69)	11 (9.84)
Total	26 (100.00)	27 (100.00)	12 (100.00)	19 (100.00)	84 (100.00)

Out of 84 beneficiaries, who contested elections, nearly three-fourth of beneficiaries contested as ward members of village panchayats. Nineteen beneficiaries contested for the position of Sarpanch and eleven as MPTC members. The number of beneficiaries who contested in elections is slightly more than that of those, who are the members of political parties. In other words, some more beneficiaries, who are not members of the political parties had contested elections. The reason would be that the Panchayat elections are fought on non-party basis in Andhra Pradesh.

The successful implementation of the women development programmes and the effectiveness of the agencies implementing the programmes can be assessed based on the perceptions of the beneficiaries. The perceptions of the beneficiaries on the utility of the benefit, benefit utilization, politics in the selection of beneficiaries, role and attitude of the officials, the problems faced by them in getting loan or any other benefit, etc. have been analysed. The opinion of the beneficiaries are also elicited on the issues like continuing the present programmes. The beneficiaries have been requested to suggest measures for more effective implementation of women development programmes. The data on these aspects have been presented in the Tables from 6.38 to 6.49.

Adequacy of Benefit

The sample beneficiaries received benefits like training on self-employment or income generating trades, accommodation in hostels, nutrients from Aganwadi centres under ICDS schemes from the DWCDA and DMSVK, and loans and training on the use of loans from DSCCSS and DBCCSS. The responses of the beneficiaries on the adequacy of the benefit are presented in the Table 6.38.

TABLE 6.38

Adequacy of Benefit

Benefit	*DWCDA*	*DRDA*	*DSCCSS*	*DBCCSS*	*Total*
Adequate	76 (58.46)	49 (40.83)	45 (47.37)	61 (76.25)	230 (54.12)
Not Adequate	54 (41.54)	71 (59.17)	50 (52.63)	19 (23.75)	195 (45.88)
Total	130 (100.00)	120 (100.00)	95 (100.00)	80 (100.00)	425 (100.00)

More than half of the sample beneficiaries had reported that the benefit was adequate. The beneficiaries of DBCCSS who expressed that the benefit was adequate constitute 76.25 per cent, while the beneficiaries of DRDA constitute 40.83 per cent. In other words, majority of the beneficiaries of DRDA felt that the loan received by them was not adequate. The respondents were asked whether the benefits received by them were relevant to their needs. Their responses have been presented in following table.

Relevance of Benefit

TABLE 6.39

Relevance of Benefit

Whether Relevant or Not	*DWCDA*	*DRDA*	*DSCCSS*	*DBCCSS*	*Total*
Relevant	92 (70.77)	77 (64.17)	74 (77.89)	60 (75.00)	306 (72.00)
Not Relevant	38 (29.23)	43 (35.83)	21 (22.11)	20 (25.00)	119 (28.00)
Total	130 (100.00)	120 (100.00)	95 (100.00)	80 (100.00)	425 (100.00)

About 72 per cent of the selected beneficiaries expressed view that the benefits given by the respective government departments or organizations were relevant to their needs. There is no significant difference in the percentage of beneficiaries of different organization who expressed this opinion. For instance, 77.89 per cent of beneficiaries of DSCCSS felt that the benefit they got was relevant to their needs whereas the beneficiaries of DRDA who expressed similar view constituted 64 per cent. The beneficiaries were asked whether they utilized the loan for which it was sanctioned or given. The responses for this question have been presented in the following table.

Utilisation of Benefit

TABLE 6.40

Utilisation of Benefit

Benefit Utilisation	*DWCDA*	*DRDA*	*DSCCSS*	*DBCCSS*	*Total*
Yes	97 (74.62)	59 (49.17)	58 (61.05)	51 (63.75)	275 (64.71)
No	33 (25.38)	61 (50.83)	37 (38.95)	29 (36.25)	160 (35.29)
Total	130 (100.00)	120 (100.00)	95 (100.00)	80 (100.00)	425 (100.00)

More than one-third of the beneficiaries reported that they had not utilized the benefit for the expected purpose. The beneficiaries of DRDA, who had not utilized the benefit for the expected purpose constitute 50.83 per cent. Three-fourth of the beneficiaries of DWCDA reported that they had utilized the benefit for which it was sanctioned. More than 60 per cent of the sample beneficiaries of DSCCSS and DBCCSS had utilized the benefit for the expected purpose. It is clear from this analysis that an overwhelming majority of the beneficiaries had utilized the benefit properly. The beneficiaries who had not utilized the benefit properly and who are 160 in number were asked why they could not do so. The reasons reported by them have been presented in the Table 6.41.

Reasons For Not Utilising Benefit

TABLE 6.41

Reasons for not Utilising Benefit

Reasons	*DWCDA*	*DRDA*	*DSCCSS*	*DBCCSS*	*Total*
Training was not useful	19 (57.58)	10 (16.39)	05 (13.51)	08 (27.59)	42 (26.25)
Utility of loan was less useful	08 (24.24)	26 (42.62)	19 (51.35)	11 (37.93)	64 (40.00)
Inadequate loan amount	04 (12.12)	19 (31.15)	06 (16.22)	08 (27.59)	37 (23.13)
Inadequate subsidy amount	02 (6.06)	06 (9.84)	07 (18.92)	02 (6.89)	17 (10.62)
Total	33 (100.00)	61 (100.00)	37 (100.00)	29 (100.00)	160 (100.00)

Out of 160 beneficiaries, 64 beneficiaries had not utilized the benefit properly as the utility of loan was less. More than one-fourth of the beneficiaries, i.e. 42 felt that the training given to them was not useful. Nearly one-fourth of the beneficiaries were unable to utilize the benefit properly because the loan amount is not adequate. The beneficiaries who reported that the subsidy amount was inadequate constitute 10.62 per cent of the total beneficiaries who had not utilized the benefit for the expected purpose.

Pattern of Benefit Utilisation

The utilization of benefit (training or loan) by the recipients is shown in Table 6.42. The benefit utilization has been categorized into three-agricultural purposes, non-agricultural purposes and business.

TABLE 6.42

Pattern of Benefit Utilisation

Activities Undertaken	*DWCDA*	*DRDA*	*DSCCSS*	*DBCCSS*	*Total*
Agricultural purpose	20 (15.38)	18 (15.00)	11 (11.58)	10 (12.50)	59 (13.88)
Non-agricultural	69 (53.08)	65 (54.17)	66 (69.47)	57 (71.25)	257 (60.47)
Business	41 (31.54)	37 (30.83)	18 (18.95)	13 (16.25)	109 (25.65)
Total	130 (100.00)	120 (100.00)	95 (100.00)	80 (100.00)	425 (100.00)

It was found that an overwhelming majority of the beneficiaries utilized benefit or invested the total loan amount in non-agricultural purposes. There is a significant difference of benefit utilization between the organisations. More than half of the beneficiaries of DWCDA and DRDA and about 70 per cent of beneficiaries of DSCCSS and DBCCSS come under this category. The non-agricultural purposes include purchase of milch cattle, repayment to old debt, repayment of previous overdue instalments, medical treatment, construction of house and others. The next highest number of beneficiaries, i.e. 109 (25.65 per cent) had undertaken with the help from the governmental organizations petty businesses like running kirana, fancy and pan shops. There is significant difference in the percentage of beneficiaries between the organizations. More than 30 per cent of the beneficiaries of DWCDA and DRDA and less than 20 per cent of the beneficiaries of DSCCSS and DBCCSS had utilized the assistance for business purposes. It is interesting to note that a very small number of beneficiaries utilized benefit for agricultural purposes, even though the majority of the beneficiaries belong to agricultural families.

Overall Opinion on the Programmes

The beneficiaries had also been requested to give their opinion on whether the government programmes are satisfactory or not satisfactory. Their responses have been presented in the following table.

TABLE 6.43

Opinion on the Programme

Opinion	*DWCDA*	*DRDA*	*DSCCSS*	*DBCCSS*	*Total*
Satisfactory	94 (72.31)	88 (73.33)	76 (80.00)	63 (78.75)	321 (75.53)
Not Satisfactory	36 (27.69)	32 (26.67)	19 (20.00)	17 (21.25)	104 (24.47)
Total	130 (100.00)	120 (100.00)	95 (100.00)	80 (100.00)	425 (100.00)

On the whole, three-fourth of the beneficiaries expressed satisfaction about the programmes of the Government. There is no significant difference between beneficiaries of different organizations. The beneficiaries who are satisfied with the governmental programmes were also requested to give the reasons why they were satisfied. Their responses have been presented in the following table.

TABLE 6.44

Reasons for Satisfaction

Reasons	*DWCDA*	*DRDA*	*DSCCSS*	*DBCCSS*	*Total*
Solved my problems	19 (20.21)	25 (28.41)	30 (39.47)	23 (36.51)	97 (30.22)
Lead to my progress	44 (46.81)	30 (34.09)	24 (31.58)	22 (34.92)	120 (37.38)
Increased my income	18 (19.15)	16 (18.18)	13 (17.11)	10 (15.87)	57 (17.76)
Improved Status in the family	13 (13.83)	17 (19.32)	09 (11.84)	08 (12.70)	47 (14.64)
Total	130 (100.00)	120 (100.00)	95 (100.00)	80 (100.00)	425 (100.00)

More than one-third of the beneficiaries reported that the benefit received from the governmental organisations had led their progress, while 30 per cent beneficiaries reported that the benefit had solved their financial problems. Fifty, seven beneficiaries (17.76 per cent) observed that the benefit received by them had increased their income. The data also revealed that the programmes of the developmental organisations had paved the way for improved status of women in the family. There is only marginal difference in the percentage of beneficiaries of different organisations, who expressed views on the reasons for their satisfaction.

Politics in Selection of Beneficiaries

The opinion of the beneficiaries on the politics in their selection has been presented in the following table.

TABLE 6.45

Politics in Selection of Beneficiaries

Politics in selecting beneficiaries	*DWCDA*	*DRDA*	*DSCCSS*	*DBCCSS*	*Total*
Yes	43 (33.08)	35 (29.17)	15 (15.79)	32 (40.00)	125 (29.41)
No	87 (66.92)	95 (70.83)	80 (84.21)	48 (60.00)	300 (70.59)
Total	130 (100.00)	120 (100.00)	95 (100.00)	80 (100.00)	425 (100.00)

On an average 70 per cent of the beneficiaries observed that there were no politics in the selection of beneficiaries. There is, however, significant difference in the percentage of beneficiaries between the beneficiaries of different organisations. The beneficiaries of DSCCSS who expressed the view that there were politics in benefit selection constitute only 15.79 per cent whereas the beneficiaries of DBCCSS, who expressed the similar view constitute 40 per cent. The data on this aspect reveal that the politics are not ruled out in the selection of beneficiaries.

Attitude of Government Officials

The role of officials is crucial for effective implementation of the programmes. Their positive, favourable and cooperative attitude towards people particularly the women beneficiaries would enhance the effectiveness of administration for women development programmes. Hence, the beneficiaries were requested to give their opinion on the attitude of the officials. The observations of the beneficiaries have been presented in the table 6.46.

TABLE 6.46

Satisfaction of Beneficiaries with the Attitude of Officials

Whether Satisfied	*DWCDA*	*DRDA*	*DSCCSS*	*DBCCSS*	*Total*
Yes	96 (73.85)	102 (85.00)	89 (93.68)	67 (83.75)	357 (84.00)
No	34 (26.15)	18 (15.00)	06 (6.32)	13 (16.25)	47 (16.00)
Total	130 (100.00)	120 (100.00)	95 (100.00)	80 (100.00)	425 (100.00)

An overwhelming majority, i.e. eighty four per cent of beneficiaries were satisfied with the attitude of the officials. There is, however, significant difference in the percentage of beneficiaries between organisations. The beneficiaries of DWCDA who expressed satisfaction about the attitude of officials constitute 73.85 per cent while the beneficiaries of DSCCSS who expressed similar opinion constitute 93.65 per cent. It is clear that only six beneficiaries of DSCCSS were not satisfied with the attitude of officials.

Visits by Government Officials

The attention of the beneficiaries was drawn to the need for officials guidance at every stage of the programme. The beneficiaries were asked to give their observations about the visit of the officials of government organizations before the programme started, during the programme and after the programme. Their replies have been presented in the Tables 6.47 to 6.49.

More than one third of the beneficiaries reported that the officials of the governmental organizations visited their places before their selection. There is, however, wide variation in the percentage of beneficiaries who expressed this opinion. About 40 per cent of beneficiaries of DWCDA gave positive reply while this percentage is as low as 19 in the case of beneficiaries of DSCCSS.

TABLE 6.47

Visit of Officials Before Programme

Whether visited	*DWCDA*	*DRDA*	*DSCCSS*	*DBCCSS*	*Total*
Yes	52 (40.00)	44 (36.67)	18 (18.95)	31 (38.75)	145 (34.12)
No	78 (60.00)	76 (63.33)	77 (81.05)	49 (61.25)	280 (65.88)
Total	130 (100.00)	120 (100.00)	95 (100.00)	80 (100.00)	425 (100.00)

TABLE 6.48

Visit of Officials during the Programme

Whether visited	*DWCDA*	*DRDA*	*DSCCSS*	*DBCCSS*	*Total*
Yes	43 (33.08)	35 (29.17)	16 (16.84)	24 (30.00)	118 (27.76)
No	87 (66.92)	85 (70.83)	79 (83.16)	56 (70.00)	307 (72.24)
Total	130 (100.00)	120 (100.00)	95 (100.00)	80 (100.00)	425 (100.00)

Out of 425 sample beneficiaries, 118 (27.76 per cent) reported that the officials visited their places during the period of programme. There is, however, significant difference in the percentage of beneficiaries of different organizations who expressed this views. The beneficiaries of DWCDA who observed that the officials visited their places during programme constitute 33 per cent whereas the beneficiaries of DSCCSS constitute as low as 16.84 per cent.

TABLE 6.49

Visit of Officials after the Programme

Whether visited	*DWCDA*	*DRDA*	*DSCCSS*	*DBCCSS*	*Total*
Yes	31 (29.23)	24 (26.67)	11 (11.58)	18 (22.50)	84 (19.76)
No	99 (70.77)	90 (73.33)	84 (88.42)	62 (77.50)	341 (80.24)
Total	130 (100.00)	120 (100.00)	95 (100.00)	80 (100.00)	425 (100.00)

The above table makes it clear that four-fifths of the beneficiaries reported that the officials had not visited their places after the programme was completed. The reply of the most of the beneficiaries is, thus, negative when their attention was drawn to the issue of visiting of government officials to the villages or houses of beneficiaries. An overwhelming majority of the beneficiaries of all organisations observed that the government officials did not visit their villages before, during or after the programme.

Continuation of Existing System

The opinion of the beneficiaries was elicited on the issue whether the present existing system of administration should be continued or not. Their opinion has been presented in the following table.

TABLE 6.50

Continuation of Existing System

Be Continued	*DWCDA*	*DRDA*	*DBCCSS*	*DSCCSS*	*Total*
Yes	86 (66.15)	92 (76.67)	80 (84.21)	61 (76.25)	319 (75.06)
No	44 (33.85)	28 (23.33)	15 (15.79)	19 (23.75)	106 (24.94)
Total	130 (100.00)	120 (100.00)	95 (100.00)	80 (100.00)	425 (100.00)

On the whole three-fourth of the beneficiaries desired that the existing system of administration should be continued. The percentage of beneficiaries who expressed this opinion varies from organisation to organisation. For instance, the beneficiaries of DCWDA who expressed this opinion constitute 66.5 per cent while the beneficiaries of DSCCSS constitute 84.21 per cent. At the same time almost all the beneficiaries desired that some more programmes should be launched for the development of women. They are, however, not sure the nature or type of new programmes to be launched by the Government.

Major Problems

The beneficiaries were requested to give the problems encountered by them in process of getting a loan and selected for training. They reported more than one problem. But they were asked to identify, among other, the most serious problem. Their responses have been presented in the Table 6.51.

TABLE 6.51

Problems Faced by Beneficiaries

Problems	*DWCDA*	*DRDA*	*DSCCSS*	*DBCCSS*	*Total*
Delay in release of loan/selecting for training	28 (21.54)	40 (33.33)	36 (37.89)	27 (33.75)	131 (30.82)
Many trips to the office	32 (24.62)	18 (15.00)	18 (18.95)	11 (13.75)	79 (18.59)
Requirement of documents/ surety	15 (11.54)	14 (11.67)	11 (11.58)	18 (22.50)	58 (13.65)
Irresponsible attitude of officials	13 (10.00)	11 11 (9.17)	02 (2.11)	04 (5.00	30 (7.06)
Non-availability of proper guidance	11 (8.46)	14 (11.67)	03 (3.16)	06 (7.50)	34 (8.00)
More household responsibilities	13 (10.00)	10 (8.33)	08 (8.42)	04 (5.00)	35 (8.23)
No Problems	18 (13.84)	13 (10.83)	17 (17.89)	10 (12.50)	58 (13.65)
Total	130 (100.00)	120 (100.00)	95 (100.00)	80 (100.00)	425 (100.00)

The beneficiaries who reported the problem of delay in release of loan sanctioned or selecting for training constitute 30.82 per cent of the total selected beneficiaries. There is, of course, some difference in the percentage of beneficiaries of different organisations. For instance, the beneficiaries of DSCCSS, who reported the problem of delay in releasing loan constitute 37.89 per cent, while the beneficiaries of DWCDA constitute 21.54 per cent. The next highest number of beneficiaries who made many trips to the office constitute 18.59 per cent. Fifty-eight beneficiaries experienced difficulty in producing required documents. The beneficiaries, who reported other problems like irresponsible attitude of officials (30), non-availability of guidance (34) and house-hold responsibilities (35) were small in number. The data presented in the above Table (6.51) also reveal that 58 (13.65 per cent) of total selected beneficiaries had not reported any problem.

Suggestions

The beneficiaries were requested to give suggestion for more effectiveness of administration of women development programmes and to make women development programmes more useful. Their suggestions have been presented in the following table.

TABLE 6.52

Suggestions for Improvement

Suggestions	*DWCDA*	*DRDA*	*DSCCSS*	*DBCCSS*	*Total*
No politics in beneficiary selection	57 (43.85)	33 (27.50)	18 (18.95)	24 (30.00)	132 (31.06)
Loan amount be increased	—	14 (11.67)	18 (19.95)	15 (18.75)	47 (11.06)
Subsidy amount be increased	—	21 (17.50)	21 (22.11)	15 (18.75)	57 (13.41)
No insistence of documents	—	14 (11.67)	12 (12.63)	05 (6.25)	31 (7.29)
Delivery of loan/selection for training be made easy	36 (27.69)	18 (15.00)	17 (17.89)	12 (15.00)	83 (19.53)
More awareness programme be organized	24 (18.46)	07 (5.83)	03 (3.16)	05 (6.25)	39 (9.18)
Officials guidance be provided during entire period of benefit	13 (10.00)	13 (10.83)	06 (6.31)	04 (5.00)	36 (8.47)
Total	130 (100.00)	120 (100.00)	95 (100.00)	80 (100.00)	425 (100.00)

On the whole 132 (31 per cent) beneficiaries felt that there shall not be politics in beneficiary selection or in sanction of a loan. The percentage of beneficiaries who expressed this views differs from organisation to organisation. The beneficiaries of DWCDA who suggested this measure constitute 44 per cent whereas the beneficiaries of DSCCSS constitute 19 per cent. Eighty-three (19.53 per cent) beneficiaries suggested that the sanction and delivery of loan or selection of a beneficiary should be made easy. There is no significant difference in the percentage of beneficiaries of different organisations, who gave this suggestion. Fifty-seven beneficiaries of DRDA, DSCCSS and DBCCSS had suggested that the subsidy amount should be increased. The other suggestions made by the beneficiaries include increase in loan amount, increase in subsidy amount, non-insistence of documents and surety, more awareness programmes and official support or guidance during the entire period of programme.

SUMMARY AND CONCLUSIONS

Women form 50 percent of the world population and contribute 50 percent of the food production. They do two-thirds of world's work hours. In other words, the sphere of activities of women is larger and wider than that of men, almost in all the societies of the world. It is necessary to ensure that this large segment of the world's population gets its rightful share out of all the development programmes and assumes its rightful role in the society. The international community has, therefore, initiated several plans of action for full, equal and beneficial integration of women in all development activities.

The UN convention on the elimination of all forms of discrimination against women on 18th December, 1979, the declaration of 1976-85 as the decade for women. The Nairobi Forward Looking Strategies adopted at the UN Decade for Women End Conference in June 1985, and the United Nations Fourth World Conference on Women in Beijing in 1995, are some of the measures initiated by the UNO for removing all obstacles to participation of women in all shapes of public and private life.

The United Nations also gave an official and global recognition to women to fulfil the long felt need that half of humanity can no longer be ignored at different levels of policy making, administration and implementation. National governments, donor agencies and women groups all over the world have started showing concern about the status and role of women in every aspect of human and economic development. In India also an enabling environment, with requisite policies and programmes, institutional mechanisms at various levels and adequate financial resources has been created to empower women. A summary of these policies, programmes, institutional mechanisms and findings of the study is given in this chapter. The concluding remarks are also presented in this chapter.

Status of the Indian Women

The present status of women in India in terms of sex-ratio, education, health, employment and political representation has been examined. The sex ratio of women in India is low. The sex ratio has been continuously declining from 1901 onwards. There was a marginal increase of one point in 1951 but thereafter it again dropped for two consecutive decades to reach 930 in 1971. Thereafter, it has fluctuated marginally around 930 in successive census. The development process of independent India has not succeeded in stopping the decline of sex ratio. Nearly 50 percent of the female population is still steeped in ignorance and illiteracy. Women have been benefited much less from educational opportunities. The female literacy rate is low when compared to the literacy rate of males. In terms of sheer volume, although the number of literate women has increased from 155 lakh in 1951 to 2,250.41 lakh in 2001, we still have 1,895.55 lakh illiterate women. This is definitely the largest number of illiterate women existing in any country of the world. The effort of the government to increase female literacy through formal and non-formal education has been tremendous. In spite of these gains we are still lagging behind in our achievements as compared to important developing countries.

An important indicator of women's health is her life expectancy at birth. The available data, which traces life expectancy for men and women, indicate that women had lesser life expectancy than men upto 1971-81. It is only now that women have a slight edge over men. There is an increase in the life expectancy of women from 31.7 years in 1941-51 to 64.2 years in 1991-2001. This has been due to the multifaceted health initiatives taken by health agencies. It is a very significant achievement. The steeply declining death rates have contributed towards increasing life expectancy. However, India still has a long way to go to achieve the standards of the developed world and even to some important developing countries.

The women's work participation rate had increased from 22.73 percent in 1991 to 28.6 percent during 2001. But the number of employed women is very less when compared with men. The Census of India 2001 statistics show that out of a total of 32.62 crores of economically active female population only 6.03 crores, i.e. 18.5 percent is employed, whereas out of 34.97 crores of economically active males, 23.63 crores representing 67.6 percent is employed in paid jobs. The employment of women in different branches of the public sector and various government agencies indicates concentration of women in state government and local bodies. The share of employment of women in central government services is very low as compared to men. If we see women's status as indicated in all sectors of employment, it would be clear that women are concentrated in low paid jobs and are low in the hierarchies of status. This compares very adversely with women's attainments in developed countries.

The right of vote was granted to women through Constitution. There has been a marked increase in the level of literacy and political awareness of women. However, the representation of Indian women in the parliament has always remained at a very low level never going beyond 10 percent at any point of time. The highest members, i.e. 49 (9.02 percent) of women were elected to thirteenth Lok Sabha. This number had declined to 45 (8.25 percent) in the next Lok Sabha. In the case of Rajya Sabha also the percentage of women members has never crossed 12 percent. Thus, the participation of women has dwindled in the country's political life.

Women Development Policies

In India, numerous policy measures had been enunciated over the years for improving the conditions of women. The various policy measures on women development include constitutional provisions, legislative measures, appointment of committees and commissions, formulation of development plans, establishment of institutions and support to voluntary organisations.

The Constitution of India marks a heyday for women. The women's right of equality with men has been embodied in the Constitution. Indian women are the beneficiaries of the fundamental rights in the same manner as men. The Directive Principles of State Policy under articles 39(a), 39(d), 39(e), 42, 44, 51A(c), etc. have a special bearing on the status of women. The Constitution of India not only grants equality to women but also empowers the state to adopt measures of positive discrimination in favour of women.

Besides providing a formal structure of equality, the government as it is found in many of third world countries used law as a major instrument to change society. One of the major planks of government activities with regard to women is legislation. The legislations such as Hindu Marriage Act 1955, Dowry Prohibition Act, 1961, Suppression of Immoral Traffic among Women Act, 1956, the Commission of Sati (Prevention) Act, 1987, etc., passed since independence have been considered quite revolutionary.

An important landmark in the history of women's welfare and development was the appointment of committees and commissions. A committee on status of Indian women under the chairmanship of Phulrenu Guha, was appointed in 1974 to undertake comprehensive examination of all the questions relating to the rights and status of women in the context of changing social and economic condition in the country and problems relating to the advancement of women. The National Commission on Self-Employed Women was constituted to collect material on socio-economic life of Indian women. The constitution of the National Commission for women is another important measure for women welfare and development. Investigation and examination of all matters relating to the safeguards provided for women under the constitution and other laws are entrusted to the Commission.

In each five year plan women development issues especially their economic and educational and health received considerable attention and a number of welfare measures were undertaken to ameliorate their conditions. The National Plan of Action for Women (NPAW) was adopted by both the houses of parliament and National Committee on women with the chairmanship of the

Prime Minister of India was formed for implementation. A national perspective plan for women (1988-2000) was drafted advocating a holistic approach for the development of women.

Another important landmark in the history of women welfare and development is the creation of institutions and setting up of organisations to implement various women welfare and development programmes. The Central Social Welfare Board was the first organisation set-up by the Union Government in 1953. The Ministry of Social Welfare created in 1979 was renamed as Ministry of Social and Women's Welfare. In 1988, the Government of India constituted a separate department in the Ministry of Human Resource Development for the development of women and children. This department executes its policies through its agencies like the Central Social Welfare Board. The department also oversees women welfare and development programmes of other ministries and departments.

Women development corporations were set-up since 1986-87 in several states to identify and assist women entrepreneurs. Rashtriya Mahila Kosh was set-up as a registered society under the Registration of Societies Act, 1960 in march, 1993 to meet credit needs of poor women, particularly in the informal sector, who have little or no access to formal credit institutions. The voluntary organisations have been encouraged to involve in the formulation and implementation of welfare programmes for women. The financial support has been extended to voluntary agencies through grants-in-aid to develop programmes and services to women. Due to the encouraging policy of the government and the initiative of the people themselves, the voluntary sector has borne rich fruit in the sense that there has been a profusion of voluntary organisations working for women.

The National Policy for the Empowerment of Women evolved in 2001 recognizes the causes of gender inequality which are related to social and economic structures. The policy underlines the need for mainstreaming gender perspective in the development process. The policy visualises the means of social and economic empowerment of women besides empowering women to participate in decision-making process.

Women Development Programmes

Government programmes for women's development began as early as 1954. Apart from giving grants to voluntary agencies, the Central Social Welfare Board initiated some new programmes of assistance which were developmental in nature such as the scheme of welfare extension projects, socio-economic programmes and hostels for working women. Thereafter, the Ministry of Social Welfare also sponsored programmes and activities of women's welfare and development, through grants-in-aid. The other ministries such as Agriculture, Health, Rural Development, Labour, etc., also contributed for the development of women in addition to the programmes and services of the Department of Women and Child Development which has the coordinating responsibilities. Some of the important official programmes for the welfare and development of women are short stay homes, hostels for working women, creches for working and aiding mothers, STEP, DWCRA, MSY and IMY.

Institutional Mechanism for Women Development

Many institutions have been created and supported for the welfare and development of women in India. As a result of the UN General Assembly Resolution of 1963 the Government of India established in 1964 a Department of Social Welfare to look after women issues from the welfare point of view, the primary focus being on women in distress. A committee called the Committee on the Status of Women was set-up in 1974 to do a complete review and bring out a report on the status of women in India. The Committee emphasized the need for a national machinery to coordinate and intensify the efforts and measures needed for women development. As a result, a Women's Welfare and Development Bureau was established in 1976 in the Ministry of Social Welfare to aid the National Committee on Women, which was constituted in September 1976 and also to act as a nodal point within the Government to coordinate policy and programmes and to initiate measures for women's development. A separate department for women and child development was set-up in 1985 in the Ministry of Human Resource Development. New structures were also created in other ministries and departments to look after the issues and programmes relevant to women. The women development programmes have been integrated into the development projects of these departments and ministries.

Separate independent departments headed by secretary level officials have come into existence in states like Haryana, Rajasthan, Maharashtra, Karnataka, Uttar Pradesh, Andhra Pradesh, Kerala and Tamil Nadu. The other states have social and women's welfare departments or only a social welfare department. The other departments at the State level, which are concerned with women development are education, health and family welfare, labour, agriculture, etc. Each one of these are equally concerned about women development, particularly in relation to female education, family size, training and employment, role of women in agriculture development, etc.

The State Department or Directorate of Women and Child Development maintains liaison with other state level departments and with other bodies like the State Social Welfare Advisory Board, Women Development Cooperatives, Khadi and Village Industries Commission, etc. The Directorates implement various central and state schemes concerning women and child development. This is done through district level Social Welfare Officers and by the Block Development Officers at the block level.

Voluntary organisations in India have undertaken several programmes for the development of women. In fact, voluntary action has been throughout a prominently visible strain of our cultural milieu. The voluntary organisations are considered as more appropriate instruments to carry out the task of women's development because of their attributes of flexibility, quickness, innovativeness and human touch. In fact, successive plan documents and reports of official commissions and committees have acclaimed positive dimensions of functioning of voluntary organisations and their increasing relevance. At present it is estimated that there are about 10,000 voluntary organisations in the country engaged in welfare and developmental work. These organisations have introduced development schemes affecting lives of rural and urban women. While some organisations like Akhil Hind Mahila Parishad (All India Women's Conference), Bharatiya Grameena Mahila Sangh (National Association for Rural Women in India) and Andhra Mahila Sabha are working exclusively for the benefit of women, other organisations are working for the development of women as one of their programmes.

Women Development Organisations

The district administration in Visakhapatnam has taken up varied measures for the overall development of the district keeping in view the requirements of all sections of the people especially the weaker sections. In Visakhapatnam district, the organisations involved in women welfare and development are not many. On thorough examination of various departments and organisations engaged in developmental activities, it is observed that the following organisations are undertaking various programmes beneficial to women:

1. District Women and Child Development Agency
2. District Rural Development Agency
3. District Scheduled Castes Cooperative Service Society
4. District Backward Classes Cooperative Service Society

District Women and Child Development Agency

The Visakhapatnam District Women and Child Development Agency started functioning from 6th October, 1997. All the women and child welfare activities in the district have been entrusted to this agency. The District Agency is headed by an officer called Project Director, drawn from Group-I Services of the State. He is assisted by the Assistant Project Officer and other staff in the office. The officials of the District Agency have been posted both under plan and non-plan expenditure. It is interesting to note that the appointment of majority of the officials is temporary. The posts of Assistant Project Officer, Superintendent, one typist and two drivers only are permanent. The remaining posts including the Project Director are temporary. The important institutions, which are working for the welfare of women and children in the district and functioning under the District Agency are 5 Children Homes, 2 Working Women Hostels, 1 Sishu Gruha, 8 Creches, 6 Balwadies, 1 Bala Vihar, 1 D.C.T.C., 2 Women and Child Welfare Centres, and 1 Durgabai Mahila Sisu Vikasa Kendram

Twenty-two I.C.D.S. projects were sanctioned to Visakhapatnam district so far. Out of 22 projects, four are urban projects, 10 are rural projects and the remaining 8 are tribal projects. A total of 3,121 Anganwadi Centers are working under these projects. About 1,30,840 children in the age group of 0-6 years and 34,000 pregnant and lacting mothers are covered under the ICDS Scheme in the district. For the management of ICDS scheme, the posts of Child Development Project Officer (CDPO), Assistant Child Development Project Officer (ACDPO), Supervisor, Senior Assistant, Junior Assistant, Typist, Driver, Attender and Watchman were sanctioned.

The Visakhapatnam District Women and Child Development Agency has been implementing the other important programmes like Girl Child Protection Scheme, Balika Mandal Scheme and Swayam Siddha Scheme. A total of 2,099 children of 0-7 age groups have been benefited from the Girl Child Protection Scheme implemented by the District Agency during the last three years. Under the Balika Mandal Scheme, 187 Balika Mandals were formed from the 17 ICDS Projects. From each mandal, three members had been selected as change agents and given training in 5 batches. The civil works like laying c.c. roads in the villages, construction of community halls, bus shelters, etc. have been undertaken by the District Agency with the cooperation of Swayam Siddha SHGs in the areas of Narsipatnam and Ravi Kamatham ICDS Projects.

District Rural Development Agency

The DRDA of Visakhapatnam came into existence in 1980 by integrating the schemes of Small Farmers Development Agency, Integrated Rural Development Programme, Training of Rural Youth for Self-Employment and Antyodaya Programme. The DRDA was registered under the Societies Act of Government of Andhra Pradesh. It is a body corporate with all characteristic features. It comprises a Governing Body, Chairman, Executive Chairman, Executive Committee and the Project Director. The Zilla Parishad Chairman is the Chairman and the District Collector is the Executive Chairman of the Governing Body. The Project Director acts as the Member-Secretary of the Society's Governing Body. The DRDA has been made the overall in-charge of the planning, implementation, monitoring and evaluation of the rural development programmes in the district. It is headed by a full-time Project Director, a senior scale officer from Group-I Service of Government of Andhra Pradesh. He is assisted by the Additional Project Director and other officers and office staff. The staff of DRDA is broadly categorized into the Executive, Office and Supporting staff.

The DRDA had undertaken many rural development programmes since its inception. The important programmes undertaken in recent years by the DRDA include Swarnajayanthi Gram Swarozgar Yojana Scheme, Pavala Vaddi (Interest subsidy) Scheme, Pension Scheme, Deepam Scheme, Indira Parspara Hami Pathakam, and Padi Pasuvula Appu Hami Pathakam. Most of these programmes are implemented under the DWACRA and SGSY. Some of these programmes are exclusively intended for women.

There are 31041 SHGs in the District. The members of all the self-help groups are women. The total members of these groups are 3,76,812. In addition to the Government grants under various schemes, the SHGs in the district received an amount of Rs. 120.26 crores from the banks during 2005-06 under the SHG-Bank Linkage Programme. During the same year an amount of Rs. 17.24 crores was released to SHGs in the district as interest subsidy under Paval Vaddi Scheme. Under Deepam Scheme, a total of 23,121 gas connections were given to the women in the district during 2004-05. Dairy activity is being encouraged in big way since 2004-05 among SHG members as income generating activities. Tie-up arrangements have been made with the private diaries for marketing the milk produced by the SHG members. Four Bulk Milk Cooling Centers have been established in the district to enable SHG members to get a substainable regular income.

The DRDA had taken up Human Insurance from 2005-06 through Zilla Samakhya under Indira Paraspara Hami Pathakam. Memorandum of Understanding was signed with the TATA-AIG and New India Assurance Company to provide insurance facility to the SHG members at low premium of Rs. 100 with the coverage of Rs. 25,000 for natural death of the insurer as well as her spouse and Rs. 50,000 for accidental death of the insurer. Another insurance scheme namely Milch Cattle Insurance was taken up during the same year under Padi Pasuvula Appu Hami Pathakam. The DRDA had entered into MoU with the New India Assurance

Company to provide insurance to the milch cattle purchased by the SHG Women at low premium of Rs. 200 with coverage of Rs. 10,000. The total milch animals covered under the insurance during 2005-06 are 10320.

The State Government released an amount of Rs. 29.67 crores during 2004-05, Rs. 30.82 crores during 2005-06 and Rs. 21.22 crores during 206-07 under Swarnajayanthi Gram Swarozgar Yojana Scheme to Visakhapatnam DRDA. The funds available with the DRDA under SGSY is being untilised on subsidy to rural poor (including women) to undertake income generating activities and training to improve the skills of the beneficiaries. The two important projects namely Fashion Technology Project and Etikoppaka Toys Project have been undertaken by the DRDA under SGSY scheme.

District Scheduled Castes Cooperative Service Society

The Visakhapatnam District Scheduled Castes Cooperative Service Society was established in 1974 and registered under Andhra Pradesh Cooperative Societies Act, 1964. The District Society receives grants from the Andhra Pradesh Scheduled Castes Cooperative Finance Corporation and implements schemes for the welfare and development of Scheduled Castes in the district. The District Society also mobilizes local resources in terms of SGSY subsidy, subsidy from DRDA, SCSP from line departments, loans from banks and 15 per cent earmarked funds from the local bodies. The task of monitoring Scheduled Caste Sub-plan allocations and expenditure is entrusted to the Society. The Society undertakes surveys and identifies the eligible SC families and motivates them to undertake suitable economic development schemes. It provides financial assistance to the SCs in the form of margin money or direct loan on low rate of interest and subsidy. The Society also imparts training in different skills to the target groups.

The District Society functions under the guidance of a committee under the Chairmanship of the District Collector. The day-to-day affairs of the Society are managed by the Executive Director, a senior officer from Group-I Service of the State. He is assisted by subject specialists and other subordinate staff in the implementation of the schemes.

The Visakhapatnam District Society of SC Corporation has been implementing SC welfare programmes in the District. The Society purchased 165 acres of land at a cost of Rs. 134.26 lakhs and allotted to 264 beneficiaries. Under the land development programme, an extent of 1098.17 acres of land was developed by the Society by spending an amount of Rs. 121.72 lakhs. The total beneficiaries of this programme is 822. The District Society had implemented various minor irrigation programmes to provide irrigation facility to 1743 acres benefiting 2617 Scheduled Caste farmers (both men and women) with an outlay of Rs. 219.76 lakhs in a period of 5 years starting from 2002-03. An amount of Rs. 185.45 lakhs was spent by the Society during 2006-07 for purchase of Cross Breed Cows and Graded Murrah Buffaloes and for fodder development. The total number of beneficiaries of dairy scheme is 672 out of which 660 beneficiaries are SC Women (98 per cent). An amount of Rs. 3001.64 lakhs was spent benefiting 12,341 SC candidates on different self employment schemes, during a period of five years from 2002-03 to 2006-07. The Society spent an amount of Rs. 160.48 lakhs on training and beneficiary awareness programmes from 2002-03 to 2006-07. The total number of beneficiaries under different training programmes is 2959.

District Backward Classes Cooperative Service Society

The Visakhapatnam District Backward Classes Cooperative Service Society is the district level agency of Andhra Pradesh Backward Classes Cooperative Finance Corporation. The Visakhapatnam District Society started its activities from the year 1976, the year of its as well as the Corporation's establishment. There is a governing body for the Society for which the District Collector is the Chairman. The administrative head of the Society is the Executive Director, a Group-I Service Officer. He is assisted by Executive Officer, Assistant Executive Officer, Loan Inspectors, and other office staff members. The main objective of the Society is to sanction the financial assistance to the BCs who are below poverty line. The main function of the Society is to implement the development programmes meant for the BCs in the district.

The Visakhapatnam District Backward Classes Cooperative Service Society had undertaken all the schemes of the Corporation for the benefit of BCs in the district. During a period of 5 years the Society had financed a total of 410 SHGs covering 6,145 beneficiaries with an outlay of Rs. 123.89 lakhs as margin money. The Society secured an amount of Rs. 17.68 lakhs during 2002-03 and Rs. 1.74 lakhs, during 2003-04 as term loan from NBCFDC. About 1,141 unemployed youth were benefited from this scheme.

Under the micro credit scheme, the Society had provided financial assistance to 176 SHGs during 2002-2003, 79 SHGs during 2003-04 and 34 SHGs during 2006-07. The poor BC women benefited from this scheme during the above three years were 4317. In a period of 5 years starting with the financial year 2002-2003, the Society had given educational loan to 191 students with a total outlay of Rs. 65.70 lakhs. Under Swarnima Scheme, the Society sanctioned an amount of Rs. 17.68 lakhs during 2002-03 and Rs. 4.35 lakhs during 2003-04. A total of 1385 B.C. women were benefited by this scheme. During the year 2003-04, the District Society had given tool kits to 4345 artisans with an outlay of Rs. 331 lakhs. The Government sanctioned Rs. 8 lakhs for construction of 8 Dhobhighats in the year 2006-07 in the District. About 1022 washermen communities were benefited from this scheme.

Perceptions of Officials

The opinion of 52 officials of 4 women development organisations in Visakhapatnam district was ascertained regarding the organisational structure, infrastructural facilities (physical resources), personnel (human resources), financial resources, process of implementation of programmes and linkages with other organisations. The officers were requested to give their opinion on the adequacy of the machinery for women development. They were also asked about the problems or challenges encountered by them or by their organisations. Finally, they were requested to suggest measures for effective implementation of women development programmes.

Three-fourths of the official respondents reported that they were satisfied with the present organisational structure of their respective agencies. However, majority of the officials wanted some changes in the structure. More than half of the respondents reported that the infrastructural facilities were adequate. About 71 per cent of the respondents observed that the existing or present institutions working for the development of women were adequate. Sixty percent of the official respondents had reported that the present staff strength was not adequate. All the respondents were unanimous in demanding for more staff. Two-thirds of the respondents felt that the funds allocated to their organisations were not adequate. More than half of the respondents (27) observed that the funds were released regularly. Two-third of the respondents reported that some more funds were required by their organisation for successful implementation of the programmes.

An overwhelming majority (86.54 per cent) of the official respondents reported that the head office is very cooperative. The official respondents who reported that the other governmental organisation were cooperating in their endeavour to uplift women constitute 80.77 per cent. More than three-fourth of respondents said 'yes', when the attention of the respondents was drawn about the cooperation from non-governmental organisations. About 69 per cent of the respondents gave positive reply about the cooperation from the beneficiaries. One-third of the respondents i.e., 17 (32.69 per cent) reported that the cooperation from higher level or head office, other governmental organisations, non-governmental organisations and beneficiaries was the most influencing factor for the efficiency of their respective organisations. The next highest number of officials, i.e. 15 (28.85 per cent) reported that availability of funds was an important influencing factor. Nearly one-fourth of the respondents, i.e. 12 (23 per cent) felt that the availability of adequate staff was the most influencing factor. The remaining 8 officials felt that the infrastructural facilities were the most influencing factor.

Nearly one-third of the officials observed that non-availability of funds was the most serious problem faced by their respective organisations. One-fourth of the respondents reported that their organisations were facing the problem of shortage of staff. The officials who reported inadequate infrastructural facilities constitute 15.38 per cent. The selection of beneficiaries (9.62 per cent), cooperation from other organisations (7.69 per cent) and political interference (11.54 per cent) are some other problems reported by the officials.

The officials gave many suggestions. Their number varies from one suggestion to the other. Those who suggested more funds constitute 26.92 per cent. The suggestion of one-fourth of the officials is for more staff. Nearly one-fourth of the officials suggested that there should not be any political influence in the selection of beneficiaries and implementation of programmes. The officials who suggested the cooperation from other organisations constitute only 9.62 per cent. The officials who suggested measures like conduct of awareness, counselling, motivation and education programmes for women constitute 15.38 per cent.

Perceptions of Beneficiaries

A sample of 425 women beneficiaries were selected to analyze the administration of women development programmes. The sample women beneficiaries are the beneficiaries of the 4 women development agencies in the Visakhapatnam district. The perceptions of the beneficiaries on the utility of the benefit, benefit utilization, politics in the selection of beneficiaries, role and attitude of the officials, the problems faced by them in getting loan or any other benefit, etc. have been analysed. The opinion of the beneficiaries are also elicited on the issues like continuing the present programmes. The beneficiaries have been requested to suggest measures for more effective implementation of women development programmes. More than half of the sample beneficiaries had reported that the benefit was adequate. About 72 per cent of the selected beneficiaries expressed view that the benefits given by the respective government departments or organizations were relevant to their needs. More than one-third of the beneficiaries reported that they had not utilized the benefit for the expected purpose. These beneficiaries had not utilized the benefit properly as the utility of loan was less. It was found that an overwhelming majority of the beneficiaries utilized benefit or invested the total loan amount in non-agricultural purposes. Three-fourth of the beneficiaries expressed satisfaction about the programmes of the Government.

More than one-third of the beneficiaries reported that the benefit received from the governmental organisations had led their progress, while 30 per cent beneficiaries reported that the benefit had solved their financial problems. Fifty-seven beneficiaries (17.76 per cent) observed that the benefit received by them had increased their income. The data also revealed that the programmes of the developmental organisations had paved the way for improved status of women in the family. On an average 70 per cent of the beneficiaries observed that there were no politics in the selection of beneficiaries.

An overwhelming majority, i.e. eighty four per cent of beneficiaries were satisfied with the attitude of the officials. The majority of the beneficiaries of all organisations observed that the government officials did not visit their villages before, during or after the programme. On the whole three-fourth of the beneficiaries desired that the existing system of administration should be continued. At the same time almost all the beneficiaries desired that some more programmes should be launched for the development of women.

The beneficiaries who reported the problem of delay in release of loan sanctioned or selecting for training constitute 30.82 per cent of the total selected beneficiaries. The next highest number of beneficiaries who made many trips to the office constitute 18.59 per cent. Fifty-eight beneficiaries experienced difficulty in producing required documents. The beneficiaries, who reported other problems like irresponsible attitude of officials (30), non-availability of guidance (34) and household responsibilities (35) were small in number. On the whole 132 (31 per cent) beneficiaries felt that there shall not be politics in beneficiary selection or in sanction of a loan. Eighty-three (19.53 per cent) beneficiaries suggested that the sanction and delivery of loan or selection of a beneficiary should be made easy. Fifty-seven beneficiaries of DRDA, DSCCSS and DBCCSS had suggested that the subsidy amount should be increased.

Conclusions

The constitutional recognition of equal status for women and legal enactments has empowered Indian women with juridical equality. Women have been inducted in some of the decision-making bodies. Many policy measures have been initiated to improve the position of women. The women's groups demand for equality and opportunities for their participation in development had been accepted by the government. To operationalise the Government's concern for equality, strategies were spelt out to improve women's economic status and to empower them with a greater say in decision-making.[1] The planning as now conceived and practiced is intended to benefit women. The poverty alleviation programmes provide the structural context within which solutions are sought for their problems. The Government have recognized them as active participation in development. The schemes specially oriented to their needs have been introduced. For instance, the Government initiated the Development of Women and Children in Rural Areas Scheme in 1982. The special components have been incorporated in various other schemes. The IRDP, TRYSEM and NREP stipulated that one-third of the beneficiaries should be women.

Several structures have been created by the Government to meet the needs of women. At the central level, there is a department, namely Department of Women and Child Development which has been entrusted with the responsibility of implementing and coordinating programmes of women's welfare and development. The Central Social Welfare Board was brought under the purview of this Department. Since its inception, the Department has initiated programmes with a view to promoting five major objectives—generating employment and income, imparting education and training, building greater awareness, providing support services and legal assistance. There is a similar set-up at the state level. At the lower echelons of administration also there are organisations for women programmes. The Women Cooperative Finance Corporations were set-up for providing institutional credit facilities exclusively for women for organizing home-based or community-based economic projects. The ministries of Agriculture, Health, Family Welfare, Industry, Commerce and Labour also have special components in their programmes. In addition, several apex organisations such as the KVIC, provide funds, training and marketing support for several socio-economic schemes. While the government provides subsidies, the banking sector is engaged in providing credit.

Despite plethora of laws, policies, plans and programmes, women suffer from exploitation because of their tardy implementation. Administrative machinery is not sufficiently adequate to meet the social and economic needs of women. A study of the historical perspective and demographic profile of

Indian women indicates their low status in society which is basically due to deep-rooted gender bias. The absence of the requisite social services coupled with their status and the socio-psychological factors hamper their development.[2] Although women contribute considerably to economic development, yet they are the worst sufferers of the present economic system because of their low employment level and absence of supportive services to them. Because of low literacy and gender bias, their political participation is very low. The development assistance has not done enough to dismantle patriarchical structures of power and to change women's gender identity of subordination both in productive and reproductive roles.[3] The poor and illiterate women have few options other than being street hawkers, becoming maids or entering commercial sex sector. The situation makes one suspect that something has been going wrong either at the top level where the policies are formulated or at the place where they are implemented in the shape of the programmes.

The district continues to be a very important level of both implementation and coordination of various programmes. Therefore, for women and child development also, it should become an important cutting edge level.[4] At present various programmes for women like the DWCRA have programme-linked officers at the district level. The National Perspective Plan for Women has suggested the appointment of district level officers called the District Coordinators for an integrated approach to the issues of women and children. This useful suggestion had been accepted by the many state governments including Andhra Pradesh and the District Women and Child Development Agencies have been formed. These agencies have been undertaking various programmes exclusively for the welfare and development of women and children. There are other agencies like DRDA, DSCCSS and DBCCSS, which were working for the development of the poor including women.

One of the main functions of women development organisations in the district of Visakhapatnam is the mobilization of institutional credit for economic development schemes for women. The function of WDOs in Visakhapatnam district also include identifying eligible beneficiaries, assessment of their felt needs and financial requirements thereof, preparation of suitable economic schemes for different occupational groups of society including SC, ST and BC women, bringing the women in contact with financial institutions and government development agencies, etc. They also undertake skill development training programmes. Under the see training schemes women are mostly given training on traditional activities like tailoring, stitching, embroidering, leather work, etc. which facilitate self-employment for women. They establish linkages with financial and technical institutions and provide technical services to women.

The WDOs are expected to widen their scope to include somewhat broader perspectives. Overall development of women is seen to include such process as awareness-raising in order to make women self-confident and self-reliant rather than simply enabling them to get some credit and acquire some skills to take up income generating activities. It becomes apparent that while access to financial services can and does make vital contributions to the economic productivity and social well-being of poor women and their households, it does not automatically empower women.[5] The other interventions such as education, political quotas, etc., seek to bring about radical structural transformation that true empowerment entail. Education increases the options of poor women. Adult or non-formal education programmes should therefore, be specially adopted to the needs of women by the WDOs. Such programmes would create awareness among women and promote the well-being of women.

Some of the beneficiaries have stated that they were not aware of the types of programmes and there was no proper guidance as how to proceed and whom to approach for a loan or benefit. Such a communication gap or unawareness created a category of middlemen (Pairavikars) who seized the opportunities to make money. They spoil the officials too. The organisations under study had not taken care of to set-up a public relations wing in their organisations and educate the people about various schemes and sources of financial assistance. Therefore, a Public Relations Officer with specialization in women development or welfare may be appointed in every organisation in the district.

The study of organisation and working of the local women development organisations also call for far-reaching changes regarding organisational structure, administrative set-up, personnel system, programme implementation and identification of beneficiaries. The main thrust of the working of development organisations is based on the identification of beneficiaries followed by the financial assistance partly from them as margin money and loan from banks and other financial institutions. The intention to create the organisations was, perhaps, to see that the benefits reach the individual beneficiary in any area in the district. The identification of beneficiaries is, however, the serious problem encountered in the administration of women development programmes. The statistics in India is notoriously poor and unreliable and the list of the poorest prepared for providing benefits to them does not always comprise the poorest only. Politically motivated inclusions and exclusions are not rare and this vitiates the rest of the process of poverty alleviation in India.[6] It is estimated that nearly 20 per cent of the beneficiaries come from better off groups but have been included in the list under pressure from the local MLA or MP. It is surprising that though no systematic survey was conducted in the whole district to identify the target groups, the women development organisations and other financial institutions advanced financial assistance. A comprehensive survey should be done every year for the identification of genuine beneficiaries. The beneficiaries, who are not eligible under the schemes, should not be mis-identified as poor.

A political functionary, like the president of Mandal Parishad, is not statutorily associated with the women development organisations. The political executives of Panchayati Raj are neither involved in the process of identification of beneficiaries nor in transmitting the cases of beneficiaries to the women development organisations. As a result, the political chief executives of the PRIs tend to become indifferent to these programmes. It may be difficult to achieve desired results unless peoples' participation is ensured in all the processes of programmes.

The organisations under study have no own machinery to fulfil their responsibility of identification of target groups. They are heavily dependent on other organisations and officers like Mandal Parishad Development Officer (MPDO) and Village Secretary. The role of MPDO and other officers, who identify the beneficiaries, finishes after just forwarding the case of beneficiary to the DRDA and other organisations. They are not entrusted with the responsibility to see whether the project is grounded properly and the necessary supplementary financial or technical assistance required by the beneficiary is extended. Thus, an organisational device is needed to identify the beneficiaries on more scientific lines. The identification of eligible beneficiaries should be the responsibility of the grassroots organisations such as Gram Sabha.

Out of 160 sample beneficiaries who had not utilized the benefit, 64 (40 per cent) beneficiaries reported that the utility of loan was less useful. Sincere efforts should be made to link the programme with the requirements of women, their skills and the economic viability of the benefit.

The amount of loans and subsidies have been reported to be inadequate. Nearly one-third of the beneficiaries had not utilised the benefit properly as the loan amount was less and subsidy was inadequate. Hence, the loan and subsidy amounts should be increased. This is the desire of more than one-fourth of the sample beneficiaries.

The governmental organisations process applications of beneficiaries verifying all the formalities completed earlier and transmits it to the concerned bank by releasing subsidy. Though applications are forwarded to various financial institutions for grant of loan, the margin money is not released by the organisastion. It is stated that there are several cases pending with the governmental organisations. The financial institutions, in certain cases, wait even for several months for release of margin money. Out of 425 sample beneficiaries of the study, 131 (30.82 percent) beneficiaries reported that there was delay in release of loan. The loaning procedure should be simplified and streamlined to reduce to the minimum time-gap between applying for the loan, after selection and the release of the loan. Credit camps should be organized for speedy process of applications. Corruption and misappropriation, wherever noticed, should be sternly dealt with. The emphasis should be on taking exemplary action against the officials, non-officials or beneficiaries engaged in this practice.

The policy or administrative framework in our country indicates that all major policy decisions and initiatives relating to women development are taken centrally and then passed down the hierarchy for implementation. Now attempts are being made to decentralize the functions as per the objective of Five-Year Plans.[7] In this direction, the administrative system of local organisations should be strengthened and it should be made autonomous system for initiating, planning, organizing and executing welfare and development programmes.

One-fourth of the official respondents were not happy with the existing organisational structure of women development agencies. Nearly 60 per cent of the officials preferred to suggest alternative structure to the existing organisational structure. An examination of the existing organisational structure as well as the observations of the officials indicate that the organisational arrangement of women development organisations is not conducive to achieving desired goals. So it is necessary to devise a structure that would remain outward looking and responsive and which would also respect the rights of women to determine local solutions as far as possible.

The DWCDA had no governing body or executive committee. All the members of the governing bodies of DSCCSS and DSCCSS are the officials. We find the representatives of people and PRIs as members only in the Governing Body of DRDA. Even in this agency also the officials constitute majority. It is, thus, clear from the above analysis that the Governing Body or Executive Committee of women development organisations is dominated by the officials of various departments. The representation of women and weaker sections for whom the schemes are intended is meagre. The most of the officials are the heads of different departments and they have their own departmental work. So most of the members of the Governing Body of developmental organisations do not always accord first priority to the functioning of development agencies. Further, there is lot of grumbling and also a strong protest from the panchayati raj political functionaries that the functions of various development agencies should have been entrusted to them instead of creating separate agencies like DRDA. They feel that much harm has been done to the development programmes than expected. The Governing Body or Executive Committee of women development organisations should, therefore, invariably include the people's representatives particularly women representatives elected for the local government institutions in the district. The women from weaker sections should be represented in these bodies particularly SC women in DSCCSS and BC women in DBCCSS.

Whether the District Collector should be associated with developmental administration or not is a question which has been debated ever since the developmental programmes were launched in the country. Some states have hived of developmental functions from the regulatory ones and have set-up an entirely new functionary chief executive officer or district development officer to look after the former set of functions. Some states have taken the view that developmental tasks would get more effectively performed by a close association of the traditionally honoured District Collector with them, and accordingly have made him the head of the agency.

Though the District Collector is the member of the IAS, the person having 4 or 5 years of service is not in a position to command the cooperation and respect of the functionaries of development organisations who possess more experience and are older in age. What is even worse, he is subject to frequent transfers, his average stay being less than two years. With all such parameters within which he has to function, he is hardly in a position to provide meaningful leadership to development administration. The larger truth today is that he is not in a position to administer even traditional regulator affairs with an acceptable level of efficiency. The state of village records can be cited for a general erosion of his efficiency.

The Government of Andhra Pradesh have realized that the District Collector has many responsibilities and as such can not devote an adequate amount of his time and energy to development administration. Hence, a full-time functionary, called Project Director or Executive Director, is made the Executive Officer of the development organisation in the district. He was, however, asked to work under the overall supervision and guidance of the District Collector. The District Collector is the chairman of the Governing Body of all the district level women development organisations. It was observed during the period of collection of field data that most of the time, head of the organisation and his staff waited for the orders of the District Collector who is busy with many other programmes. As a result, the launching or even initiating a programme was delayed. This situation may be changed and the executive head of the organisation may be given freedom to plan and implement the programmes of his organisation.

The number, qualifications and skills of officials have greater importance for performance of local organisations. The task of implementing a development programme is difficult and time-consuming and requires large number of dedicated and hard working employees. The staff have to take up many tasks, besides managing the office, like identification of beneficiaries, distribution of benefits, evaluation of the programme, etc. The study reveals that the women development organisations are facing the problem of shortage of staff. When the officials were asked about the problems faced by them or their organisations, one-fourth of the respondents reported the problem of shortage of staff. When they were requested to give their opinion on the adequacy of staff strength, 60 per cent of the officials respondents had reported that the present staff strength was not adequate.

On an examination of the staff position of women development organisations, all the four agencies are better equipped with adequate and well qualified officials. Some of them say DRDA are equipped with more than sufficient staff. However, the problem boils down to the field level machinery which needs reorientation and strength. There is no machinery at mandal and village levels for DSCCSS and DRDA. For DWCDA and DBCCSS, the mandal level and village level functionaries form a small nuclear staff. Consequently, the implementation process got considerably weakened due to the dearth of local functionaries. Therefore, arrangements should be made for the appointment of staff at these levels.

The strategies and approaches of women development in India have been changing from time to time, but the bureaucratic system, the instrument of implementation, has remained more or less stable, notwithstanding changes in nomenclatures and matters of such kinds. This factor alone calls for efforts to keep the bureaucracy in good form and sensitive to environment, implying due cognizance of the multiple environmental factors, such as stages of development, levels of education, social structure, etc. These get often overlooked. Thus, one comes across the spectacle of male dominated delivery system. Women are not well represented in senior management and decision-making, and are still under-represented in staff positions within government and business agencies in most of the world.[8] Where women do appear, they are small in number. The same situation is prevalent in the three out of four women development organisations. The most of the employees working in ICDS and DMSVK and other units of DWCDA are women. The other organisations namely DRDA, DSCCSS and DBCCSS are, however, dominated by male officers. Even the District Office of DWCDA is dominated by the male officers. Men simply cannot establish any rapport with the women beneficiaries. To build organisational capacity to implement gender-inclusive policies, women must be included, as policy implementers in the decision-making ranks as well as at the client-contact levels. As already stated, the women development organisations are facing the problem of shortage of staff. So the number of women staff members may be increased and they may be posted at field levels of these agencies.

The properly selected and trained personnel fulfil the mission of development efficiently. The level of an individual's knowledge affects his attitudes, which in turn affects his behaviour. Thus, for staff who most implements gender-inclusive policies, gender awareness training would seem to be an important step in moving them toward changes in attitudes and behaviour so that they can support and perhaps even become change agents for gender-inclusive policies. Staff training to increase gender sensitivity among policy implementers was rarely conducted.[9] In the present study, it was found that 75 per cent of the officials received training. Some of them (44 per cent) were trained more than once. There is, however, considerable number (i.e. one-fourth) of officials who did not receive training even once. There is, therefore, a need for their training and necessary arrangements for periodic re-training or job training to the staff may be made.

The policies and programmes must ensure that the results should reach the targeted population. A first step to ensure that such programmes and policies are indeed meeting the specified objective is to monitor their results.[10] The next step is the evaluation of the programmes in terms of whether they contribute positively to progress. The present study reveals that the programmes of the DCWDA, DSCCSS and DBCCSS and their performance were never monitored and evaluated. It is only in one instance that the programme of DRDA was evaluated. The Deepam scheme of DRDA was evaluated during 2005-06. Based on the findings, the gaps in the programme were filled in the year 2006-07. The success of the women development programmes has been measured in terms of amounts disbursed, number of facilities provided and the number of beneficiaries covered, but the questions of how far the beneficiaries utilized the loans and benefits and to what extent they could improve their income and employment levels, etc. have never been investigated with thoroughness. The beneficiaries' observation on the role of officials are relevant in this context. Nearly two-thirds of beneficiaries reported that the officials did not visit their villages before the programme. The beneficiaries who reported the officials did not visit their areas during the programme constitute 72.24 per cent. The percentage of beneficiaries who reported that the officials did not visit their areas after the programme is as high as 80 per cent.

It is clear from the above analysis that important aspects of programme implementation like supervision, monitoring and evaluation had been neglected by all the women development organisations. Even the results of the programmes were not assessed. Similar shortcomings were observed in many studies conducted earlier.[11] In the absence of follow-up visits the beneficiaries may not utilise the benefit for the expected purpose and they simply enjoy subsidy benefit. In fact, the financial allocation to DSCCSS and DBCCSS also include assistance for administrative costs particularly for supervision, monitoring and evaluation. The task of monitoring and on-going evaluation of the governmental programmes may be entrusted to any agencies or officers. The training given and loan or benefit extended to the beneficiaries should be regularly followed up by the officers. This would keep the beneficiaries alert and also help to solve their problems, thereby reducing the chances of misusing or diverting the benefit.

Different agencies have been set-up at the district level to meet the needs of and implement various programmes for the benefit of different sections of society. Though one of the motivations behind the setting up of an agency has been to curb departmentalism in the execution of programmes, the problem of coordination at the district level looms large with each organisation preferring to hoe its own row, an administrative behaviour reinforced in no inconsiderable measure by both development and democracy. The officers of particular organisation or department are zealously assertive of their organisational independence. They dislike comments and suggestions from other departments and organisations. The coordination was inadequate with other departments and agencies as also among the organisations involved in developing the poor women in Visakhapatnam district. Coordination was also inadequate among the bankers and WDOs and lack of coordination is the most important bottleneck, which rise to poor implementation of programmes. There is, therefore, a need for coordination among all the developmental organisations in the district. The District Collector can solve the problem of coordination as he is the head of all the agencies in the district. He may, however, be empowered to solve the issues related to women development through a district level coordination committee.

The women development organisations had received significant cooperation from their respective head offices, other governmental organisations, non-governmental organisations and beneficiaries. The WDOs may continue to seek cooperation from different organisations in the district particularly the PRIs and NGOs.

In rural areas, PRIs are already working towards women's empowerment by reserving not less than one-third of total number of seats and offices at all the three levels. The PRIs have the responsibility to formulate and execute various programmes of economic development and social justice.[12] The panchayati raj system is not only an excellent system for ensuing the people's participation in planning and implementation of rural development schemes but also an excellent system of checks and balances on the bureaucracy. The PRIs have necessary infrastructure and experience in development functions.

Today, there is also a widespread appreciation of the work done by local NGOs. Very often government officials try to interact with NGOs as a result of their contributions to development activities. Voluntary efforts have succeeded in encouraging women to break traditional notions of the division of labour between men and women. For example, women have learnt to weave, a skill which has always been considered a male preserve.[13] SEWA, for example, has achieved major breakthroughs in organizing cooperatives of vegetable sellers, kerosene vendors, rag-pickers and those engaged in cleaning services. Though planning for various development programmes will have to be borne by the official machinery, yet whenever possible the services of suitable voluntary agencies may also be utilized. The women development organisations should, therefore, work in coordination with PRIs and voluntary organisations. In many countries such an effort has resulted in a formidable source of support for women issues.

Notes and References

1. Uma Ramaswamy, "Women and Development" in A.M. Shah, B.S. Baviskar and E.A. Ramaswamy (eds.), *Social Structure and Change*, Sage Publications, New Delhi, 1996, p. 88.
2. Paul D. Chowdary, *Women Welfare and Development*, Inter-India Publications, New Delhi, 1992, p. 347.
3. Govind Kelkar, "Development Effectiveness through Gender Mainstreaming: Gender Equality and Poverty Reduction in South Asia", *Economic and Political Weekly*, Vol. 40, No. 39, October 29, 2005, p. 4693.
4. Sudhir Varma, "Women in Development: Need for a Strong National Machinery", *Administrative Change*, Vol. XIX, Nos. 1-2, July 1991-June 1992, p. 27.
5. Naila Kabeer, "Is Microfinance a Magic Bullet for Women's Empowerment? Analysis of Findings from South Asia", *Economic and Political Weekly*, Vol. 40, No. 39, October 29, 2005, p. 4709.
6. Sriram Maheswari, "Rural Development and Bureaucracy in India", *The Indian Journal of Public Administration*, Vol. XXX, No. 4, October-December, 1984, p. 1102.
7. Hoshiar Singh, *Administration of Rural Development*, Sterling Publishers, New Delhi, 1995, p. 48.
8. United Nations, *Women: Challenges to the Year 2000*, United Nations, New York, 1991.
9. Monteze Snyder, Fran Berry and Paul Mavina, "Gender Policy in Development Assistance: Improving Implementation Results", *World Development*, Vol. 24, No. 9, 1996, p. 1490.

10. Meena Acharya and Puspa Ghimire, "Gender Indicators of Equality, Inclusion and Poverty Reduction: Measuring Programme/Project Effectiveness", *Economic and Political Weekly*, Vol. 40, No. 39, October 29, 2005, p. 4719.
11. For details of one of the studies see Mohinder Singh, *Rural Development Administration and Anti-Poverty Programmes*, Deep & Deep Publications, New Delhi, 1988.
12. For details see Gautam Vohra, *Women in Bihar*, Vikas, Delhi, 1988.
13. J. Bhagya Lakshmi, "Women Empowerment: Miles to Go", *Yojana*, Vol. 48, No. 10, August 2004, p. 41.

BIBLIOGRAPHY

Books

Afshar, W., *Women Development and Survivals in the Third World*, Longman, London, 1991.

Altekar, A.S., *The Position of Women in Hindu Civilization*, Motilal Banarsidas, Delhi, 1978.

Andhra Pradesh Scheduled Castes Cooperative Finance Corporation, *Action Plan, 2007-08*, Hyderabad, 2007.

——, *Marching Towards Economic Upliftment of Scheduled Castes*, Hyderabad, 2007.

Andhra Pradesh Women Co-operative Finance Corporation, *Taruni-Educating, Enlightening, Enriching and Empowering*, Hyderabad, 2006.

Anju Bhatia, *Women's Development and NGOs*, Rawat Publications, New Delhi, 2000.

Appa Rao, T., *North Andhra: Industries, Institutions and Cultural Heritage*, Sarvani Printers, Visakhaptnam, 2004.

Baig, Tara Ali (ed.), *Women of India*, Puoiications Division, Government of India, New Delhi, 1990.

Bakshi, S.R., and Kiran Bala, *Development of Women, Children and Weaker Sections*, Deep & Deep Publications, New Delhi, 1999.

Bhandari, R.K., *Educational Development of Women in India*, Ministry of Education and Culture, New Delhi, 1982.

Bhatia, S.C., *Social Justice in Health*, New Delhi, IUACE, 1988.

Boserup, Ester and Christian Liljenerants, *Integration of Women in Development: Why, When and Why*, UN Development Programme, New York, 1975.

Buhler, G., *The Laws of Manu: Sacred Books of the East*, Trans, Vol. 25, Motilal Banarsidass, New Delhi, 1964.

Cernea, Michael M., *Putting People for Sociological Variables in Rural Development*, Oxford University Press, New York, 1985.

Chandrasekhar, B., *Women Development and Welfare Schemes*, Lakshmi Publications, Hyderabad, October, 2002.

Chowdhry, Paul D., *Women Welfare and Development: A Source Book*, Inter-India Publications, New Delhi, 1992.

David Colman and Frederick Nixon, *Economics of Change in Less Developed Countries*, Halstead Press, John Wiley and Sons, New York, 1978.

Deolalikar, Anil B., *Attaining the Millennium Development Goals in India*, Oxford University Press, Delhi, 2005.

Devaki Jain and Nirmala Benerjee (eds.), *Women in Poverty: The Tyranny of the Household*, Vikas Publishing House, New Delhi, 1985.

District Backward Classes Cooperative Service Society, *Note on Developmental Activities*, Visakhapatnam, 2004.

——, *Targets and Achievements on Various Schemes from 2002-03 to 2006-07*, Visakhapatnam.

District Rural Development Agency, *Brief Note on DRDA Activities*, Visakhapatnam, 2007.

District Scheduled Castes Cooperative Service Society, *Brief Note on S.C. Action Plan 2002-03*, Visakhapatnam.

——, *Performance under S.C. Action Plan 2003-04*, Visakhapatnam.

Dixan, R. Mueller, *Women's Work in Third World Agriculture: Women, Work and Development*, ILO, Geneva, 1983.

Everett, Jana Matsan Everett, *Women and Social Change in India*, Heritage Publishers, New Delhi, 1979.

Fuchs, Victor R., *Women's Quest for Economic Equality*, Harward University Press, London, 1988.

Gail Omvedt, *We Will Smash This Prison*, Orient Longman, New Delhi, 1979.

Gautam Vohra, *Women in Bihar*, Vikas Publishing House, Delhi, 1988.

Gita Sen and Caren Grown, *Development Crisis and Alternative Vision: The Third World Women's Perspectives*, Institute of Social Studies Trust, New Delhi, 1984.

Government of Andhra Pradesh, *Strategy Paper on Backward Classes*

Welfare in Andhra Pradesh, Department of B.C. Welfare, Hyderabad, February 2001.

Government of India, *Blueprint of Action Points and National Plan of Action for Women,* Department of Social Welfare, New Delhi, 1976.

——, *Challenge of Education,* Ministry of Education, New Delhi, 1985.

——, *First Five Year Plan (1951-56),* Planning Commission, New Delhi, 1951.

——, *National Perspective Plan for Women's Education 1988-2000 A.D.,* Ministry of Education, New Delhi, 1988.

——, *National Plan of Action: Sixth Five Year Plan 1978-83,* Planning Commission, New Delhi, 1975.

——, *National Policy for Empowerment of Women,* Department of Women and Child Development, New Delhi, 2001.

——, *National Policy on Education,* Ministry of Education, New Delhi, 1986.

——, *Policies and Programmes for the Advancement of Women in India,* Department of Women and Child Development, New Delhi, 1993.

——, *Third Five Year Plan (1961-66),* Planning Commission, New Delhi, 1961.

——, *Women in India: A Statistical Profile,* Department of Women and Child Development, New Delhi, 1988.

——, *Women's Activities in Rural India, A Study Based on NSS, 32nd Round,* Department of Statistics, Government of India, New Delhi, June, 1981.

Gupta, Amit Kumar (ed.), *Women and Society,* Criterion, New Delhi, 1986.

Harshad Trivedi, *Scheduled Caste Women: Studies in Exploitation,* Concept Publishing Company, New Delhi, 1977.

Hate, A. Chandrakala, *Changing Status of Women in Post-Independent India,* Allied Publishers, Bombay, 1969.

Hoshiar Singh, *Administration of Rural Development,* Sterling Publishers, New Delhi, 1995.

Indian Council of Social Science Research, *Status of Women in India: A Synopsis of the Report of the National Commission on the Status of Women 1971-74,* New Delhi, 1975.

Institute of Social Studies Trust, *A Study of Women Development*

Corporations in India, Women's Studies Resource Centre, New Delhi, 1995.

——, *Institutional Mechanism for Women's Advancement*, Women's Studies Resource Centre, New Delhi, 1995.

Jacobson, J. and Susan Wadley, *Women in India: Two Perspectives*, South Asia Books, Columbia, 1977.

Jean Dredz and Amartya Sen, *India Development and Participation*, Oxford University Press, Delhi, 2002.

Kala Rani, *Role Conflict in Working Women*, Chetna Publications, New Delhi, 1976.

Kalpana Shah, *Women Liberation and Voluntary Action*, Ajanta Publications, New Delhi, 1984.

Kamaladevi Chattopadhya, *Indian Women's Battle for Freedom*, Abhinav Publications, New Delhi, 1983.

Khanna, S.K., *Women and Human Rights*, Commonwealth Publishers, New Delhi, 1998.

Kiran Devendra, *Changing Status of Women in India*, Vikas Publishing House, New Delhi, 1994.

Krishna Raj, Maithreyi, *Women and Development: The Indian Experience*, Subhadra Prakashan, Bombay, 1988.

Lakshmi Mishra, *Education of Women in India, 1921-66*, Macmillan, Bombay, 1966.

Leela Dube and Rajini Parliwala (ed.), *Women and Household in Asia: Structures and Strategies—women, work and family*, Oxford University Press, London, 1986.

Malavika Karlekar, *Poverty and Women's Work: A Study of Sweeper Women in Delhi*, Delhi, Vikas Publishing House, 1982.

Mira Seth, *Women and Development: The Indian Experience*, Sage Publications, New Delhi, 2000.

Mishra, R.B., and Chandrapal Singh (eds.), *Indian Women: Challenges and Change*, Commonwealth Publishers, New Delhi, 1992.

Mitra, A., *Implications of the Declining Sex Ratio in India's Population*, Allied Publishers, Bombay, 1979.

——, *Status of Women: Household and Non-Household Economic Activity*, Allied Publishers, Delhi, 1978.

——, *The Status of Women Literacy and Employment*, Allied Publishers, Delhi, 1971, 1979.

Mitra, A., L.P. Pathak, and S. Mukerji, *The Status of Women: Shifts in Occupational Participation, 1961-71*, New Delhi, Abhinav Publications, 1980.

Mohinder Singh, *Rural Development Administration and Anti-Poverty Programmes*, Deep & Deep Publications, New Delhi, 1988.

Molly Mathews, *Woman Workers in the Food Processing Industry in Kerala* (mimeo), Indian Institute of Regional Development Studies, Kottayam, 1983.

Momsen, Janet Henohall, *Women and Development in the Third World*, Routledge, London, 1991.

Narayana Reddy, G., *Women and Child Development: Some Contemporary Issues*, Chugh Publicaitons, Allahabad,1987.

Neera Desai, *Women in Modern India*, Vora & Co., Bombay, 1977.

——, *Review of Studies on Middle Class Women in India*, MSS Research Centre on Women's Studies, Bombay, 1993.

Neera Desai and Maithreyi Krishna Raj, *Women and Society in India*, Ajantha Publications, Delhi, 1987.

Neera Desai and Vibhuti Patel, *Indian Women: Change and Challenge in the International Decade 1975-85*, Popular Prakashan, Bombay, 1985.

Neeta Tapan, *Need for Women Empowerment*, Jaipur, Rawat Publications, 2000.

Nirmala Benerjee, *Women in the Unorganised Sector, The Calcutta Experience*, Orient Longman, Hyderabad, 1984.

——, *Indian Women's Experience of Development—An Analysis*, ISST, New Delhi, 1990.

Ostergaard, L., *Gender and Development: A Practical Guide*, Routledge, London, 1992.

Padma, A., *Women in Medieval Times*, G.V. Graphics, Hyderabad, 2001.

Parmar, P.M., *Social Work and Social Welfare in India*, Sublime Publications, Jaipur, 2007.

Patel, Krishna Ahooja, *Women and Sustainable Development: An International Dimension*, Ashish Publishing House, New Delhi, 1995.

Prabhati Mukherjee, *Hindu Women: Normative Models*, Orient Longman, New Delhi, 1978.

Project Director, District Rural Development Agency, *Brief Note on DRDA Activities*, Visakhapatnam, 2007.

Project Director, District Women and Child Development Agency, *Department Note*, Visakhapatnam, 2006.

Rajakumari Chandrashakar (ed.), *Women Resources and National Development: A Perspective*, Gourav Publications, New Delhi, 1992.

Ralhan, O.P. (ed.), *Indian Women Through Ages*, Anmol Publications, New Delhi, 1995.

Reed, Evelyn, *Women's Evolution*, Path Finder Press, New York, 1976.

Rehman, M.M., and Kamalakant Biswal, *Education, Work, and Women: An Enquiry into Gender Bias*, Commonwealth Publishers, New Delhi, 1991.

Rekha Mehra and K. Saradamoni, *Women and Rural Transformation*, Concept Publishing Company, New Delhi, 1983.

Rose, Aileen D., *Hindu Family in an Urban Setting*, Oxford University Press, Delhi, 1961.

Sabala Sangh Saheli, *Development for Whom—A Critique of Women's Development Programmes*, Action India, Delhi, 1991.

Sakuntala Narasimhan, *Empowering Women: An Alternative Strategy for Rural India*, Sage Publications, New Delhi, 1999.

Sarala Ranganathan, *Women and Social Order: A Profile of Major Indicators and Determinants*, Kaushik Publishers, New Delhi, 1998.

Shanta Krishna Swamy, *Glimpses of Women in India*, Ashish Publishing House, New Delhi, 1983.

Singh, Andrea Manefee and Anita Kelles Vitanen (eds.), *Invisible Hand: Women in Home Based Production*, Sage Publications, New Delhi, 1987.

Singh, Indu Prakash, *Indian Women—The Power Trapped*, Galaxy Publications, New Delhi, 1991.

Sivard, R.L., *Women—A World Survey: World Priorities*, Washington, D.C., U.S.A., 1985.

Srinivas, M.N., *The Changing Position of Indian Women*, Oxford University Press, Bombay, 1978.

Staudit, K.A., *Women in Development: Women's Organisations in Rural Development*, Washington, D.C., USAID, 1980.

Sumitra Gupta, *Social Welfare in India*, Allahabad, Chugh Publications, 1989.

Suseela Kaushik (ed.)., *Women's Oppression, Patterns and Perspectives*, Vikas Publishing House, New Delhi, 1989.

Susmita Chandra, *Women and Economic Development: A Case Study of U.P.*, B.R. Publishing Corporation, Delhi, 2001.

Tandon, R.K., *Status of Women in Contemporary World*, Commonwealth Publishers, New Delhi, 1998.

Tinker, Irene and Bo Bromsen, *Women and World Development*, Overseas Development Council, Washington, D.C., 1978.

United Nations, *Directory of Focal Points for the Advancement of Women*, 1985.

United Nations, *The Beijing Declaration and Platform for Action*, Department of Public Information, New Delhi, 1995.

United Nations, *Women: Challenges to the Year 2000*, United Nations, New York, 1991.

United Nations, *World Survey on the Role of Women in Development*, New York, UN, 1989.

United Nations, *World's Women: Trends and Data, 1970-90*, New York, 1990.

United Nations Development Programme, *Human Development Report*, Oxford University Press, Bombay, 1995.

United Nations Division for the Advancement of Women, *Beijing Plus Five Draft Political Declaration*, 1999.

Upadhyay, Bhagavat Sexsena, *Women in Rigveda*, S. Chand and Co., New Delhi, 1974.

Upadhyay, H.C., *Status of Women in Indira*, Anmol Publications, New Delhi, 1977.

Usha Narayanan, "Women's Political Empowerment: Imperatives and Challenges", *Mainstream*, April 16, 1999.

Usha Rao, N.J., *Women in a Developing Society*, Ashish Publishing House, New Delhi, 1983.

Usha Sharma, *Women's Emancipation: Rights Vs. Population Control*, Author's Press, Delhi, 2001.

Vanitha Viswanath, *NGO's and Women's Development in Rural South India: A Comparative Analysis*, Vistaar Publications, New Delhi, 1993.

Vijay Sharma, *Protection to Women in Matrimonial Home*, Deep and Deep Publications, New Delhi, 1994.

Vina Mazumdar, *Emergence of Women's Questions in India and the Role of Women's Studies*, Centre for Women's Development Studies, New Delhi, 1985.

——, *Role of Rural Women in Development*, Allied Publishers, New Delhi, 1978.

——, *Symbols of Power: Women in Changing Society*, Allied Publishers, Bombay, 1979.

——, *Women in Changing Society*, Allied Publishers, Bombay, 1979.

Articles

Ackerley, B., "Testing the Tools of Development Credit Programmes: Loan Involvement and Women's Empowerment", *IDS Bulletin*, Vol. 26, No. 3, 1995.

Asaiah, K., "Status of Backward Classes" in R.S. Rao *et. al.* (eds.), *Fifty years of Andhra Pradesh 1956-2006*, Centre for Documentation, Research and Communication, Hyderabad, 2007.

Bhagyalakshmi, J., "Women's Empowerment: Miles to Go", *Yojana*, Vol. 48, No. 10, August, 2004.

Chandra, Shanta Kohli, "Women and Empowerment", *The Indian Journal of Public Administration*, Vol. XLIII, No. 3, July-September, 1997.

Chinnadurai, R., "Women Entrepreneurship and Service Sector", *Kurukshetra*, Vol. 54, No. 2, November 2005.

Devaki Jain, N. Singh, and M. Chand, "India: Status and Role of Women", in R. John (ed.), *Women in Asia*, Minority Rights Group, London, 1980.

Gail Omvedt, "Women in Governance in South Asia,", *Economic and Political Weekly*, Vol. 40, No. 39, October 29, 2005.

Gita Sen, "Whither Women's Health", *Seminar*, 537, May 2004.

Govind Kelkar, "Development Effectiveness through Gender Mainstreaming: Gender Equality and Poverty Reduction in South Asia", *Economic and Political Weekly*, Vol. 40, No. 39, October 29, 2005.

Kamalnath, "Female Work Participation and Economic Development—A Regional Analysis", *Economic and Political Wekly*, Vol. 5, No. 27, May 23, 1970.

Karuna Chanana, "The Education of Women in Pre-Independence India" in A.M. Shah, B.S. Baviskar, E.A. Rama Swamy (eds.), *Women in Indian Society*, Sage Publications, New Delhi, 1996.

Koteswara Rao, M.V.S., "National Policy for Empowerment of Women" in M. Lakshmipathi Raju (ed.), *Women Empowerment: Challenges and Strategies*, Regal Publications, New Delhi, 2007.

Largnia, Isabel, "The Economic Basis of the Status of Women", in

Ruby Rohrlich-Levitt (ed.), *Women Cross – Culturally: Change and Challenge*, Mouton, The Hague, 1975.

Leela Gulati, "Female Work Participation", *Economic and Political Weekly*, Vol. 10, No. 2, January 17, 1975.

Maya Ghosh, "Human Face of Indian Women: A Policy Approach Towards Correcting Imbalance", *Administrative Change*, Vol. XXXII, No. 2, Vol. XXXIII, No. 1, January-December, 2005.

Meena Acharya and Puspa Ghimire, "Gender Indicators of Equality, Inclusion and Poverty Reduction: Measuring Programme/Project Effectiveness", *Economic and Political Weekly*, Vol. 40, No. 39, October 29, 2005.

Monteze Snyder, Fran Berry and Paul Mavina, "Gender Policy in Development Assistance: Improving Implementation Results", *World Development*, Vol. 24, No. 9, 1996.

Naila Kabeer, "Is Microfinance a Magic Bullet for Women's Empowerment? Analysis of Findings from South Asia", *Economic and Political Weekly*, Vol. 40, No. 39, October 29, 2005.

Narayana, E.A., "Women Empowerment: The Need for Strong Institutional Mechanism" in M. Lakshmipathi Raju (ed.), *Women Empowerment: Challenges and Strategies*, Regal Publications, New Delhi, 2008.

Neera Desai, "Women's Employment and their Familial Role in India" in A.M. Shah, B.S. Baviskar and E.A. Ramaswamy (eds.), *Women in Indian Society*, Sage Publications, New Delhi, 1996.

Pandimuruga Chinnan, K., "Women's Education as a Tool for Rural Development", *Kurukshetra*, Vol. 53, No.11, September 2005.

Pearson, R., "Gender Matters in Development", in T. Allen and A. Thomson (eds.), *Poverty and Development in the 1990s*, Oxford University Press, Oxford, 1990.

Peerzade, Sayed Afzal and Prema Parande, "Empowerment of Women—As Lady", *Kurukshetra*, Vol. 54, No. 1, November, 2005.

Phillip Klein, "An Institutionalist View of Development Economics", *Journal of Economic Issues*, Vol. XI, No. 4, 1979.

Prema Ramachandran, "Nutrition in Pregnancy" in G. Gopalan and Surinder Kaur (eds.), *Women and Nutrition in India*, Nutrition Foundation of India, New Delhi, 1986.

Rajyalakshmi, K., "Development Through Education" in Rajakumari Chandrasekhar (ed.), *Women Resources and National Development: A Perspective*, Gaurav Publications, New Delhi, 1992.

Robins Sherman, and Davis Kemal, "Income Distribution and Socio-Economic Mobility", *Journal of Development Studies*, Vol. 13, No. 4, 1977.

Roopa Sharma, "The Women's Reservation Bill: A Crisis of Identity", *The Indian Journal of Public Administration*, Vol. XLVII, No. 1, January-March 2005.

Sarojini Varadappan, "Women's Development: A National Perspective" in Rajakumari Chandrasekhar (ed.), *Women's Resources and National Development: A Perspective*, Gaurav Publications, New Delhi, 1992.

Singh, J.P., "Indian Democracy and Empowerment of Women", *The Indian Journal of Public Administration*, Vol. XLVI, No. 4, October-December 2000.

Sita Lakshmi, S., and K. Thangamani, "Organisational Support for Rural Women", *Report of the Seminar on Role of Rural Women in Development*, NIPCCD, New Delhi, 1988.

Snehalata Panda, "Reservations for Women in Union and State Legislatures", *The Indian Journal of Public Administration*, Vol. XLVII, No. 4, October-December 2001.

Sriram Maheswari, "Rural Development and Bureaucracy in India", *The Indian Journal of Public Administration*, Vol. XXX, No. 4, October-December 1984.

Sudhir Varma, "Women in Development: Need for a Strong National Machinery", *Administrative Change*, Vol. XIX, Nos. 1-2, July, 1991; June, 1992.

Thaper, Romila, "Looking Back in History", in Devaki Jain (ed.), *Indian Women*, Publication Division, Ministry of Information and Broadcasting, Government of India, New Delhi, 1975.

Tomsic, V., "Policy of Non-Alignment Struggle for the NIEO and the Role of Women in Development", paper presented at Golden Jubilee Symposium on Women, Work and Society, I.S.I., New Delhi, 1982.

Uma Ramaswamy, "Women and Development" in A.M. Shah, B.S. Baviskar, E.A. Ramaswamy (Eds.), *Women in Indian Society*, Sage Publications, New Delhi, 1996.

Upreti, H.C., "Role of Rural Women in Development: Some Structural and Cultural Constraints", *Report of the Seminar on Role of Rural Women in Development*, NIPCCD, New Delhi, 1988.

Usha Narayanan, "Women's Political Empowerment: Imperatives and Challenges", *Mainstream*, April 16, 1999.

Vana Mala, "Employment of Women in Andhra Pradesh Public Enterprises", in K. Murali Monohar (ed.), *Women's Status and Development in India*, Society for Women's Studies and Development, Warangal, 1984.

Veena Das, "Indian Women, Work, Power and Status" in B.R. Nanda (eds.), *Indian Women*, Vikas Publishing House, New Delhi, 1976.

Verma, Ravinder K. and Gyanender K. Verma, "Women in Bihar Politics", *Economic and Political Weekly*, April 13, 1996.

Vina Majumdar, "Historical Soundings", *Seminar*, 457, September, 1977.

Vina Mazumdar, "The Social Reform Movement in India from Ranade to Nehru" in B.R. Nanda (ed.), *Indian Women: from Purdah to Modernity*, Vikas, New Delhi, 1976.

Wadley, Susan, "Women and the Hindu Tradition", in Jacobson and Susan Wadley (eds.), *Women in India: Two Perspectives*, Manohar, Delhi, 1977.

Yogendra Narian, S.N. Sahu and L. Lakshmi, "Political Empowerment of Women", *The Indian Journal of Public Administration*, Vol. LI, No.1, January-March, 2005.

Reports

District Scheduled Castes Cooperative Service Society, *Progress Report under S.C. Action Plan 2006-07*, Visakhapatnam.

Government of India, *Annual Report, 1984-85*, Ministry of Social and Women Welfare, New Delhi, 1985.

——, *Annual Report 1999-2000*, Ministry of Health and Family Welfare, New Delhi, 2000.

——, *Report of the National Commission on Self-Employed Women and Women in the Informal Sector*, New Delhi, 1988.

——, *Report of the National Committee on Women Education*, Ministry of Education, New Delhi, 1959.

——, *Report of the Working Group on Health for All by A.D. 2000*, Ministry of Health and Family Welfare, New Delhi, 1981.

——, *Shramshakti: Report of the National Commission on Self-Employed Women and Women in the Informal Sector,* Department of Women and Child Development, New Delhi, 1988.

——, *Towards Equality: Report of the Committee on the Status of Women in India,* Ministry of Education and Social Welfare, New Delhi, 1975.

His Majesty's Government of Nepal, *Beijing Plus Five Country Report,* Kathmandu,1999.

SNDT University, *Report of the First National Conference on Women's Studies,* Bombay, 1981.

UNESCO, *Women's Studies and Social Sciences in Asia: Report of a Meeting of Experts,* Bangkok, 1983.

United Nations, *Report of the World Conference to Review and Appraise the Achievements of the United Nations Decade for Women: Equality, Development and Peace,* Nairobi, 15-26 July, 1985.

INDEX